CHANCE AND CIRCUMSTANCE

LAWRENCE M. BASKIR

CHANCE AND

THE DRAFT, THE WAR AND

WILLIAM A. STRAUSS

CIRCUMSTANCE

THE VIETNAM GENERATION

Vintage Books
A Division of Random House, New York

First Vintage Books Edition, October 1978

Copyright © 1978 by Lawrence M. Baskir and William A. Strauss
All rights reserved under International and Pan-American Copyright
Conventions. Published in the United States by Random House, Inc., New
York, and simultaneously in Canada by Random House of Canada Limited,
Toronto. Originally published by Alfred A. Knopf, Inc., in April 1978.

Library of Congress Cataloging in Publication Data
Baskir, Lawrence M.
Chance and circumstance.
Bibliography: p.
Includes index.
1. Vietnamese Conflict, 1961-1975—Draft resisters—United States.
2. Vietnamese Conflict, 1961-1975—Desertions—United States.
3. United States—History—1945-
I. Strauss, William A., joint author.   II. Title.
[DS559.8.D7B37 1978b]   959.704'38   78-55717
ISBN 0-394-72749-5

Manufactured in the United States of America

To Cecily and Melanie we dedicate this book
with a father's prayer of peace

CONTENTS

ILLUSTRATIONS

FOREWORD

This is the first comprehensive study of the Vietnam generation, those 53 million young Americans who came of age—draft age, that is—between 1964 and 1973, roughly the decade of the Vietnam war. Because of the lingering unpopularity of that war, it may well be the only such study written, the single contemporary historical record, since the American people tend to put unpleasant and unsuccessful events far behind them as quickly as possible. While the decade was in progress, one heard or spoke of the war many times every day. It was an omnipresent incubus. Now one rarely speaks about the war or hears about it, unless something unusual happens, like another presidential pardon or a commission to search for those still "Missing in Action."

However, the American people cannot commit to oblivion the malevolent experience of the quarter of all Americans who directly confronted that war and the many heartrending personal decisions it demanded. Granted that half of the more than fifty million coming of draft age were women. They were also sweethearts, sisters, classmates. Granted that more than 60 percent of the 27 million men escaped service by a variety of legal and illegal means. That action, too, left its moral scars when one views the composition of those who were drafted, the quarter of a million who were wounded in Vietnam, the more than fifty thousand who died, the hundreds of thousands who became legally entangled in resisting the draft, and the other hundreds of thousands who, mainly for family and not antiwar reasons, committed military offenses, many after serving a full year in Vietnam.

The great bulk of all these Americans deeply scarred by Vietnam were those already economically, socially, and educationally disadvantaged. They not only carried the burden of the fighting and dying, they now bear the lion's share of the penalties occasioned by the war and its aftermath. One often hears shocked people excoriating the President for pardoning deserters and draft resisters, but do these self-righteous critics ever advert to the fact that 15 million men of draft age completely avoided even one day of military service without penalty, and that only twenty-four soldiers were convicted of deserting under fire in Vietnam, fewer than three a year?

What occurs to me in commending this unique study to Americans is the key sentence in the authors' opening chapter: "Until Americans evaluate the conduct of these men [deserters and draft resisters] in the context of the entire generation's response to the war, there can never be any real understanding of the tragedy of Vietnam."

I should perhaps add a personal note regarding how this book came to be written and why I am writing this introduction. I lived out the war in a university and had my share of antiwar protests in ever-growing crescendo. One would think that it was a students' war but, in fact, only a minuscule percentage of college graduates ever saw service in Vietnam. I had my own change of heart and conviction during the war years, coming at last to hate the whole involvement with a passion. Once the war ended, although I had come out for unconditional amnesty, I was invited by President Ford to serve on his original nine-member Presidential Clemency Board to administer, case by case, his well-intentioned program of conditional clemency for convicted draft offenders and military deserters. After one year and several thousand case studies, I had become profoundly moved by the basic injustice and all-pervading inequity of closing one's eyes to the great majority of young Americans (mostly white and advantaged) who protested but did not serve, while lowering the boom on those who protested and took their punishment here or in exile, or who served and deserted mainly when called by a higher duty to their family in crisis. Poor families are almost always in crisis.

Granting that there are a few thousand out of millions whose felonious behavior in or out of service does not deserve forgiveness, the great, great majority of the hundreds of thousands scarred one way or another by the war they did not create deserve relief from this one more burden, since they are already carrying so many burdens. Read the book and see for yourself what I am saying—the evidence is all here.

At the conclusion of the one year's activity of the Ford Presidential Clemency Board, it appeared to me, and to my generous good friend Mr. McGeorge Bundy, president of the Ford Foundation, that we might use much of the monumental evidence assembled by the Presidential Clemency Board to strike a well-deserved blow for justice and equity. The Foundation provided the modest funds needed, and I persuaded the two most talented and dedicated members of the Clemency Board staff to make the study and to draw the public policy conclusions that were otherwise likely never to come to light. It was not, and is not today, the most popular of enterprises, but to their credit, Larry Baskir and Bill Strauss did it, with the help of a very balanced and wise committee that we assembled to counsel them along the way.

Already this study and a preliminary publication, *Reconciliation After Vietnam,* have influenced the courageous actions of President Carter to address some legal aspects of the problem. It is our present hope that *Chance and Circumstance* will contribute to the solution of the more intractable side of the problem, the need for the American people to find a true measure of compassion in their hearts.

In the end, it is justice that really counts. Americans are, in my view, a fair people. If enough of them read this book and ponder its implications, I am sure we may then legitimately put the Vietnam experience behind us, for we will have restored justice to what is now a very unjust residue of a very unpopular war.

Rev. Theodore M. Hesburgh
University of Notre Dame

PREFACE

As we complete this book, it is almost exactly two years since three decades of America's Vietnam involvement ended with the entry into Saigon of North Vietnamese and Viet Cong troops. To most Americans, Vietnam already belongs to another era. It is hard to remember how our national soul was wracked, so quickly and so eagerly have we put those years behind us. Yet nations have psyches just as do individuals. And this conscious effort at forgetting may only mask a period of internal healing. The time will come when we openly begin to reexamine Vietnam and try to digest that experience as a people. We have written this book as our contribution to that effort.

Chance and Circumstance focuses on that part of the American people who were confronted most immediately with the reality of Vietnam—the 27 million draft-age men we call the Vietnam generation. Yet this book is not about those who actually fought the war. Their firsthand accounts are eloquent, tortured, and tragic, and are perhaps the most important single chronicle of the Vietnam experience. We have written instead about the 25 million men who did not fight. Our purpose is to show who they were and how they escaped the war—and yet, in truth, did not escape it. Vietnam was, as a Washington *Post* editorial once observed, "a generation-wide catastrophe." In its wreckage lay an astonishing variety of victims.

It is altogether fitting that we be the authors of such a book. Had our luck been different, or had government policies been otherwise, we might have written a firsthand account of Vietnam. As it is, California is the closest we have ever been to Southeast Asia.

One of us (Baskir) finished law school in 1962, in those prewar days when the draft kindly permitted young men to continue in school as long as they wished and were able, until the magic age of twenty-six. Yet the law degree came at twenty-four. Wishing to avoid two more years of education or the indignity of two years as an enlisted man, he took one of the routes especially designed for the thinking man and joined the reserves. Basic training at Fort Dix, New Jersey, was no more distasteful than it had to be. The training company was composed exclusively of reservists, and all were recent college or professional school graduates. The unit was well insulated from the real army of draftees, volunteers, and lifers. The final two months of active duty were spent as a battalion clerk, sufficiently free from the rigors of military life to spend every day reading Gibbon and every night at Princeton, playing bridge. The one clinker in the reserves was the fact that for six years you were liable to call-up in an emergency. The example of the Berlin crisis hung like a pall for all that time, a danger made increasingly real by the escalation in Vietnam. But it was not like Korea this time. President Johnson found his soldiers elsewhere.

The other (Strauss) lived for years with the threat of the draft, but good luck kept him away from a personal confrontation with Vietnam. He graduated from college in 1969, six months before the first Selective Service lottery. While his friends were under pressure from their draft boards, his San Mateo, California board mysteriously left him alone. Meanwhile, he cooked high-calorie meals to help a friend eat his way over the weight limit and out of the draft. The first draft lottery designated his February 5 birthday as #214. The government later announced that #215 would be the cutoff number, and he lived for months with the lonely horror that he might be among the last to be drafted. On a hot July evening on a subway station outside Yankee Stadium, he saw a folded New York *Post* under a man's arm with the partial headline "195" in ten-point type. An instant later, he learned that his escape from the draft was as narrow as nineteen pellets in a scrambled drum. But this was not just luck; statistics experts later proved that the first lottery had a bias in favor of January and February birthdays, whose pellets had been put in the drum first and ended up at the bottom.

Neither of us can say what we would have done had we actually been faced with orders to Vietnam. Would we have had the courage to go, or the courage to refuse? We could not answer that question then, and we still cannot. But we strongly suspect that even without the luck of the lottery, or Johnson's reserve policy, we would have avoided combat via some other manifestation of chance and circumstance.

Our involvement with President Ford's clemency program gave us an opportunity to consider our personal experiences in a broader context. We were both senior officials with the Presidential Clemency Board, Baskir as general counsel and chief executive officer, and Strauss as director of planning and management and editor of the Board's final report. During our year with the program, we came to recognize how much we, like so many Americans, had misunderstood the amnesty issue. The clemency program, despite the President's good intentions, was an inadequate solution.

Among those who shared our opinion was Father Theodore M. Hesburgh, president of the University of Notre Dame and a member of the Clemency Board. At his urging, and supported by a special grant from the Ford Foundation, we undertook this "Vietnam Offender Study" as faculty fellows of the University of Notre Dame, working through the law school's Center for Civil Rights. In January 1977, the University of Notre Dame Press published our report, *Reconciliation After Vietnam*, in which we recommended a specific program of relief for draft and military offenders.

President Carter's response was less comprehensive than we proposed, especially for Vietnam veterans, and we persist in the belief that the wounds of the war have been more covered over than healed. Just as the government proved incapable of punishing draft resisters and deserters as effectively as most Americans believed, so has it been unable to devise an adequate means of relieving the punishment it did impose. Yet the most severe punishment suffered by draft resisters and deserters has been the condemnation and misunderstanding of their fellow citizens. No government program can remedy this. True forgiveness can come only from understanding.

As we began our study, we were surprised at how little careful analysis had ever been given the subject. To get the necessary background information, we visited several military bases to learn about past and current disciplinary problems; we interviewed hundreds of counselors, lawyers, government officials, draft resisters, and deserters throughout the United States; and we visited Canada and Sweden to speak with exiles. With the aid of the University, we researched draft and military law and analyzed the raw data that emerged from President Ford's program.

Finally, we conducted our own survey of 1,586 men who were of draft age during the Vietnam war to learn of their experiences with the draft and military. This "Notre Dame survey" was not a national sample. It consisted of roughly equal groups of men from South Bend, Indiana; Ann Arbor, Michigan; and Washington, D.C. Subjects were chosen through neighborhood spot-samples, with a special effort to get a representative number of interviews in low-income or minority neighborhoods. We have used the findings of the Notre Dame survey to draw conclusions about the entire draft-age generation, recognizing that there is some margin of error.

The nine flowcharts have been constructed through analysis of the best available data, much of which is not very good. But we are confident that the data is sufficiently accurate to put all issues in proper perspective. Some of our statistics conflict with those commonly cited elsewhere—for example, the number of Vietnam troops or the number of Vietnam-era bad discharges. This is generally because we have defined our terms differently from other sources. The notes should help explain any discrepancies.

To protect the privacy of individuals whose cases we describe, we have used fictitious names. The only exceptions are well-known legal cases, public figures, and persons who requested that their real names be used.

We wish to thank the many people who have given their time, energy, interest, and advice in the preparation of this book. We are especially indebted to the members of our advisory committee, Hon. Charles McC. Mathias, Jr., Professor Morris Janowitz, Professor Jefferson Fordham, William Klaus, Eddie Williams, Roger Kelley, and the chairman, Father Hesburgh; to McGeorge Bundy, Peter Bell, and Sandy Jaffe of the Ford Foundation; to Dr. Donald Kommers, director of the Civil Rights Center of the University of Notre Dame; to the university's provost, Rev. James Bertchaell; to Mike Wise, Tom Linn, Dave Curry, Jim Carr, Susan Zwick, Barbara Gaal, Bonnie Katz, Bill Miller, Bill Valentine, Rick Drucker, and the many other fine people who helped immeasurably with our research; to Rick Tropp, Bob Knisely, Rob Quartel, Neil Broder, Tom Alder, Ed Sherman, and Henry Schwarzschild for their editorial help; to Ash Green and Lee Goerner, our editors at Alfred A. Knopf; and above all to our secretaries, Paddy Shakin, Anita Listman, and Harold Peltz, and our research assistant, Larry Vogel. For the support of our wives, Marna and Janie, we can only offer a special thank you.

Lawrence M. Baskir
William A. Strauss

CHANCE AND CIRCUMSTANCE

I | THE VIETNAM GENERATION

When John F. Kennedy was inaugurated on January 20, 1961, the new President told the nation and the world that "the torch has been passed to a new generation of Americans," under whose leadership America would "pay any price, bear any burden . . . to assure the survival and the success of liberty." These were brave words, very well received.

This "new generation," described by Kennedy as "tempered by war, disciplined by a hard and bitter peace," consisted of World War II veterans then in their late thirties and forties. Their "best and brightest" would later steer the nation through a very different, much more controversial war in Vietnam. Yet this time it was not they who had to do the fighting. Fewer than five hundred members of this generation died in Southeast Asia, most from accidents, diseases, and other causes that had nothing to do with combat. The rest paid the taxes to finance this $165 billion venture. It was their children, the baby-boom generation —the product of an enormous jump in the birthrate between 1946 and 1953—who paid the real price of Vietnam.

Fifty-three million Americans came of age during the Vietnam war. Roughly half were women, immune from the draft. Only six thousand women saw military service in Vietnam, none in combat. But as sisters, girl friends, and wives, millions of draft-age women paid a heavy share of the emotional cost of the war.

For their male counterparts, the war had devastating consequences. As Figure 1 illustrates, 26,800,000 men came of draft age between August 4, 1964, when the Tonkin Gulf Resolution marked the nation's formal entry into the war, and March 28, 1973, when the last American troops left. Fifty-one thousand died—17,000 from gunshot wounds,

7,500 from multiple fragmentation wounds, 6,750 from grenades and mines, 10,500 from other enemy action, 8,000 from nonhostile causes, and 350 by suicide. Another 270,000 were wounded, 21,000 of whom were disabled. Roughly 5,000 lost one or more limbs in the war. A half million were branded as criminals, more than two million served in the war zone, and millions more had their futures shaped by the threat of going to war.

These were the sons of parents reunited after a long but victorious war, parents who, in columnist George Will's description, "were anxious to turn from the collective task of history-making to the private task of family-making. Like Studebakers and toothpaste, the next batch of children would be 'new and improved.' " Having faced depression and war, they wanted their children to know nothing but peace and prosperity. As William Manchester noted in *The Glory and the Dream*, their offspring would be "adorable as babies, cute as grade school pupils, and striking as they entered their teens. After high school they would attend the best colleges and universities in the country, where their parents would be very, very proud of them." They were the Dr. Spock generation, the Sputnik generation, the Pepsi generation, and eventually the Woodstock generation. But above all else, they became the Vietnam generation.

As children and teenagers, they had grown accustomed to the existence of the draft. Some looked forward to military service as an exciting and potentially valuable experience—a chance to demonstrate their manhood, serve their country, and get some adventure before settling down. Others saw the draft as an unpleasant but nonetheless tolerable demand on two years of their lives. Many, especially those from well-to-do families, looked upon the draft as something to avoid, an unwelcome interference with their personal plans. But most never thought much about it. Consciously or unconsciously, they put the draft out of their minds; it was something that happened to someone else, never to them.

But when the generation and the Vietnam war collided, the draft became a preeminent concern. In 1966, a survey of high-school sophomores found that only 7 percent mentioned the draft or Vietnam as one of "the problems young men your age worry about most." But when the same question was asked of the same individuals after their

FIGURE 1: VIETNAM GENERATION

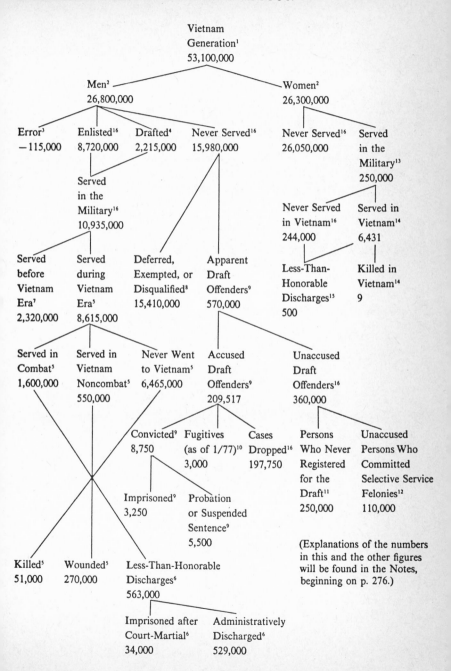

Vietnam
Generation[1]
53,100,000

Men[2]
26,800,000

Women[2]
26,300,000

Error[3]
—115,000

Enlisted[16]
8,720,000

Drafted[4]
2,215,000

Never Served[16]
15,980,000

Never Served[16]
26,050,000

Served
in the
Military[13]
250,000

Served
in the
Military[16]
10,935,000

Never Served
in Vietnam[16]
244,000

Served in
Vietnam[14]
6,431

Served
before
Vietnam
Era[7]
2,320,000

Served
during
Vietnam
Era[5]
8,615,000

Deferred,
Exempted, or
Disqualified[8]
15,410,000

Apparent
Draft
Offenders[9]
570,000

Less-Than-
Honorable
Discharges[15]
500

Killed in
Vietnam[14]
9

Served in
Combat[5]
1,600,000

Served in
Vietnam
Noncombat[5]
550,000

Never Went
to Vietnam[5]
6,465,000

Accused
Draft
Offenders[9]
209,517

Unaccused
Draft
Offenders[16]
360,000

Convicted[9]
8,750

Fugitives
(as of 1/77)[10]
3,000

Cases
Dropped[16]
197,750

Persons
Who Never
Registered
for the
Draft[11]
250,000

Unaccused
Persons Who
Committed
Selective Service
Felonies[12]
110,000

Imprisoned[9]
3,250

Probation
or Suspended
Sentence[9]
5,500

(Explanations of the numbers
in this and the other figures
will be found in the Notes,
beginning on p. 276.)

Killed[5]
51,000

Wounded[5]
270,000

Less-Than-Honorable
Discharges[6]
563,000

Imprisoned after
Court-Martial[6]
34,000

Administratively
Discharged[6]
529,000

high-school graduation in 1969, that number had grown to 75 percent. Few nineteen- to twenty-six-year-olds were eager to risk their lives in Vietnam.

Although only 6 percent of all young men were needed to fight, the Vietnam draft cast the entire generation into a contest for individual survival. The draft was not, however, an arbitrary and omnipotent force, imposing itself like blind fate upon men who were powerless to resist. Instead, it worked as an instrument of Darwinian social policy. The "fittest"—those with background, wit, or money—managed to escape. Through an elaborate structure of deferments, exemptions, legal technicalities, and noncombat military alternatives, the draft rewarded those who manipulated the system to their advantage.

Among this generation, fighting for one's country was not a source of pride; it was misfortune. Going to Vietnam was the penalty for those who lacked the wherewithal to avoid it. A 1971 Harris survey found that most Americans believed that those who went to Vietnam were "suckers, having to risk their lives in the wrong war, in the wrong place, at the wrong time."

Much of this sentiment reflected the public's growing disenchantment with American involvement in Vietnam. The outspoken antiwar views of many young people helped sway public opinion and turn around the nation's policies. Their activism involved moral courage, but little concrete sacrifice. Except for occasional individuals who, on principle, abandoned deferments and exemptions to go to prison or take exile, opposing the war was in every draft-age man's self-interest. The sooner the war ended, the less likely it was that he would bear personal hardship.

This sense of self-interest was best illustrated by the attitude of antiwar collegians toward their student deferments. Harvard College graduate James Glassman recalled that in 1966, before the draft calls began to rise, "students complained that the system was highly discriminatory, favoring the well-off. They called the II-S an unfair advantage for those who could go to college." But as the war escalated, "the altruism was forgotten. What was most important now was saving your own skin." In 1967, when graduate-school deferments were abolished, the Harvard *Crimson* published an editorial entitled "The Axe Falls," accusing the government of "careless expediency" which was "clearly unfair to students."

Many students defended their deferments—and their draft avoidance —with a measure of class arrogance. A Rhodes scholar, now a corporate lawyer, observed that "there are certain people who can do more good in a lifetime in politics or academics or medicine than by getting killed in a trench." A University of Michigan student commented that "if I lost a couple of years, it would mean $16,000 to me. I know I sound selfish, but, by God, I paid $10,000 to get this education." These attitudes were shared by millions of draft-age men with other deferments and exemptions. "I got a good steady job," a Delaware defense worker said. "I'm making good money and having a ball every weekend. Why the hell should I want to go?" Why should he have wanted to go? Vietnam veterans were held in no esteem, and the fate of the nation hardly lay in the balance.

"The result," as Yale University president Kingman Brewster noted, was "a cynical avoidance of service, a corruption of the aims of education, a tarnishing of the national spirit, . . . and a cops and robbers view of national obligation." Avoiding Vietnam became a generation-wide preoccupation. According to the Notre Dame survey, approximately 15 million (60 percent) of the draft-age men who did not see combat took positive steps to help fate along. More than half of all men who escaped the draft, and almost half of all servicemen who escaped combat, believe today that the actions they took were wholly or partly responsible for keeping them away from the fighting.

Avoiding Vietnam did not necessarily mean emerging unscathed. For one in four, it meant hurried marriages, unwanted children, misdirected careers, or physical impairments. But millions emerged untouched, triumphant in what New Orleans draft counselor Collins Vallee called a "victory over the government." They never went to war, and they never faced the costly alternatives of prison, exile, or court-martial.

Avoidance was available to everyone. Ghetto youths sidestepped the draft by failing to register. High-school dropouts married and had children. But by far the greatest number of escape routes were open to youths from privileged backgrounds. Through status deferments, physical exemptions, or safe enlistments, they had little difficulty staying far from Vietnam. Even doctors, who were subject to special draft calls, were seldom involved in the war. Fewer than one of every ten medical-school graduates was drafted; many of the rest found refuge in the National Institute of Health, Public Health Service, or the reserves.

The draftees who fought and died in Vietnam were primarily society's "losers," the same men who get left behind in schools, jobs, and other forms of social competition. The discriminatory social, economic, and racial impact of Vietnam cannot be fairly measured against other wars in American history, but the American people were never before as conscious of how unevenly the obligation to serve was distributed. Few of the nation's elite had sons or close friends who did any fighting. Leslie Fiedler, commenting about his university community, wrote that he

> had never known a single family that had lost a son in Vietnam, or indeed, one with a son wounded, missing in action, or held prisoner of war. And this despite the fact that American casualties in Vietnam are already almost equal to those of World War I. Nor am I alone in my strange plight; in talking to friends about a subject they seem eager not to discuss, I discover they can, they must, all say the same. . . .

The racial inequities became a major scandal of the late 1960s. General S. L. A. Marshall commented that he had seen

> too many of our battalions come out of line after hard struggle and heavy loss. In the average rifle company, the strength was 50% composed of Negroes, Southwestern Mexicans, Puerto Ricans, Guamanians, Nisei, and so on. But a real cross-section of American youth? Almost never.

At the end of World War II, blacks comprised 12 percent of all combat troops; by the start of the Vietnam war, their share had grown to 31 percent. In 1965, blacks accounted for 24 percent of all Army combat deaths. The Defense Department undertook a concerted campaign to reduce the minorities' share of the fighting. That share was reduced to 16 percent in 1966, and 13 percent in 1968. In 1970, the figure for all services was under 9 percent.

Over the course of the war, minorities did more than their share of the fighting and dying. Yet the most serious inequities were social and economic. Poorly educated, low-income whites and poorly educated, low-income blacks together bore a vastly disproportionate share of the burdens of Vietnam. The Notre Dame survey found that men from disadvantaged backgrounds were about twice as likely as their better-off peers to serve in the military, go to Vietnam, and see combat. (See the table below.) These were the men President Eisenhower once called "sitting ducks" for the draft.

LIKELIHOOD OF VIETNAM-ERA SERVICE

	Military Service	Vietnam Service	Combat Service
Low-Income	40%	19%	15%
Middle-Income	30%	12%	7%
High-Income	24%	9%	7%
High-School Dropouts	42%	18%	14%
High-School Graduates	45%	21%	17%
College Graduates	23%	12%	9%

The government did not undertake any wartime studies of the social and economic incidence of military service. The only contemporary evidence was scattered and anecdotal. A 1965–66 survey discovered that college graduates made up only 2 percent of all draftees. Congressman Alvin O'Konski took a personal survey of one hundred inductees from his northern Wisconsin district. Not one of them came from a family with an annual income of over $5,000. A Harvard *Crimson* editor from the class of 1970 tallied his twelve hundred classmates and counted only fifty-six who entered the military, just two of whom went to Vietnam. By contrast, thirty-five men from the Harvard class of 1941 died in World War II, and hundreds more saw combat duty. Not many

Vietnam-era troops were college graduates, and even the relatively few who joined the service had a better-than-normal chance of avoiding Vietnam.

After the war was over, however, the evidence began to mount. Postwar Army records showed that an enlisted man who was a college graduate had a 42 percent chance of going to Vietnam, versus a 64 percent chance for a high-school graduate and a 70 percent chance for a high-school dropout. Surveys in Long Island, Wisconsin, and Salt Lake City found a very heavy incidence of combat deaths among disadvantaged youths. In the most significant study thus far, Gilbert Badillo and David Curry analyzed casualties suffered by Chicago neighborhoods with different socioeconomic characteristics. They discovered that youths from low-income neighborhoods were three times as likely to die in Vietnam as youths from high-income neighborhoods. They also found youths from neighborhoods with low educational levels to be four times as likely to die in Vietnam as youths from better-educated neighborhoods.

During World War II, conscription and combat service were matters of personal honor. Men bent the rules to get into military service. Patriotism knew no class boundaries; Winthrop Rockefeller and the president of the New York Stock Exchange volunteered to be among the first ten thousand to submit to induction. Returning veterans were public heroes. Prisoners of war were more an embarrassment than the object of national pride. But among the tragic ironies of Vietnam, the only real heroes of the war were POWs. Ordinarily, they were not members of the younger generation; they were Air Force and Navy pilots, officers well beyond draft age. The youths returning as combat veterans were easily forgotten.

America was not winning the war, and many people were ashamed of what was happening. With the war calling into question so much of America's self-esteem, and with so many young men resisting the war, the nation needed assurance that patriotism still had meaning. Draft resisters and deserters thus became the folk villains of the times. John Geiger of the American Legion spoke for a great many Americans when he called them "a mixture of victims of error, deliberate conspirators, and professional criminals." Their detractors insisted that their numbers were small—Richard Nixon referred to them as "those few hundreds"—and that the judicial system dealt with them swiftly and severely. None of this was true, but it helped reaffirm traditional values.

The national conscience was also salved by comparing the cowardice of draft resisters and deserters with the courage of combat soldiers. This helped blind the nation to the fact that 25 million men of military age did not serve in Vietnam, and that relatively few were touched directly by the sacrifices of those who did.

After the fighting was over, draft resisters and deserters served one last, tragic purpose. They became scapegoats, much like Eddie Slovik, the only soldier executed for desertion in World War II. Slovik was a misfit totally incapable of being a combat soldier. He performed so poorly in basic training that his commanding officer tried, without success, to get him discharged or transferred to a noncombat unit. Slovik never actually ran away, but he confessed to desertion as a way of staying out of the fighting. On the day of his execution, a few months before the end of the war, Slovik told a reporter, "They are not shooting me for deserting the U.S. Army. Thousands of guys have done that. They just need to make an example out of somebody, and I'm it."

Those who feel a deep, unarticulated resentment about what happened to America in Vietnam have made whipping boys of the draft resisters and deserters. They are the ones to blame for the tragedy of a lost war and lost illusions, symbols of the nation's lack of resolve to win. For those who condemn the antiauthoritarian values of the generation, the resisters and deserters represent the worst of a bad lot. For those who suffered personal tragedies in the war, these are the men who should have gone in place of loved ones.

As important a symbol as the draft resisters and deserters have been, Americans know little about them. They are, like the draftees who saw combat, society's "losers"—disproportionately black, poorly educated youths from low-income families. Had they been better advised or more clever, most could have found one of the escape routes used by so many others. The disadvantaged not only did more than their share of the fighting; they also paid too much of the penalty for not fighting.

Vietnam-era draft and military offenders number more than a million. An estimated 570,000 men committed draft violations that could have sent them to prison for five years. Yet fewer than half were reported to federal prosecutors, only some 25,000 were indicted, and fewer than 9,000 convicted. Just 3,250 went to prison, most of whom were paroled within a year. In the military, a quarter of a million men were punished with Undesirable, Bad Conduct, or Dishonorable Discharges, branding them as deserters or military criminals of other sorts. Yet only 13 percent of them were convicted by court-martial, and even they seldom spent more than a few months in prison. Another 300,000 servicemen were sent home with General Discharges, which are technically given "under honorable conditions," although they are nonetheless a handicap in these men's search for jobs.

A great many escaped the brunt of the law because of legal or administrative problems. More than 100,000 draft cases were dismissed because of draft boards' failure to obey court-imposed rules. The overburdened military justice system gave 130,000 servicemen undesirable discharges as plea bargains, sparing the armed forces the expense of trying and imprisoning them. But, in part, this leniency reflected the views of many prosecutors, judges, and military officers that these individuals did not deserve the stiff punishments the public thought they were getting.

It is inaccurate to assume that the "evaders," as a group, did anything fundamentally worse than their 24 million peers who also escaped Vietnam, but by legal means. The term "evader" says little about each individual's attitude toward his responsibility to serve in the military. A great many men who legally avoided combat service would have been evaders had the necessity arisen; the Notre Dame survey found that 15 percent of all draft avoiders would have seriously considered breaking the law if that had been their only recourse. As one resister commented, "Almost every kid in this country [was] either a draft evader, a potential draft evader, or a failed draft evader." According to Michael Brophy, a Milwaukee draft counselor, the epithet has been misapplied:

> To evade is to avoid something by deceitful means. The draft evaders are in the Reserves and the National Guard, seminaries, and other educational institutions. . . . A man who [breaks the law] may do so to avoid the draft, but he is not deceiving anyone.

The opprobrium of "evader" is inappropriate for large categories of Vietnam-era offenders. About one-third of all draft resisters could have avoided the draft through deferments, exemptions, and legal loopholes, but they insisted on accepting exile or punishment as the consequence of their beliefs. One-fifth of all deserters never actually evaded Vietnam service. They finished full combat tours before running afoul of military discipline back home, often because of postcombat readjustment problems.

The law has worked its will on these men. By the mid-1970s, all but a few thousand had paid the legal penalty. They were prosecuted, punished, and officially forgiven. Still, the question remains whether the American people will continue to condemn them.

Until Americans evaluate the conduct of these men in the context of the entire generation's response to the war, there can never be any real understanding of the tragedy of Vietnam. The memory of the war may be too bitter for any to be cast as heroes. But perhaps the American people can begin to understand the extent to which so many young men, veterans and law breakers alike, were victims. And, with the passage of time, critics of the generation may stop setting victim against victim, fixing blame that only exacerbates the tragedy of the war.

Vietnam wrought havoc on millions of lives in a manner that most Americans may never understand. The war was, at root, the personal calamity of the generation called upon to fight it. They are the ones who faced the terrible choices, and they are the ones who suffered. "You were damned if you did go and damned if you didn't," said Ursula Diliberto, whose son was killed in Vietnam two weeks before the end of his tour. "My son was a victim, my family was a victim, all boys of draft age were victims in one way or another."

II | AVOIDERS

Channeling

In the summer of 1968, Paul Milligan received an induction order from his Des Moines draft board. On the day he reported, no military transport was available to take him to Fort Polk for basic training, so he was given a job for the day filing case histories in the local draft office. He read about young men who had avoided the draft through one ruse or another. At first, Milligan resented what others had done, but later he began to feel the fool. That night he telephoned his mother: "The whole setup is corrupt. I don't need to *be* here! I don't need to *be* here! I don't need to *be* here! I simply didn't *need* to be drafted!"

Paul Milligan became one of the 2,150,000 draft-age men who went to Vietnam, and was one of the 51,000 of his generation who sacrificed their lives in the war. He had been chosen from among 27 million men by military manpower policies that did not care who was drafted as long as enough people were drafted.

Combat was the basic mission of the war, but even at the height of American involvement fewer than 1 percent of all draft-age men were needed to fight at any one time. For every combat soldier, many others had to perform support functions in Vietnam and in the United States. Troop commitments had to be fulfilled in Germany, Korea, and American bases in other parts of the world. The Navy, Air Force, Coast Guard, and National Guard had to maintain readiness for an emergency. Civilians also had functions to perform for the nation's long-term security. Scientists and engineers had to stay on the job in vital defense industries. Students had to complete their education to become the next generation of doctors, scientists, and engineers, and to provide the quality officer corps needed by a technologically oriented military. Because Vietnam was a limited war, civilian society had to operate with as few disruptions as possible. Family life had to go on, and as many people as possible had to stay financially self-sufficient. And, of course, no person with a severe mental or physical handicap could be asked to do anything beyond his abilities.

That was the plan. Manpower policies were designed to allocate the draft-age generation among these different functions, in addition to combat, the least desirable job in the minds of most young men. The nation might have relied on the marketplace, paying whatever was necessary to attract qualified applicants for every position. But Vietnam was already costly. Even paying combat soldiers the federal minimum wage would have made the war prohibitively expensive. The nation was not ready to experiment with a volunteer military in time of war. Alternatively, selection could have been left to chance, using a lottery to assign men to military service. Eventually, both of these policies were implemented, but too late in the war to make much difference for the draft-age generation. Through most of the war, men were directed into desirable civilian and military avenues through a comprehensive manpower policy that Selective Service Director Lewis B. Hershey called "channeling." The draft system, and to a somewhat lesser extent the armed forces personnel system, used the threat of induction to "channel" people into a variety of more attractive civilian and military pursuits that were considered to be in the national interest.

General Hershey became director of Selective Service in 1947. He had been heavily involved in the total mobilization of World War II, and had seen the nation mortgage its future by depleting its colleges of students and emptying its laboratories of scientists. The lesson of that experience was that future military manpower procurement had to be viewed in a larger context. According to Hershey, "we are [not] so rich in human resources that we can afford deliberately to ignore opportunities we have to channel people into training and the application of training."

The Selective Service, in Hershey's view, was an instrument of human resource planning, exerting "pressurized guidance" to encourage young people to enter and remain in study, in critical occupations, and in other activities in the national health, safety and interest. . . . The psychology of granting wide choice under pressure to take action is the American or indirect way of achieving what is done by direction in foreign countries where choice is not permitted. . . . From the individual's viewpoint, he is standing in a room which has been made uncomfortably warm. Several doors are open, but they all lead to various forms of recognized, patriotic service to the Nation. Some accept the alternatives gladly—some with reluctance. The consequence is approximately the same. . . . The club of induction [could thereby drive men] out of areas considered to be less important to the areas of greater importance in which deferments were given.

During General Hershey's tenure, he expanded the functions of Selective Service so that the drafting of soldiers was only an incidental part of its mission:

> Delivery of manpower for induction . . . is not much of an administrative or financial challenge. It is in dealing with other millions of registrants that the [Selective Service] System is heavily occupied, developing more effective human beings in the national interest.

In his twenty-two years of leadership, Lewis B. Hershey came to personify the draft system much as J. Edgar Hoover did the FBI. He shaped it to his own image, converting what was originally a civilian agency into a paramilitary organization, 90 percent of whose top-ranking officials and state directors were officers in the armed forces. In turn, they appointed local board members with perspectives like their own. At all levels of Selective Service, turnover was low and morale high.

Hershey was a master at the skills of politics and bureaucracy, and for years he withstood attacks by his critics. Four Presidents and a long string of Congresses gave him frequent praise and near-total support. By the 1960s, however, the consequences of one-man rule, low personnel turnover, and a dated philosophy left Selective Service extremely vulnerable to criticism. Hershey might still have weathered the assault had the Vietnam war been more popular. As it was, the controversy about the war put the draft system in the public spotlight, and Hershey was discredited. Reform was exceedingly gradual, however, and the remnants of channeling persisted throughout the war.

General Hershey and other supporters of the traditional system failed to foresee the extent and the implications of the Vietnam generation's compliance with the channeling policy. For seven years, millions of draft-age men looked for doors out of Hershey's "uncomfortably warm" room. Draft critics marshaled their forces and, through a nationwide network of counselors, took advantage of every imaginable weakness in the system. The draft became a sieve for men who got the right advice at the right time, or who were clever enough to wage an independent fight against the system.

Like the tax system, the draft was seen as an instrument of public policy capable of inducing socially acceptable behavior. But unlike the tax system, little care was given to fashion incentives to ensure that lawful avoidance served useful national purposes. And unlike the Internal Revenue Service, the Selective Service System never made a serious effort to keep pace with sophisticated efforts which enabled people to distort the process to their personal advantage.

Aside from giving the armed forces the soldiers needed to fight the war, the draft did little to "channel" a generation of draft-age men in directions that served the national interest. Instead, it created distortion, dislocation, and above all, class discrimination. This cannot be blamed on General Hershey alone; he was merely the most vocal advocate of a manpower policy deeply rooted in American history.

The Civil War provided the first American experience with the draft as part of a national manpower policy. The first Confederate conscription law exempted whole classes of citizens from military service—railway employees, minor government officials, lawyers, newspapermen, schoolteachers, druggists, and others. Plantation overseers were exempted at the rate of one overseer for every twenty slaves, through the notorious "20-Nigger Law." The purpose of these exemptions was to maintain a functioning civilian economy, but the effects were scandalous. Schools were established without pupils, newspapers without readers, and drugstores without customers. Wealthy landowners were able to take advantage of the "20-Nigger Law" to keep their sons home from the front. It was not until late in the war, with the Confederacy facing a shortage of able-bodied men, that most of these exemptions were canceled.

Draft avoidance was rampant in the Union. More than 750,000 names were selected by lot, but only 50,000 were conscripted. In the Confederacy and Union alike, a man could avoid military service by hiring a substitute at a price agreed on by the two. In the North, this served the same purpose as the southern exemption of professionals and plantation overseers; the well-to-do could avoid the draft simply by using the marketplace to their advantage. The fees for substitutes ran as high as $1,500 in the Union and $600 in the Confederacy, the equivalent of several years' earnings for most. The Union policy prompted draft riots in many states, including one in New York City that caused 1,200 deaths. The Confederacy abandoned this practice entirely in 1863, but the Union made it cheaper and easier by enabling any person to avoid the draft by paying a $300 fee.

In 1866, General James Oakes, assessing the experience of the Union draft, recommended that any future system be administered by civilian boards composed of friends and neighbors of draft-eligible men to assure that decisions would be fairly made. His report lay dormant for fifty years, but it was the origin of twentieth-century America's conscription policies.

The 1917 Selective Service Act created a structure of local boards, deferments, and exemptions as an integral part of the World War I system of conscription. According to President Wilson, the draft had to be used as a comprehensive manpower policy so that Americans could

speak, act, and serve together. . . . The nation needs all men, but it needs each man not in the field that will most pleasure him, but in the endeavor that will best serve the common good. . . . People who work in deferred occupations will be serving the country and conducting the fight for peace and freedom as effectively as the men in the trenches.

More than half of those in the first draft call of World War I made formal claims for exemption, usually for occupational or physical reasons. A hundred thousand shipbuilders were given a blanket exemption because of the need to enlarge the nation's merchant fleet. So many registrants had their teeth extracted to avoid induction that the War Department publicly warned that dentists could be prosecuted for aiding draft evasion. A "Student Army Training Corps" enabled 145,000 students to defer their service for three years; by the time deferments had expired, the war was over. Throughout the war, no one was reclassified from his original deferment or exemption, no matter how much his personal circumstances had changed.

By all contemporary accounts, the World War I draft was a great success. It registered nearly 24,000,000 men, and it drafted 2,700,000 soldiers, two-thirds of the manpower needed to fight the war. The only acknowledged problems were nonregistration and "draft desertion," the willful refusal of induction. Two years after the war was over, the War Department tallied 325,000 individuals who were still wanted for those offenses. Those who could not be found and those whose offenses were not considered "willful" were given military discharges *in absentia* ("this man . . . performed no military service whatsoever . . .") and forgotten.

World War II required a much more complete mobilization. In all, 10 million men were drafted. Only the most essential jobs in war industries qualified for exemptions, but a great many draft-age men maneuvered their way into deferred jobs or safe military duty at the homefront. As General Hershey recalled, "we deferred more damn people to build battleships." The most common way to avoid World War II was to fail the preinduction physical exam. Almost one-third of all registrants were exempted for physical, emotional, or mental defects; in some southern states, the rejection rate exceeded 50 percent.

Student deferments were a matter of considerable controversy before World War II. In France and England, college students had been among the first to fight and die in World War I. This left these countries with severe shortages of skilled professionals and potential leaders. America did not want to repeat that mistake, so the 1940 draft law deferred anyone whose activity was considered essential to the nation's welfare. Higher education was included in the definition, and more than 100,000 college students were deferred when the Japanese attacked

Pearl Harbor. As manpower needs increased, however, student deferments were restricted to men preparing for critical occupations in
engineering, science, and medicine. Some inductees were assigned to
college ROTC units, but the overall college enrollment tumbled
sharply. By 1944, the male college population was less than one-third
its prewar level.

When the war ended, there was widespread concern that the nation's
survival had been jeopardized by the depletion of the colleges. One
prominent scientist accused World War II draft policies of causing
"great difficulty and hazard to the war effort itself" by impeding the
nation's ability to assemble highly qualified people for such tasks as
the Manhattan Project's atomic bomb research. Another observed
that the war had left the United States in a poor position to compete
with the Soviet Union in the postwar era: "We were extremely fortunate that the war years were followed by a five-year period of peace
which, combined with the GI Bill, allowed us to recover at least in
part from this serious mistake [of not deferring college students]."

The postwar years witnessed a spirited debate between the advocates
of universal military training, including President Truman, and advocates of a limited system of conscription. The debate was framed entirely in terms of national priorities, with little attention given such
notions as social equity or individual liberty. The line between civilian
and military service to the country was never more blurred. President
Truman acknowledged that universal military training had only an
"incidental" military purpose, as its real goals were "to develop skills
that could be used in civilian life, . . . to develop citizenship responsibilities, and to foster the moral and spiritual welfare of our young people."
The other side argued for World War I–style policies that would meet
military and civilian needs at the same time, without expanding the size
of the armed forces.

The latter side won the debate, and one of its chief proponents—
Lewis B. Hershey—was appointed director of Selective Service. At
about the same time (1948), Congress enacted America's first peacetime
conscription law. The President was authorized to defer any category
of persons whose activity he deemed essential to the national interest.
The new law also created two special enlistment options for draft-age

men who wanted to minimize their risk of combat. Eighteen-year-olds were allowed to enlist for one year, and anyone could avoid induction by joining the reserves for six years. But the most significant new feature was the student deferment. Congress had rejected a specific proposal to defer all students until graduation, not wanting to engage in what one member called "a highly preferential action which would benefit only the sons of wealthy men." However, a special committee of educators convinced President Truman that college students should be selected for deferment on the basis of their performance, and given four months after graduation to find employment that would qualify them for further deferments. Starting in 1950, college students could avoid the draft either by ranking in the top half of their class or by scoring well on a special aptitude test. Within a year, more than three-fourths of the nation's college students were deferred or exempted from the draft.

These expanded deferments and exemptions survived the Korean War intact. Even though 1,500,000 men were drafted between 1951 and 1953, enlistments and reserve call-ups were large enough to ease the pressure on the overall manpower supply. College graduates joined the service, typically as officers, in rough proportion to their numbers. Throughout the 1950s and early 1960s, the main criticism of the channeling concept was that the underprivileged were too often barred from the benefits of military service by unrealistically high mental and physical standards.

Special interest groups sprang to the support of deferments and exemptions every time there was talk of a change. Medical, scientific, engineering, union, and farm organizations were covetous of occupational deferments. According to General Hershey, "Business was all over my back, agriculture wanted this that and the other thing, and education wanted their PhD's." The Scientific Manpower Commission suggested in 1955 that the military obligation be eliminated altogether for men trained in science and engineering. Educators joined the National Student Association in arguing vigorously on behalf of student deferments, warning that their removal could have "a devastating effect on the morale of the campuses and on the financial integrity of institutions."

Between 1954 and 1964, draft quotas were low. The operating policy was to draft all or almost all registrants classified as available for immediate induction (I-A). In this way Selective Service maintained the fiction of a universal obligation for all registrants. The draft system then controlled the size of the I-A pool by liberalizing the rules for exemptions and deferments. Preinduction physical rejection rates reached all-time highs. Deferment for postgraduate study was allowed for the first time, and the total number of all student deferments grew by 900 percent between 1951 and 1966. The most important new development was the expansion of hardship and dependency deferments to include fatherhood. General Hershey defended these deferments as necessary "to strengthen the Nation's civilian economy . . . [and to] foster the family life of the Nation."

By 1963, the draft system faced an unusual problem: the number of draft-eligible men was increasing as the postwar baby boom matured, and Selective Service was running out of defensible ways to limit its I-A pool. The notion of the draft as a universal obligation was in immediate jeopardy. A lottery was one possible solution, but Hershey strongly resisted the idea. In his eyes, the difference between the existing system and a lottery was "at bottom the difference between a human being and a machine. The people on local boards have more compassion than a machine . . . [which] cannot tell whether a man is more valuable as a father or student or scientist or doctor than as a soldier."

Hershey convinced President Kennedy to put all married men in a special low-priority I-A category, and the problem was averted. By 1966, hardship, fatherhood, and marital deferments outnumbered student deferments by almost two to one. Draft calls remained relatively low, however, and a Selective Service official acknowledged that "we have got more people than we can induct unless the inductions go up."

President Johnson's escalation of the Vietnam war solved this problem. Almost immediately, monthly draft calls rose from fewer than ten thousand to more than thirty thousand. So rapid was the escalation that Selective Service soon found itself with a shortage of I-A registrants. Even the large numbers of the baby-boom generation could not prevent retrenchment from the exemptions and deferments of the preceding fifteen years. Occupational deferments were made harder to get. Fatherhood deferments were limited to those who had never been granted student deferments. Most draft boards no longer gave new deferments to married men and graduate students, but registrants who already held them were generally allowed to keep them.

Selective Service resumed its Korean-era practice of limiting student deferments to those with good grades or high scores on a special aptitude test. A college student with a low class ranking had to take the Selective Service Qualifying Test, which General Hershey admitted was "cocked over toward the mathematical, because it's easier to grade for one thing." Three-quarters of a million students took the test in 1966 and 1967, and many who scored poorly were reclassified and drafted. The test became a rallying point for antiwar activists, who boycotted it and threatened sabotage by shouting answers aloud in the exam room. An antiwar National Vietnam Examination was published, with questions like "Who said 'I have only one hero—Hitler'? (Answer: South Vietnam President Nguyen Cao Ky)." Eventually, Selective Service abandoned the special test, and educational deferments remained available to college students who maintained respectable grades.

The Vietnam war put unaccustomed pressure on the nation's four thousand local draft boards, who had long understood the necessity of applying the rules flexibly. One draft board member described the system as "sort of like an accordion. Sometimes you stretch it out and get generous with deferments, and then other times you squeeze it up tight." Before the war escalated, most draft boards had willingly given deferments and exemptions to anyone who presented a reasonable case; when faced with borderline cases, they tended to give registrants the benefit of the doubt. Social scientist Roger Little observed a number of boards at work, learning that "many cases considered 'too hot,' 'too puzzling,' or 'too troublesome' [were] handled by granting a deferment with the statement that 'he's got several years to go to reach 26, so we'll try to nail him later.'" Once the Vietnam escalation began, the benefit of the doubt was not given so easily.

Despite the rapidly changing environment in which Selective Service now functioned, General Hershey resisted reform. Local boards consisted predominantly of older, white, middle-class men with military backgrounds from World Wars I and II. Part-time, unpaid volunteers, they were poorly trained and ill-equipped to cope with a decentralized system of subjective decision-making in the midst of unprecedented challenges. But Hershey refused to issue specific rules that would intrude upon local discretion. "Once you train them, once they learn the business, you can't meddle around in their affairs," he observed. He remained confident that board members knew enough about each registrant "to know whether he is putting something over on them."

Draft board meetings were typically held one or two evenings a month. During each meeting, board members had to determine the appropriate classification for hundreds, even thousands, of young men. They were usually able to spend only a few moments on each case and relied heavily on the recommendations of their clerks, who were lower-grade civil service employees.

Left to their own devices, the four thousand draft boards developed four thousand very different policies. Each board's monthly induction quota bore only a loose relationship to the size of its total manpower pool, and its day-to-day interpretation of the rules was often strongly affected by its own administrative requirements. Consciously or not, a board's policy usually reflected its members' traditional values, treating deferments and exemptions as rewards for young men who shared these values. According to Roger Little,

> Registrants were often lectured or quizzed on the values of thrift, hard work, obedience to the law, morality, and concern for parents. . . . They probed into many irrelevant aspects of the registrants' lives in an effort to find something on which to base a decision. Typical queries were such as these: "What do you do with your spare time?" "You don't like to submit to authority, do you?" "What kind of car do you drive?" "Were you ever in the Boy Scouts?"

As implemented by the local boards, channeling became less a means of allocating manpower to different beneficial national pursuits than a means of enforcing a set of political and social mores. Roger Little heard comments like the following:

"You ought to see this guy. . . . Well, this is the sort of guy you would take down to the latrine and scrub down with a wire brush. . . . Let's make this baby I-A. We'll fix his trolley."

This distortion of channeling reached an extreme with the practices of punitive reclassification and accelerated induction employed by Selective Service to enforce the government's Vietnam policy. In December 1965, thirty-five University of Michigan students staged a sit-in at the Ann Arbor draft board, and General Hershey recommended that they be drafted as a lesson to other would-be demonstrators: "Reclassification is quicker at stopping sit-ins than some indictment that takes effect six months later." Within a month, several of the Ann Arbor students lost their student deferments.

The policy of punitive reclassification used Hershey's "club of induction" as retaliation against dissenters who opposed an unpopular war. The armed forces strongly resisted the idea of military service as punishment, prompting Hershey to comment, "I'm as popular as a bastard at a family reunion with the military because they don't want to run a correctional institution. But they have the know-how to teach discipline." Many judges agreed with Hershey that military service was a good way to rehabilitate social misfits and petty criminals. They sometimes gave convicted offenders a choice between joining the military or going to jail. Before appeals courts rejected these practices, thousands of war resisters and convicted criminals were channeled into uniform.

Under pressure from the courts, draft boards increasingly took exactly the opposite approach with registrants they considered to be troublemakers. A good strategy for avoiding the draft was to harass local boards with antiwar leaflets, postage-due packages with bricks inside, or letters declaring an intent to refuse induction. Roger Little found that draft boards often responded by putting the registrant "into some slot . . . [where] he was no longer problematic for them." Mark Rudd, the leader of Students for a Democratic Society at the height of the war, asked his draft board for an occupational deferment as a professional revolutionary. His board refused, declaring that his occupation was not "in the national health, safety, or interest," whereupon Rudd advised them that he intended to pursue the same occupation in the Army. He was later found physically unfit under circumstances which suggested that his draft board was eager to keep him out of the military.

General Hershey's ill-fated effort to use the draft to punish his critics galvanized national opposition to his administration of Selective Service. But it was the treatment of conscientious objection that set in motion the forces that eventually undermined the system Hershey had created over the course of two decades.

Before the Vietnam war, courts had given local boards considerable leeway in making classification decisions, including requests for CO exemptions. Combined with the vague rules issued by headquarters, this led many boards to feel that they enjoyed total discretion in deciding these cases. Different standards were applied by every local board. For example, Lake Charles, Louisiana, had three draft boards: one gave CO exemptions to almost every applicant, another gave them to no one, and the third looked at the merits of each case.

The draft system quickly got into trouble with the courts for its casual procedures and inconsistent treatment of CO applicants. The resulting court-imposed rules had to be applied to all cases, not just to conscientious objectors. By the late 1960s, draft boards had to grant full due-process safeguards in every case to make their induction orders safe from legal challenge. This made them inclined to defer, exempt, or simply ignore registrants who presented legal or administrative problems, and they concentrated their attention on other, more easily draftable people.

In effect, stricter procedural requirements created a new door out of General Hershey's "uncomfortably warm" room. At the height of the war, the rules for setting deferments and exemptions had become so technical that the draft system worked more than ever to the advantage of the astute.

By 1969, the pressure on the manpower supply began to ease; draft calls peaked, and the number of draft-vulnerable men was increasing sharply. But unlike earlier times, Congress and the public were unwilling to let Selective Service keep the system in balance by liberalizing deferments and exemptions. In fact, the draft had by this time become so discredited that the public was demanding a fundamental restructuring of the system. General Hershey was replaced by Curtis Tarr, and the path was clear for the introduction of the Vietnam war's first draft lottery, the end to student and occupational deferments, and the post-war abolition of conscription.

Under Tarr's leadership, Selective Service sought to regain the trust that had been lost over the past several years. However, many problems continued unabated, and the draft still had an "open door" quality. Tarr's reforms did not stem the flood of judicial challenges and the resulting overlay of legal technicalities that the courts imposed on local boards. Knowledge about the draft's vulnerability to sophisticated legal attack continued to spread, and registrants increasingly sought help from skilled draft attorneys. As it became evident that the war was winding down, more and more draft-age men began to realize that they could outlast the war by exercising their legal rights and slowing down the processing of their cases.

With the reduction in American combat involvement and the lowering of draft calls, local boards could ignore complicated cases and be lax about reclassifying those whose deferments had expired. They still had more than enough I-A registrants to meet monthly quotas. Induction stations stiffened the physical standards, and the nationwide rejection rate jumped from 37 percent in 1967 to 58 percent in 1973.

One of the most remarkable escapes of the Vietnam-era draft was a direct result of the reforms that followed Hershey. It was, as one draft counselor called it, the "great lottery loophole." President Nixon was determined to abolish student deferments in 1971, but he did it in a way that enabled the entire freshman class to escape the draft permanently. With the 1972 election just a year away, Nixon's motive may have been political. He was able to take credit for making the draft more equitable without actually drafting college students, which might have alienated a large bloc of newly enfranchised eighteen-year-old voters.

This loophole resulted from a bizarre combination of bureaucratic technicalities. In late September of 1971, Congress passed amendments to the Selective Service law giving the President the power to terminate student deferments. By the time the deferments were actually abolished on December 10, all induction orders for the calendar year had been issued, so no student could be drafted until January. Under the rules of the lottery, individuals who lost deferments late in the calendar year could not be drafted any later than March of the following year. However, there were no induction calls for January, February, or March of 1972. As a result, no member of the freshman class of 1971 could legally have been issued an induction order, even if his lottery number was 1. More than 600,000 men with low lottery numbers benefited from this combination of events.

The December 28 announcement by Secretary of Defense Melvin Laird that there would be no draft calls in early 1972 was an unexpected Christmas gift for tens of thousands more who held other kinds of deferments. There was a nationwide scramble to drop deferments before the December 31 deadline for 1971 draft vulnerability passed. Bulletins were posted everywhere, phone lines to draft boards were jammed, and last-minute appeals were made at New Year's Eve parties urging people voluntarily to renounce their deferments. Many who took advantage of this loophole were the most hopeless cases, the ones who otherwise had no alternatives to the draft but prison or Canada.

The final quirk of the draft came, fittingly enough, during the last induction call of the war. Three hundred men were ordered to report to various induction stations on December 28, 1972. But the twenty-eighth was declared a national day of mourning for Harry Truman, who had just died. Those who reported on the twenty-eighth were sent home to await further instructions, which never came. Secretary Laird announced the end of the draft less than a month later.

Artful Dodgers

Many of the 16 million men who escaped the draft during Vietnam were just plain lucky. Some were the beneficiaries of a poorly administered system which lost or mishandled their cases. Four million were fortunate enough to get high lottery numbers. Millions more, as Figure 2 (pp. 30–31) indicates, were excused because of hardship, family dependency, physical, or mental reasons. For most, the structure of deferments and exemptions worked to their benefit without requiring them to take any significant steps to manipulate the system.

Yet the draft's channeling policy encouraged individuals to take fate in their own hands by rearranging their personal circumstances. According to the Notre Dame survey, three-quarters of those who never served admitted that they tried to avoid the draft. A majority (55 percent) believed that the action they took may have been responsible for keeping them out of the military.

Many, of course, did nothing more than exercise their legitimate rights under the law. They applied for deferments, documented cases for physical exemptions, applied for CO status, or made other claims and appeals. But others took far more drastic steps, often under the impression that they had no other alternative. To stay away from Vietnam, they "channeled" themselves in directions that were in neither the country's interests nor their own.

Many young men went to college solely to escape the draft. Nationwide enrollment statistics throughout the Vietnam years, along with the findings of the Notre Dame survey, suggest that male college enrollment averaged 6–7 percent higher than normal because of the draft. Additionally, 12 percent of the survey respondents said the draft kept them from taking one or more years off from college to work or travel, and another 5 percent changed their courses of study to keep their deferments. A student deferment was not a permanent escape, because it was almost always necessary for a student to acquire some other deferment or exemption between graduation and age twenty-six, when vulnerability ended.* Without these deferments, however, millions of college students would have faced induction before they got high lottery numbers or discovered other ways to work the system to their advantage.

The importance of II-S deferments to college students was demonstrated by a prank at Emory University. One day in 1966, the college humor magazine took over the newspaper presses, printing a special edition to announce that Selective Service had ordered local boards to deny deferments to all Emory students. In the hours before the prank

---

*Legally, a registrant was vulnerable to age thirty-five if he had ever received a deferment, but only in a true national emergency. During the Vietnam era, no person was drafted unless he received an induction order before his twenty-sixth birthday.

FIGURE 2: CIVILIAN AVOIDERS

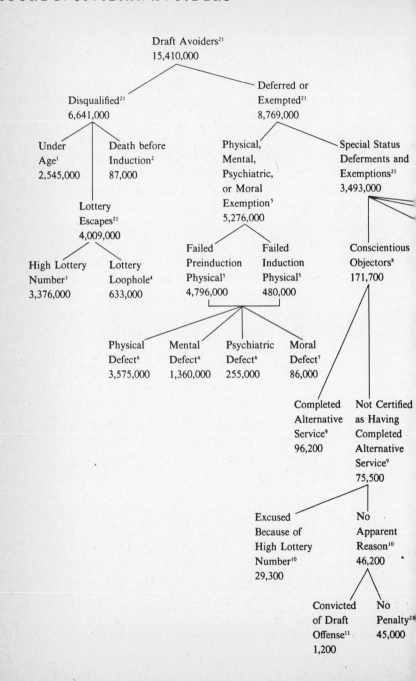

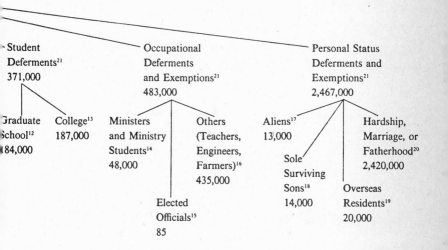

Student
Deferments[21]
371,000

Occupational
Deferments
and Exemptions[21]
483,000

Personal Status
Deferments and
Exemptions[21]
2,467,000

Graduate
School[12]
184,000

College[13]
187,000

Ministers
and Ministry
Students[14]
48,000

Others
(Teachers,
Engineers,
Farmers)[16]
435,000

Aliens[17]
13,000

Hardship,
Marriage, or
Fatherhood[20]
2,420,000

Sole
Surviving
Sons[18]
14,000

Overseas
Residents[19]
20,000

Elected
Officials[15]
85

was discovered, a number of students telephoned or mailed applications for immediate transfer to schools they thought were not affected by the order.

Before 1968, graduate schools were also havens from the draft. Three or four years in graduate school were often enough to enable a man to reach the magic age of twenty-six. In 1966 and 1967, graduate schools were besieged with draft-motivated requests for admission. The head of one well-known graduate school of business administration took a personal survey of twelve hundred male candidates for admission and found that 90 percent had applied at least partly because of the draft. Noting how the Vietnam-era draft affected higher education in the exact opposite way from the World War II draft, General Hershey said that "I feel very good about a lot of these draft-dodging PhD's, but there were some that didn't have a brain in their head. God help us."

After the end of graduate school deferments in 1967, divinity schools became increasingly popular as draft shelters—especially those that did not require strict sectarian courses of study. Some Jewish yeshivas were ideal; they offered a complete range of secular degrees, enabling students to study what they pleased while their draft boards believed they were preparing to be rabbis.

According to the channeling theory, the national interest justified inducing men to further their education. However, many university officials accused the II-S deferment of having a corrupting influence on their institutions, perhaps even contributing to the campus unrest of the period. The baby boom, along with a rapid expansion in higher education facilities, put a strain on the job market for educated people. The draft simply added to the problem.

The employment picture was especially bleak in fields like engineering or teaching, which earned almost automatic deferments from draft boards. By the late 1960s, both fields were glutted with recent college graduates. In 1968, the year New York City draft boards confirmed that all full-time teachers qualified for deferments, the city's board of education received twenty thousand more applications for teachers' licenses than the year before. By 1969, 85 percent of New York City's teacher trainees were draft-age men, and some city universities were reporting an 800 percent increase in men taking teacher education courses. Nor was this phenomenon limited to education and teaching. Ten percent of the Notre Dame survey respondents admitted that the draft influenced their choice of careers.

As an instrument of human resource allocation, the draft produced personal as well as social distortions. Bob Johnson lost his student deferment when he graduated from Yale, and his Maryland draft board promised him an occupational deferment if he taught science at a local high school. Johnson wanted to go to graduate school to study chemistry, but he decided to teach school as long as necessary to stay out of the war. By the time his draft vulnerability had passed, Johnson had married and become a father; it was too late for him to go back to school.

Altering one's family circumstances offered another way to avoid the draft. Military pay was low throughout the war, and most draft boards gave hardship deferments to people who provided the sole support for widowed mothers, younger brothers and sisters, or other dependents. A person could qualify for a deferment by inviting an unemployed or disabled dependent to live in his house. It was not necessary to be poor; George Hamilton, the actor, received a hardship deferment because his mother lived in his Hollywood mansion and relied on his $200,000 income for support.

Two common stratagems were what President Eisenhower called "babying out" and its corollary, "marrying out." Ten percent of the Notre Dame survey respondents—three of every ten fathers—said that their decision to have children was influenced by the draft. This was especially common among men who never went to college. Special draft treatment for married men existed only between 1963 and 1966; during those years, there was an immediate 10 percent rise in the marriage rates for twenty- and twenty-one-year-olds. Many marriages were hastily arranged. Colonel Harry Smith, the Georgia state director of Selective Service, recalled one week in which forty-six men who had been ordered to report for induction suddenly got married. Six percent of the Notre Dame survey respondents—one of every eight husbands—admitted that they married early as a means of avoiding the draft.

The preinduction physical, in addition to its basic function of excluding the unfit from military service, was considered a valuable means of identifying young people with serious untreated physical problems. A government manpower report, "One Third of a Nation," even hinted that the process could be used to direct people to the medical care they needed. But instead of helping identify the medically unfit, it gave the medically fit another way to avoid the draft. According to the Notre Dame survey, the preinduction screening process drove almost a million men to manipulate their health as a way of avoiding the draft. Many of their ploys were harmless, like jabbing forearms with pins to fake a heroin problem. But some tried so hard to be convincing that they risked serious harm to themselves; for example, some men injected heroin to make the addiction "act" harder to uncover.

There were dozens of ways to get an exemption by abusing one's body. Individuals who suffered from asthma, allergies, and other minor ailments often aggravated their conditions right before their physicals. Some athletes with old joint injuries deliberately reinjured themselves, hoping they would later reheal. A common tactic was to gain or lose enough weight to get outside the military standards. A University of Michigan football player ate three large pizzas every night for six months, gaining 125 pounds and the sought-for physical exemption. The grandson of a Russian immigrant pushed his body to extreme limits by staying awake for over a week before taking his preinduction physical. He could have avoided the draft in easier ways, but he felt honor-bound to use the same technique his grandfather had used to avoid conscription in the Russian army.

Some were so desperate to avoid Vietnam that they willingly suffered permanent injury. The easiest way to do this was by slicing off half a thumb, or by asking a friend to punch one's nose hard enough to cause a deviated septum. A nineteen-year-old shot himself in the foot with a .22 caliber rifle, smashing several bones and leaving himself with a permanent limp. Another youth partially blinded himself by staring at the sun.

One little-known evasion tactic, capitalizing on a loophole in the registration rules, bore an ironic similarity to the action that thousands took who fled the country illegally to avoid the draft. If a young man left the United States after his eighteenth birthday and stayed away, he faced a serious threat of prosecution for draft evasion. But if he left before turning eighteen, he acted within the law. All eighteen-year-olds living abroad were required to register with Draft Board #100 in Washington, D.C. Until mid-1971, Selective Service regulations did not allow Draft Board #100 to induct any of its registrants as long as they stayed outside the country. Teenage exiles were not the only ones who took advantage of this loophole. Sons of overseas military personnel and corporate officials were able to avoid the draft simply by going to foreign universities until they were twenty-six.

At the height of the war, Draft Board #100 had twenty-eight thousand registrants and was drafting only about two hundred per year. One board member admitted that "an awful lot of kids played games with us." By the time the law was changed in mid-1971, most of the Draft Board #100 registrants who might earlier have been drafted had turned twenty-six, had high lottery numbers, or were able to stall out the war with help from draft counselors. No one knows why this loophole ever existed, but one board member said, "It would have been unfair to make these boys travel thousands of miles just to report for induction."

In this generation-wide scramble for survival, millions of men were prepared to do whatever was necessary to avoid the war, as long as it was within (or not too far outside) the law. Many of those who manipulated their draft status were given only temporary deferments or exemptions. They were duty-bound, under penalty of law, to inform their local boards of any change in their circumstances. They seldom did.

With the war and its casualties confronting draft avoiders in every newspaper they read and every television news program they watched, many could not ignore the social and ethical implications of their conduct. Milwaukee draft counselor Michael Brophy considered each man's experience with the draft to have been his "rite of passage" into adulthood. For many men, Vietnam was their first test of personal integrity. "The long-term casualties are unbelievable," Brophy recalled. "I know someone who ate six dozen eggs and got an exemption for excessive albumin. Now, for as long as he lives, he has to maintain the lie that he is allergic to eggs." Brophy and other draft counselors still get calls from Vietnam-era clients asking for reassurance that they did the right thing.

Aid and Comfort

Beating the draft was by no means a lonely endeavor; in fact, it became more of a status symbol than did fighting for one's country. "If you are I-A, you are a nobody," observed Congressman Alvin O'Konski. "You happened to get caught because you didn't know any better. If you are not I-A, you have status." President Johnson's daughter Luci defended student efforts to keep their deferments: "Some of the students are fighting just as hard to get their education as . . . you could expect them to." A mother of a draft-deferred son spoke the minds of millions when she boasted of him as "a boy who knows how to take advantage of his opportunities." One of every four Notre Dame survey respondents had parents who openly encouraged him to avoid the draft. Outside the family, people from the most respected elements of society—teachers, employers, doctors, and lawyers—provided important help, without which millions of men might never have stayed out of the military.

Colleges were the main sanctuary from the draft, and many teachers and administrators did what they could to help their students. College grades were referred to as "A, B, C, D, and Nam," and antiwar professors sometimes adjusted their grading policies accordingly: "It's a rotten, stinking war, and I'll be damned if I'll help it along by sending over more cannon fodder. Unless he's clearly an idiot, . . . I intend to pass every able-bodied man in my class." Some professors even gave all A's in their courses, since even a B or C could affect a student's draft status.

The well-connected working man could stay away from Vietnam by getting timely help from the right people. Farmers often convinced draft boards that their sons were essential to the continued operation of the family farm. Plumbers, electricians, and other craftsmen lobbied local boards for automatic deferments for union apprentices. Employers could guarantee deferments for favored employees by designating them as supervisors of four or more full-time workers, making them "indispensable" according to the draft system's rule-of-thumb. Employers wrote letters like the following to local boards: "Braking systems for railroads and mass transit systems have been judged as essential to the welfare and safety of the nation, and our contribution as a primary supplier [is] vital for Selective Service purposes." Rural draft boards regularly granted deferments to truck drivers, laborers, and others whose employers were close friends of board members. A presidential commission reviewing the files of 199 local boards around the country in the late 1960s found that "about half" of all registrants with occupational deferments "were in neither a critical occupation nor an essential industry as defined by the Department of Labor."

Family doctors contributed to the exemption of many long-time patients. Anyone who had seen the same doctor for years had a medical history that was likely to document some kind of physical defect, and most doctors were inclined to cooperate. They gave extra tests to find heart murmurs or other minor conditions that qualified for IV-F or I-Y exemptions. As one doctor commented, "The traditional doctor-patient relationship is one of preserving life. I save lives by keeping people out of the Army." However, some doctors were staunchly against helping patients avoid the draft, even those with grounds for legitimate physical exemptions. One Bloomington, Indiana, doctor promised his patients he would write letters in their behalf, but he confidentially alerted their local boards that they were physically fit, and he urged that they be drafted as punishment.

The primary source of help came from an unprecedented network of counselors, lawyers, and other professionals with special expertise on the draft. More than one-fourth of all Notre Dame survey respondents consulted with experts, many of whom flatly guaranteed that anyone who followed their advice could avoid military service. By the late 1960s, the only real challenge left to the draft was to find the right advice in time.

Draft counseling had its roots in the pacifist movement of earlier wars. Conscientious objectors were the pariahs of the First and Second World Wars; sometimes they were jailed, sometimes they were isolated in special work camps, but always they were looked upon with suspicion by their draft boards and most of the public. Pacifist religious organizations gave them counseling and protected their rights, an unpopular task at the time.

In the early 1960s, these same groups helped establish conscientious objection as a commonly sought alternative to military service. CO exemptions were generally limited to Jehovah's Witnesses, Quakers, and members of other recognized pacifist religions, but a growing number of young people were citing personal, nonsectarian reasons for refusing to take arms. In 1965, the Supreme Court declared in the *Seeger* case that CO exemptions had to be granted to all confirmed pacifists, regardless of their religious backgrounds. To qualify, an individual's beliefs had to conform to legal standards, and he had to convince his local board of his sincerity.

Religious organizations like the Catholic Peace Fellowship and American Friends Service Committee provided the bulk of counseling in the early war years. At first, they concentrated on helping confirmed pacifists, but the growing unpopularity of the war brought an increasing number of "selective objectors" to their offices. These individuals objected only to the Vietnam war and did not qualify for exemption under the law. However, every counselor knew that CO status was only one of several ways of staying out of the military, and they rarely turned away people without giving some helpful advice.

As the war progressed, draft counseling became increasingly comprehensive, expanding well beyond conscientious objection. By the late 1960s, churches, colleges, high schools, and antiwar groups were offering a variety of counseling services. Most cities and university towns had at least one full-time counseling center. The typical center had one bona fide expert on the draft, aided by a number of paraprofessionals who relayed advice to walk-in clients. Some were volunteers, and others were paid out of church funds or donations from people they helped. A few universities hired their own full-time draft counselors, gave them clerical help, and paid for their office space. Through its legal assistance program, the Office of Economic Opportunity provided federal funds to pay salaries of lawyers engaged in draft counseling.

From the earliest days, counselors were enormously successful. Through newsletters and word of mouth, they learned each others' tactics. It was rare for a counselor to have a success rate of under 90 percent. The Catholic Peace Fellowship in New York City advised thousands of draft-age men, and all but a handful received deferments or exemptions. Even in the South and other parts of the country where public sentiment was strongly in favor of the war, counselors did extremely well.

Attorneys made especially good draft counselors. In San Francisco, Los Angeles, and other cities, lawyers' committees steered clients to participating attorneys while providing backup legal services to keep the local bar well ahead of draft boards in its knowledge of the law. Fees were fairly reasonable—usually about $200, and rarely more than $1,000. For anyone who found a competent lawyer, avoiding the draft was virtually assured. William Smith, the chairman of the Los Angeles draft attorneys' panel, told the local press that "any kid with money can absolutely stay out of the Army—with 100 percent certainty." A local prosecutor agreed with him: "If you got the dough, you don't have to go." Attorneys who charged nominal fees could represent hundreds of clients. All that was generally required was a quick interview, a standard letter, and one or two follow-up phone calls.

Expert advisers were not hard to find. They were cross-referenced with local service agencies, covered by the press, and known to most community leaders. Every state except North Dakota had at least one walk-in center, and more than half of all draft-age men had a center within a two-hour drive of their home. At the peak of the war, thousands of lawyers and paraprofessionals were doing draft counseling, serving about a million clients every year.

Most of the clients were surprisingly ill-informed about the draft and unaware of their most fundamental rights under the law. Some knew nothing about deferments or exemptions for which they were obviously qualified. Others were discouraged from filing legitimate claims by draft board clerks who misunderstood the law. Some youths were even mistaken about what their lottery numbers were. Without a visit to a draft counselor, these men might have been drafted or pressured into enlisting in the service.

Frequently, the first question a counselor heard was, "Can I qualify for a CO exemption?" Many draft-age men knew that conscientious objection was one way to avoid the war, but they had little idea about how to apply or how to qualify. The counselors' main role was to help CO applicants articulate and document their beliefs in a way that would convince draft boards of their sincerity. One organization advised people to

> sit down and think about why you are against killing people in war. Write down short sentences or ideas (for instance: love . . . brotherhood . . . peace . . . equality . . . personal responsibility . . .). Let your mind work freely, and you will probably get down on paper most of the ideas that will make a good CO case.

CO applicants were encouraged to get people they knew, especially clergymen, lawyers, or educators, to discuss their beliefs with them, and then write letters of reference attesting to the firmness of their convictions. Clients were sometimes referred to clergymen who were adept at writing letters supporting CO claims. Through schools like the Jane Addams Peace Center in Philadelphia, CO applicants were prepped on the questions that were commonly asked by local draft boards in personal interviews.

Most counselors who specialized in conscientious objection believed that no one could fabricate sincerity, but some draft board members were not so sure. Over time, CO applications became so standardized that it was hard for draft boards to tell who was sincere and who was not. As the chairman of a Denver board complained, "So many of these CO's—you could tell they were so cleverly coached. We could tell outside forces were directing these boys."

In the view of most draft counselors, almost all conscientious objectors were spurred by deep principle, not by a shallow desire to avoid going to war; some even did their alternative service by working for civilian agencies in Vietnam. A large number of CO's were Jehovah's Witnesses, Quakers, Mennonites, Muslims, and others whose churches preached total pacifism. Many others were Catholics who had to overcome their draft boards' knowledge that the Catholic church was not pacifist. One Samoan was exempted by his California draft board because of his sincere belief that if he killed anyone, his pagan god would cause a volcano to erupt. Others belonged to no established religion, but convinced their boards of their moral and ethical opposition to all wars.

However, a few saw conscientious-objector status as nothing more than a convenient way to avoid the draft. They copied examples of successful personal statements, falsified ministers' names, and wrote their own letters of reference. Draft boards rarely had time to check up on them.

Most draft counselors knew there were better ways to avoid the draft and refused to prepare a fraudulent CO claim as a matter of principle. They tried to discourage the insincere by describing CO status as a bleak alternative to military service. The Central Committee for Conscientious Objection published a handbook which *Newsweek* magazine described as "enough to convince all but the most determined malingerer that only confirmed, absolute pacifists need apply for the dirty details, civilian volunteer work, or jail terms that conscientious objection invites."

Conscientious objection did involve considerable hardship. Almost all of the 172,000 Vietnam-era conscientious objectors were asked to do alternative service in lieu of induction. CO's had to work for two years in low-paying jobs beyond commuting distance from their homes. Many worked as hospital orderlies or as conservation workers in wilderness camps. However, most draft boards were so overloaded with inductions and reclassifications that they kept only very loose contact with CO's, and alternative service was often very casually supervised. "Many of these local boards couldn't stand the sight of CO's and wanted nothing to do with them," recalled a top-level Selective Service official. "They didn't realize that they were doing these boys a favor." Almost fifty thousand CO's dropped out and were never certified as having fulfilled their obligations. Refusing to do alternative service was a federal crime, punishable by up to five years in prison, but only about a thousand individuals were convicted of this offense.

For a number of persons, a conscientious-objector claim was only the first step in a long procedural tangle with the draft system. Even a CO application that had no chance of succeeding could tie up a draft board for months or sometimes years. By pyramiding claims and appeals, a skillful counselor could enable his client to outlast his draft vulnerability. After years of exchanging paperwork with draft boards, clients turned twenty-six, received high lottery numbers, took advantage of the lottery loophole, outlasted the draft itself, or goaded their local boards into procedural errors that made induction orders unenforceable. Stalling tactics were often expensive and always the cause of great personal anxiety, making them usually the strategy of last resort. According to New Orleans counselor Collins Vallee, "The system was full of escape valves, and all we had to do was try one tactic after another until something finally worked."

By far the biggest escape valves were the preinduction and induction examinations. Every prospective draftee had to be examined twice, once before his draft board could classify him I-A and again when he reported for induction. On either occasion, he could be given a IV-F or I-Y exemption for mental, physical, psychological, or "administrative" reasons. The mental exam was hard to fake, and examiners were quick to question anyone with a peculiarly low score. But other aspects of the examination process were extremely vulnerable to manipulation and fabrication.

Young men could qualify for an administrative exemption by admitting membership in any subversive organization listed on the Armed Forces Security Questionnaire. If a person refused to fill out the questionnaire, Army regulations required that he undergo further investigation before he could be drafted. Sometimes these men were exempted without further inquiry. As one official at Selective Service headquarters admitted, "As long as there are plenty of men available, no one's going to spend any time investigating hippies." One youth was exempted simply because he claimed that his father was a member of the Communist Party.

A person could also get what one handbook called a "draft immunization" by developing a history of petty criminal behavior. Notwithstanding the movie *Alice's Restaurant,* dumping trash by a roadside was not enough—but cattle rustling, killing an eagle, or engaging in what the rules called "sexual misconduct" could qualify a person for a I-Y exemption on the grounds of "questionable moral character." In New York City, one arrest for marijuana possession was sometimes enough to keep a person home from the war. Some men were rejected for administrative reasons upon nothing more than a subjective determination that they would not make good soldiers. "The I-Y classification is sort of a dumping ground," explained one draft counselor. "It's a place for guys the Army just doesn't want, and it's often very hard to find out why they were put there."

The physical part of the exam was easy to fake. The military knew this was a serious problem, yet it was never able to solve it. According to Colonel William G. Peard, head of the Army department which set medical standards for induction:

> Even when we suspect malingering, to prove it is very difficult. A registrant may play upon some defect which might be minor, and it's almost impossible for a physician to say he's lying. . . . Only when fakery is flagrant is . . . any detective-type investigation of a registrant's claimed defect undertaken.

To help registrants fail the preinduction physical, many draft counseling centers organized special clinics, often staffed by antiwar medical students or doctors at university health centers. A careful examination by a knowledgeable specialist and an equally careful choice of a preinduction physical site guaranteed an exemption for nine clients out of ten.

The military's stringent standards required that each inductee meet the physical requirements of an infantryman under stress. This precluded the induction or enlistment of anyone with a defect that might impair training, be aggravated by military duty, or interfere with military routine. Trick knees, flat feet, skin rashes, even excessive or obscene tattoos were enough to qualify for a IV-F or I-Y exemption. As Los Angeles attorney David Caplan explained, "There are thousands of disqualifying physical and mental conditions, and it's a rare case that someone does not have *one* of them." Roughly half of all draft-age youths failed to meet physical standards, two to three times the rejection rates for other NATO countries.

Even well-conditioned athletes in apparent good health could qualify for physical exemptions, since many of them had some history of bone or joint injuries. As described in the House Armed Services Committee's 1967 report on the draft, many military experts believed that "the chronically injured, deferred athlete is not physically able to meet the full demands of service in a combat zone. . . . [Without] quick access to whirlpool baths and other modern and elaborate therapeutic devices,

... [he] would become a quick liability to a military unit." The public's attention focused on Joe Namath and his IV-F knees, but thousands of hometown high-school athletes got similar exemptions.

Medical counselors stretched the rules as far as their imaginations allowed. "I just follow the Army's own standards," one commented sarcastically. "I'm sure the Army appreciates my help in screening out unsuitable prospects." They helped document disqualifying conditions, and sometimes advised clients of the necessary symptoms. Some conditions had symptoms that no civilian or military doctor could disprove if a person complained of them convincingly. Ménière's syndrome, for example, could be faked by attesting to persistent dizziness, nausea, ringing in the ears, and an inability to concentrate.

A determined individual with strong fortitude could fake a gastrointestinal ulcer. A few hours before his preinduction physical, he had to borrow a syringe and extract a pint of his own blood, making sure that the needle mark was in an inconspicuous place. Just before entering the examination center, he had to drink the blood. This induced vomiting a few minutes later, ideally in the presence of a military doctor. He then had to complain of severe stomach pains. When tests confirmed that his blood pressure was down and the vomited blood was his own, a IV-F exemption was guaranteed.

One draft manual, *IV-F: A Guide to Exemption,* described how a number of people could "very likely" be exempted for a defect that only one of them actually possessed:

> Since civilian doctors know their patients only by the names they give, a registrant bent on fraud with a bona fide disqualifying defect which was either intermittent (such as asthma) or unverifiable by objective tests (such as Ménière's syndrome) might receive treatment from several doctors using the names of several conspirators.

The law provided an exemption for anyone under orthodontic care, and almost every draft-age person had teeth sufficiently crooked to give braces some therapeutic value. In the Los Angeles area alone, ten dentists willingly performed orthodontic work for anyone who could pay a $1,000–$2,000 fee. Wearing braces was a common last-minute tactic for registrants who faced immediate call-up. According to one youth who wore unneeded braces, this "dental cop-out" was "very expensive and very uncomfortable. But it sure beat KP, getting up at 4 A.M., and going to Vietnam."

One could also look to a sympathetic psychiatrist or psychological therapist for another costly escape from the draft. Through a series of visits, a patient could translate his anxiety about being drafted into a psychological trauma that qualified him for an exemption. Mindful of military standards, therapists probed for a variety of mental problems: "You could theoretically be rejected for any neurotic trait from bedwetting to nail-biting." Sometimes, therapists coached patients about the necessary symptoms. "I had only one patient who was denied a psychiatric exemption," a psychiatrist recalled. "He wanted me to say he was crazy, but he wouldn't take the responsibility of acting crazy." A Washington, D.C., psychologist recalled writing a letter for one of his patients:

> I described his anxiety and periods of deep depression, but there wasn't any reason why he couldn't have served in Vietnam. The day before his interview, he accidentally cut his wrist opening a jar of pickles. He went to the examination center with my letter and a bandage on his wrist, but he never told anyone how it happened. He got an exemption.

Homosexuality was a common ground for a psychiatric exemption, and one antidraft pamphlet advised how to fake it:

> Dress very conservatively for the Army shrinker. Act like a man under tight control. Deny you're a fag, deny it again very quickly, then stop, as if you're buttoning your lip. But find an excuse to bring it back into the conversation again and again, and each time deny it and quickly change the subject. And maybe twice, no more than three times over a half hour interview, just the slightest little flick of the wrist. But above all, never admit it. Even after they're hooked, keep up the denials.

San Francisco draft counselor Paul Harris recalled that "all of my clients who faked it got their exemptions, but they drafted the one fellow who really was gay." One antiwar protester in Chicago was exempted as a homosexual, but he later married and was threatened with induction. He replied that if drafted, he would demonstrate his tendencies beyond any possible doubt at his induction physical. No one called his bluff.

The preinduction physical was a highly regimented process, with long lines of men receiving very brief attention from military doctors. Anyone who drew special attention to himself improved his chances of getting an exemption, if only because he slowed the process down. Peter Simpson suffered from a minor skin rash which he knew was, at best, borderline grounds for an exemption. While everyone else was walking around undressed, he kept wearing his business suit and carried a *Wall Street Journal* under his arm. Simpson displayed so much confidence in his claim that the examiners gave him an exemption.

One way to get special attention was to disrupt the process. Radical draft counselors often encouraged this tactic, "not only because it obstructed the smooth operation of the criminal war machine, but also because it might impress the examiners with your undesirable character traits." One San Francisco youth, tentatively stamped I-A, made a desperate visit to a draft counselor during the lunch recess from his physical. He was advised to "piss on the table" when he saw the psychiatrist. He did, and he got an exemption. In Chicago, an antiwar activist brought seventy-five demonstrators to picket outside during his examination. To keep them from storming the building, examiners summoned the military police, gave the activist a I-Y exemption, and asked him to leave.

Documenting a disqualifying condition or disrupting the process was not necessarily enough to guarantee exemption. Every preinduction examination center interpreted official standards differently, and some were alert to tricks that were popular in their areas. For these reasons, counselors often advised their clients to take advantage of a major loophole in the draft law which existed throughout the war: the right of every registrant to choose the site of his preinduction physical.

The examination process had a built-in bias which favored out-of-state examinees. Examiners had no quotas of their own, but they knew if they failed an unusually large percentage of local youths, they would draw a reaction from nearby draft boards, which did have quotas to fill. However, examiners almost never heard complaints when they disqualified out-of-state youths. Besides, many of the latter were politically oriented students whose disruptive tactics could be avoided if they got what they wanted. At the Boston examination site, for example, graduate students from Harvard and MIT were told, "If you cooperate with us, we'll cooperate with you."

The counselor network kept an up-to-date "book" on which centers were receptive to particular claims. For most of the war, Butte, Montana, was considered an easy mark for anyone with a letter from a doctor, and Little Rock, Arkansas, for anyone with a letter from a psychiatrist. Beckley, West Virginia, was well-known for giving exemptions to "anyone who looked freaked out." A number of famous rock stars avoided the draft by going to Beckley incognito with beads, bare feet, and long hair. By far the most popular place to go for a preinduction physical was Seattle, Washington. In the latter years of the war, Seattle examiners separated people into two groups: those who had letters from doctors or psychiatrists, and those who did not. Everyone with a letter received an exemption, regardless of what the letter said.

The preinduction examination process rewarded careful planning, guile, and disruptive behavior. But if a person came without a letter from his doctor, he was very likely to be declared fit for induction, regardless of any actual medical problem. All but the most obvious physical defects were easy to overlook in the confused environment and mass processing of the examination center, and disadvantaged youths who had not received adequate medical care were often classified I-A. One draftee from a low-income family spent three months in the Army before it was discovered that he was an extreme diabetic. At his preinduction physical, his urine sample had been confused with that of another person, who got the exemption. Blacks and members of other minority groups were the most common victims. In 1966, the only year for which racial data was published, a mentally qualified white youth was 50 percent more likely than his black counterpart to fail the preinduction physical.

Many doctors, dentists, and psychiatrists who specialized in draft avoidance now feel a sense of disquiet about their role during the war. The people they most wanted to help—blacks, low-income youths, and conscientious war resisters who had been denied CO status—were rarely the ones who came to see them: "The people we saw were all middle class. It wasn't that the others didn't have the money. They just never thought of going for professional help." Even at the draft-counseling medical clinic of predominantly black Fisk University, walk-ins were overwhelmingly well-educated, middle-class whites. At a large Chicago clinic, doctors refused to help any white who failed to bring at least one black with him for a medical interview.

Professionals were especially discouraged by the self-centered attitudes of many of the young men who came for help. Dr. Peter Bourne, a psychiatrist working at the time in Atlanta, commented that "some people acted as though all doctors had a moral obligation to help them dodge the draft for nothing." Dr. Bourne counseled people for free, but he sometimes had to refer them to specialists who knew more about certain disqualifying conditions. Later, he heard complaints when the specialists charged $25 to write letters to draft boards. Dr. Herbert Schwartz of Hartford, Connecticut, refused to do draft counseling after consistently encountering "opportunists who felt threatened by the war, but did not oppose the war. They were people without ideals or principles who were just looking for an easy way out."

Yet a number of the professionals were themselves opportunists. Many were far too willing to bend professional principles to help clients connive their way out of the draft. Others had a false view of what they were accomplishing. One counselor said that his goal was to encourage draft avoidance until the government could be provoked into rescinding all deferments and exemptions. "When that happens," he commented, "the sons of the rich will be drafted right along with those of the poor. And then the shoe will begin to pinch the wrong foot." But the impact of draft counseling was exactly the opposite. The burdens of war were shifted even more to the socially and economically disadvantaged.

Safety in Service

In 1966, Major General George Gelson, Jr. of the Maryland National Guard was photographed by *Life* magazine wearing a Baltimore Colts uniform, a football tucked under his arm. "We have an arrangement with the Colts," he commented. "When they have a player with a military problem, they send him to us." In Detroit, an Army reserve unit found room for the Lions' star halfback and tight end, in return for fifty-yard-line tickets and a chance to serve as the honor guard during flag ceremonies at home games. The Dallas Cowboys had ten players assigned to the same National Guard division at one time. "If we had been called up," recalled a Philadelphia reservist, "the Eagles would have been left without a backfield."

Except for one instance in 1968, reservists and guardsmen were not called up during the Vietnam war, so the Colts, Lions, Cowboys, Eagles, and dozens of other professional sports teams were able to protect their players from active military service. The Miami Dolphins almost lost a key linebacker to the draft until a club official intervened with Selective Service headquarters in Washington to get him a temporary deferment until his National Guard appointment could be arranged.

At the peak of the war, waiting lists were long, reflecting the popularity of the National Guard and reserves as sanctuaries from the draft. Many draft-vulnerable men who became guardsmen or reservists were able to leapfrog these lists by having influential persons nominate them to fill the rare vacancies. The FBI once investigated the relationship between the New York Jets and a go-between who, for a fee, could arrange for players to be put at the top of local reserve waiting lists.

Because of the difficulty in getting a position with the National Guard or reserves, not many youths from disadvantaged backgrounds were able to join. Most recruits were recent high-school graduates, but a disproportionate number were college graduates. In 1969–70, for example, 28,000 more college-trained men entered the National Guard or reserves than were enlisted or inducted into all active forces combined. Only about 1 percent of all guardsmen were black.

Guardsmen and reservists had a four-to-six-month active-duty obligation, plus yearly summer camps and monthly unit meetings over a six-year period. If they failed to show up for meetings, they were technically AWOL and subject to immediate call-up for active duty—but that did not often happen. A Wisconsin reservist (who was also a draft counselor) stopped going to meetings with three years left on his term. He never heard a word until, on schedule, he received his discharge by mail. For years, the Defense Department considered taking legal action against delinquent reservists—but, as of 1977, the matter was still under study.

Training for the National Guard or reserves was neither as rigorous nor as thorough as that given the active forces. Often, reservists had to train with outmoded equipment and then read books or watch movies to learn how to use the modern equivalents. After the National Guard was criticized for its 1967 handling of the Newark and Detroit riots, units devoted much of their training to riot control, which, according to a Defense Department report, came "at the expense of combat mission training time."

The Guard and the reserves were subject to activation and extended periods of service, including combat. Almost 700,000 guardsmen and reservists were called up during the Korean war. Most units consisted of men from the same localities, and the casualties devastated some communities. President Kennedy's call-up of the reserves during the Berlin crisis in 1961 had severe political repercussions. The lesson of that experience was that mobilizing the reserves was a drastic step with profound domestic and international implications, a step to be avoided if at all possible.

For the first three years of the war, President Johnson steadfastly refused to activate guardsmen or reservists, and the government relied on increased draft calls to fill the expanding need for troops. This was consistent with Johnson's efforts to picture Vietnam as a limited war of short duration, which could be fought with little domestic dislocation and without interfering with his administration's war on poverty. Reservists and guardsmen were better connected, better educated, more affluent, and whiter than their peers in the active forces, and the administration feared that mobilizing them would heighten public opposition to the war. Instead, they were called upon only for domestic service, during natural disasters, urban riots, and antiwar disturbances.

In 1968, a commission headed by Burke Marshall warned that the National Guard and reserves were becoming major refuges from the draft. Led by Senator Richard Russell of Georgia, chairman of the Senate Armed Services Committee, Congress made activation easier. After the 1968 *Pueblo* incident, 37,000 guardsmen and reservists were called to active duty, largely for symbolic purposes. About fifteen thousand were sent to Vietnam. But the pressure to activate them eased as the war stopped escalating, and no guardsmen or reservists were again called upon to fight.

The National Guard and reserves were attractive avenues for avoiding Vietnam. A 1966 Pentagon study found that 71 percent of all reservists were draft-motivated, and James Cantwell, president of the National Guard Association, claimed in 1970 that as many as 90 percent of all Guard enlistments were draft-motivated. At the end of 1968, with the draft still in full force, the Army National Guard had a waiting list of 100,000. After two years of shrinking draft calls, that waiting list vanished. Six months later, the Guard found itself forty-five thousand men under strength.

The nation's 1 million Vietnam-era guardsmen and reservists performed a measure of national service, as contrasted with those who avoided the military entirely. Guardsmen and reservists were willing to train, interrupt their lives, help disaster victims, and offer a show of force during inner-city riots. But they served in a way that involved much less personal hardship than did active military duty. As observed by the Gates Commission in recommending the all-volunteer force, the Guard and reserves were used by recruits to "minimiz[e] the cost of fulfilling millitary service." Draft-vulnerable men who joined the National Guard or reserves were, in one basic respect, like the millions of others who avoided the draft by letting themselves be channeled into jobs, marriages, or other situations they did not especially like; they left the fighting and dying to others.

The National Guard and reserves were not the only examples of how individuals could perform military service while minimizing the risks of Vietnam. Throughout the armed forces, there were a great many "Sergeant Bilkos," as one Pentagon manpower official described them, "men who try to look brave while making sure that someone else does the fighting." Six out of seven servicemen were never involved in actual combat. Usually, this was just a matter of chance or the military's judgment that these men had more important roles to play elsewhere. Millions of recruits did whatever they were asked to do. If ordered to Vietnam, they went to Vietnam. If ordered elsewhere, they went elsewhere. However, the findings of the Notre Dame survey suggest that a great many troops were not willing to leave things to chance. Just under half (47 percent) of all servicemen admitted trying to manipulate their military careers. They spent two, three, or four years of their lives in military duty, but they did what they could to stay far from the action.

Compared with America's other twentieth-century wars, Vietnam required the deployment of a relatively small number of front-line troops. As shown in Figure 3, about 30 percent of the 7,500,000 Vietnam-era troops went to the Southeast Asia war zone, but of these, only 1,600,000 engaged in combat. At the peak of the fighting, fewer than 250,000 troops were engaged in combat operations at any one time; that amounted to only about 6 percent of active-duty troops and 3 percent of available forces, including reserves. Overall, the risk of combat service was so low for Vietnam-era servicemen that life insurance companies did not charge extra premiums for military personnel, except for pilots and others on unusually hazardous missions.

The military's rear-echelon staff requirements grew considerably in the half-century before the outbreak of the Vietnam war. During the Spanish-American War, 13 percent of all troops were trained for noncombat roles; during World War II, 61 percent were noncombat. Yet at the 1968 height of the Vietnam war, 88 percent of all servicemen were assigned to noncombat occupational specialties. All kinds of manual, technical, and clerical skills were necessary to support combat troops. Recruits with above-average aptitude or ability were skimmed from the personnel pool and assigned special functions, often far from the combat zone. The fighting was left to those of lesser talents.

This made good management sense. The military naturally tried to use people where they would be the most productive. A college graduate with an IQ of 110 and a high-school dropout with an IQ of 85 might shoot a rifle equally well. But it made sense to give a clerical job to the college graduate, who would probably perform it better. Random assignments might have been more equitable but would have interfered with military efficiency.

The fear of combat was a powerful inducement for recruits to seek the more attractive opportunities on their own. One wartime survey

FIGURE 3: MILITARY AVOIDERS

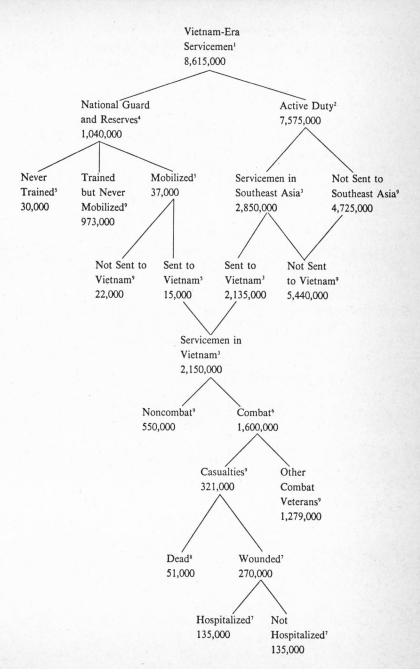

found that "less chance of death or injury" and "dislike of fighting and killing" were the two most common reasons why recruits were attracted to noncombat specialties. As a Defense Department manpower expert admitted, "We've studied this problem very carefully. People don't seem to enlist in the Army to fight. We recognize the inequity this causes in a shooting war, but we don't know what to do about it."

Sixty percent of all college-graduate enlistees were draft-motivated and not true volunteers. Competing against one another, all branches of service tried to convince the potential draftee that he had a lot to gain by enlisting. Various officer recruitment programs—especially the Reserve Officers Training Corps and the Judge Advocate General Corps —wooed university students with promises of safe assignments and deferred enlistments.

If he had sufficient education and a high enough IQ to meet their tougher enlistment standards, a draft-vulnerable man could also reduce his chances of engaging in combat by joining the Coast Guard, Navy, or Air Force. The Coast Guard lost only seven men during the entire war. Navy ships were stationed off the coast of Vietnam, but they rarely lost men to hostile fire. Almost three-quarters of the eighteen hundred Air Force casualties involved pilots, navigators, and others well beyond draft age. The Air Force's strategic bases were in places like Thailand and Guam, immune from rocket attacks or other enemy shelling. Generally, combat missions in these services involved volunteers—officers who had become pilots or patrol boat commanders with full knowledge of the risks involved, or enlisted men who willingly accepted hazardous duty. For others, the risk of combat was minimal. Altogether, the risk of dying in Vietnam was nineteen times as great for Marine and Army troops as for Navy and Air Force men.

The Coast Guard, Navy, and Air Force were well aware of these facts. Like the Air Force recruiter in Connecticut who wrote the following letter to a prospective inductee, they drove the point home that theirs were the "safe" branches of service:

Did you know that the vast majority of the U.S. forces killed in Southeast Asia have been draftees? Wouldn't you rather take advantage of the opportunity to join the branch of service that has lost the least amount of men

in Southeast Asia as opposed to being drafted into the branch of service that
has lost the most?

The Notre Dame survey found that two-thirds of all enlistees in these
branches were motivated, at least in part, by the desire to avoid Vietnam, even if this meant a three- or four-year enlistment instead of the
two years served by most draftees. As one sailor commented, "There
ain't no Viet Cong submarines."

A Marine slogan boasted of the corps' combat mission: "Every enlisted man is a rifleman, and every officer is a platoon leader." All
Marines, even members of the band, were trained as infantrymen. Yet
even in the Marine Corps, a high-aptitude recruit had a good chance
to be screened out of combat duty. A Marine general explained that "a
computer simply and fairly assigns [them] to billets where their higher-
level skills can be put to the best use for the Corps. And that's why so
few of them are being killed."

The Army, home for 90 percent of all inductees, offered many opportunities for avoiding combat. In its recruiting efforts it suggested to
draft-vulnerable men that they could avoid risks by enlisting. So they
could: At the peak of the war, Army draftees were getting killed at
almost twice the rate of volunteers. Recruitment ads hinted broadly
that enlisting was the only way to avoid infantry duty in Vietnam:
"Make your choice now—join, or we'll make the choice for you." As
Peter Barnes noted in *Pawns,* they promoted "the image of a new
'Action Army' in which there seemingly are no foot soldiers; men work
with advanced equipment, develop their bodies and leadership abilities,
study, and prepare for future success."

There were opportunities in the Army, but no guarantees. Throughout the war years, enlistees were promised only that they would be
enrolled in the training program of their choice, but not that they would
be assigned to any specialty. Many young men complained bitterly
when they passed a technical training program only to be assigned to
combat units as "Eleven-Bravo" infantrymen.

"In the Army," a personnel officer acknowledged, "we plan on
spaces, not faces." Beginning in 1965, the Army used computers to
match soldiers with occupational specialties. In the peak years of the

war, the Army had a surplus of qualified applicants for most noncombat specialties, and the computer was programmed to select the best-qualified applicants to fill quotas. Aptitude test scores, educational levels, language proficiencies, and physical skills were all important factors. An individual soldier's prospect for assignment to a noncombat function also depended greatly on when he enlisted. Most of the better-educated, high-IQ enlistees joined the service in the summer or early fall, making the competition especially fierce in those months. Recruits who enlisted in the winter or spring had a better chance.

Vietnam assignments were handled in much the same way. The standard policy of rotating soldiers out of Vietnam after one year in the war zone required a constant replenishment of troops trained in the combat arms—infantry, armor, and artillery. For them, avoiding Vietnam was usually the consequence of sheer luck. As one personnel officer explained, "A lot of guys, by the toss of the dice, went to Europe —and by the time their tours were over, there was not enough time to send them to Vietnam." Of course, some combat-trained troops volunteered for Vietnam. So many West Point graduates asked to go to Vietnam in 1966 that the Army had to select them on the basis of their class standing.

Servicemen in noncombat specialties were much less likely to be ordered to Vietnam, and not many volunteered. Periodically, recruitment shortages or heavy combat casualties required some noncombatants to be transferred to the infantry. The least productive, most expendable troops were the ones reassigned, less as punishment than as an exercise of management principles. Like regular combat troops, they tended to be low-IQ, poorly educated men from disadvantaged backgrounds.

Despite the impersonal quality of the combat selection process, there were many ways a soldier could manipulate the system to his advantage. One counseling manual advised calling the Pentagon on an Army trunk line to get special treatment:

Don't worry about someone in the Pentagon getting angry that you're calling from Fort Sill, Oklahoma, or Fort Lewis, Washington. . . . He might just be helpful. It is possible to find the person who has your [form] on his desk and to find out the chances of its being approved, whether it's a request to be stationed in Germany, for Warrant Officer Flight Training, for the Defense Language Institute's Swahili course, or for the Army cross-country ski team.

Not all noncombat jobs were filled by computer, and many better-educated soldiers were skimmed out of the manpower pool by officers who wanted reliable clerks, messengers, servants, or other helpers. Soldiers were given the chance to reenlist early in their terms, extending their service obligations but giving them new and better opportunities to be assigned to noncombat specialties.

Like draft registrants, soldiers could formally apply for designation as conscientious objectors, entitling them to noncombat assignments or, less often, immediate discharges. Application procedures were rigorous, requiring a lot of paperwork and interviews with chaplains, psychiatrists, and senior officers. Usually, the process took months to complete. Throughout the Vietnam era, only seventeen thousand servicemen applied for CO status.

In the early years of the war, the military approved less than 30 percent of the few hundred CO applications that were submitted. In the late 1960s, interest in CO status grew dramatically. CO applicants began to seek help from attorneys and other counselors, trying to take advantage of the same case law that courts were applying to civilian CO cases. However, the military continued to turn down most CO applicants, in the belief that it was not bound by these court-imposed rules.

Federal judges decided otherwise in 1971. In a series of circuit court opinions, they held that the military had to follow the *Seeger* rule, which entitled sincere pacifists to CO status even if they were not motivated by orthodox religious beliefs, and they further held that no serviceman could have his CO application turned down unless there were some factual basis in his military record to support that conclusion. Suddenly the armed forces found themselves defending an unmanageable number of lawsuits. In 1971 and 1972, two-thirds of all CO applicants were successful—and by 1975, 99 percent were successful.

Applying for CO status was never a good way of avoiding Vietnam.

In 1970, the Pacific Counseling Service temporarily seized upon the CO process as a Vietnam avoidance tactic. For several weeks, its counselors conducted an extensive leafleting campaign for soldiers passing through the Oakland Army Base, a primary embarkation point for Vietnam. Within a few weeks, they persuaded about twelve hundred troops to apply for CO status, postponing their orders to Vietnam. But the Pentagon quickly changed the regulations to prohibit soldiers from applying for CO status while en route to Vietnam, and the soldiers were shipped out.

In the first several years of the war, a CO applicant had very little chance of getting an outright discharge. If a CO applicant was unsuccessful—or only partly successful—his chances of going to Vietnam increased. He had to notify his commanding officer of his intent to apply for CO status, which sometimes led to expedited orders to Vietnam. Those who were granted noncombatant status were often retrained as medics and sent into the combat zone.

For the soldier who wanted to avoid Vietnam, it was better to take advantage of other opportunities for discharge provided by military regulations. A civilian counselors' handbook entitled "Getting Out" told how discharges were sometimes given "to the person who is too fat, has four or more dependents even though they don't create a hardship, is an alien, gets seasick, works for a foreign government, is becoming a minister or entering a religious order, flunks out of officer training, or has a very unusual and important civilian skill." The same booklet described how "political dissenters" could sometimes get honorable discharges for "substandard personal behavior [which] reflects discredit upon the service."

Many soldiers became increasingly restive as their Vietnam service neared. They no longer had confidence that "it can't happen to me," and they had a heightened awareness of the political controversy about the war. At antiwar coffeehouses outside their bases, and especially at embarkation points, they were urged to boycott the war. At the Oakland Army Base, a fourteen-year Army veteran sat on an upturned garbage can and exhorted troops in transit to injure themselves, engage in homosexual acts, commit crimes, or take other last-minute steps to save themselves. He was arrested and discharged from the Army, but many did what he described. Frank Paquin, a Vietnam-bound Green Beret, intentionally aggravated an old knee injury during a parachute jump. Ralph Oberstrom drove out in the countryside with a friend, shot two holes in his windshield, and had his friend shoot him in the left leg. Claiming to be the victim of sniper fire, he was sent to the Oak Knoll Naval Hospital and kept home from Vietnam. Fred Patterson tried to get discharged for enuresis (bed-wetting), but without success. He wet his bed for forty nights, and all his commander did was transfer him to a lower bunk.

A soldier with orders to Vietnam was not necessarily bound for combat. Servicemen with technical specialties were often sent directly to Saigon to serve in administrative capacities. Others underwent a series of interviews, any one of which could bring an assignment to a rear-guard support unit. According to the Notre Dame survey, almost half of all Vietnam-based troops tried to avoid combat, usually by arranging for relatively safe assignments.

The first screening took place on the airplane en route to Vietnam, where senior officers identified soldiers they considered dangerously immature and unfit for combat. After the plane arrived at Cam Ranh Bay, Tan Son Nhut, or Bien-Hoa, new troops were interviewed by personnel officers from the divisions with which they had been matched by computer. The officers had to sort incoming soldiers into four or five brigades, one of which was a noncombat supply brigade. Troops assigned to combat brigades were reinterviewed for battalion assignments upon reporting to the brigade personnel officer, and again they had about a one-in-four chance of going to a noncombat unit. Finally, they had one last chance to be assigned to a support company when they arrived at their battalions. In all, a soldier had a better-than-even chance of getting an assignment away from the search-and-destroy missions and other field operations. Anyone who made a good impression had a good chance of staying out of combat. As Pat Brannigan, now a career Army officer, recalled: "When I landed, I talked about computers to anyone who would listen. I knew that computers were always kept air-conditioned and far from combat areas. As it turned out, that's how I spent my year."

The assignment process was vulnerable to corruption. Interviewing officers occasionally arranged things to make some money or help their friends. One interviewing sergeant sold noncombat orders for $100. Others punished soldiers they disliked by sending them to the most dangerous places.

Young lieutenants and captains virtually exercised a veto over their own combat assignments. If they asked to be assigned away from combat, superior officers usually complied "out of concern for the troops they had to lead," as one battalion commander recalled. "A lot of experienced captains wanted to be company commanders until a combat opening arose. Then they suddenly became much less interested." John Markus, a West Point graduate, "went forward as an officer and gentleman" to ask to be kept out of combat duty because "I just couldn't handle the fighting." At his request, he was made a battery commander in the rear. Another West Point cadet relied on his postgraduate degree from Harvard to stay in the rear, where he helped map the day-to-day tactics of the war.

Noncombat assignments never came with guarantees. Emergencies like the 1968 Tet offensive brought massive reassignments of troops to the front lines. However, more than a half million troops in Vietnam never saw any fighting.

Throughout the war, 83 percent of all American casualties resulted from search-and-destroy missions or other combat operations. Over the course of his twelve months in Vietnam, a combat soldier faced about a 3 percent chance of death, a 10 percent chance of suffering a serious wound requiring hospitalization, and almost a 25 percent chance of getting enough of a wound to earn a Purple Heart. But those odds were not unalterable. Some soldiers committed petty AWOL offenses, staying away just long enough to miss the start of a field patrol mission. Usually, the only punishment was a small fine. Others bribed company clerks or other soldiers to find someone else to take their place, or they feigned shell shock to get sick leave.

Out on patrol, company or platoon officers were sometimes intimidated into turning their search-and-destroy patrols into "search-and-evade" missions. Faced with gross disobedience, or threatened with physical assault, they conformed their orders to the wishes of their troops, avoiding situations likely to produce casualties. One lieutenant learned of a $350 bounty placed on his head because his unit thought he was a hard-liner too eager to send them into combat. When he refused an order to attack, the bounty was lifted. Entire units sometimes wore red bandannas, signaling to the enemy that they would not fight unless attacked. The catchword was "CYA [cover your ass] and get home."

Before 1970, soldiers could get out of combat by reenlisting for a longer tour of duty. According to one account, recruiting officers were airlifted to remote firebases to greet combat patrols that had suffered exceptionally heavy losses, offering exhausted troops an immediate trip home in return for a four-year service commitment. The longer tour usually meant a return trip to Vietnam, but some soldiers were willing to do anything to get on the next plane home.

Others found easier ways to shorten their tours. Tony Palazzi wrote home to his mother, asking her to have the family doctor write an exaggerated account of her illness. Palazzi showed the letter to his commanding officer, left Vietnam eight months ahead of his rotation date, and completed his tour of duty at a missile base a few miles from his home. One combat-weary sergeant refused to take his antimalaria pills and slept with his arm outside his tent. He fell ill, had to be hospitalized, and was permanently reassigned out of the combat zone.

A few men were so desperate they deliberately tried to get a "million-dollar wound"—serious enough for evacuation, but minor enough to heal completely in a few months. Desperate to get out of combat, some soldiers asked friends to shoot them, or they took extra risks in the field. One soldier recalled that several men in his unit

. . . tried deliberately to get wounded. I saw one man casually stand up in a fire fight and get it through the head. Another stood up too, and only got it in the leg and the arm. He was sent to the hospital in Japan, and everybody thought he was the luckiest guy in the world because he was safe and free again.

III | EVADERS

The Resistance

In electronic circuitry, the ohm is a measure of resistance to the induction of electric currents. Its symbol, the Greek letter omega, became the symbol for resistance to the induction of troops for the Vietnam war. Inspired by Mario Savio's plea to "put your bodies upon the gears" to stop the machine, the organized Resistance movement hoped to end the war by provoking a breakdown of the draft—a breakdown that would dramatize the tragedy of the war and prevent conscription of the army necessary to fight it.

In 1964, three St. Louis men signed a pact of joint resistance, promising that if one went to jail for refusing induction, the others would follow. All three spent eighteen to twenty-three months in prison for refusing induction, and one of them later observed:

> I believe the most important thing about our pact was that we were translating a principle into action—not only draft resistance itself, but effective solidarity with a person who is prosecuted for acting in accord with conscience. I believe that any time anyone is arrested for any such cause, there should immediately be five or ten or a hundred or more who will say "Set him free or take us too" and proceed to enter prison to show they are not merely talking or signing their names.

Another collective act of draft resistance inspired the imagination of the antiwar movement in 1964. In May of that year, twelve students burned their draft cards at a New York rally as a general protest against American military policies. They coined the slogan "We Won't Go," and the list of places where they wouldn't go included the Dominican Republic and Cuba, along with Southeast Asia.

Out of the New York rally, a May Second Movement petition was circulated, calling upon its signers to refuse induction if called. The act of resistance would occur only as a matter of last resort, enabling deferred students to voice their opposition to American foreign policy without immediate self-sacrifice. Other "We Won't Go" petitions were circulated in the next two years, but the feeling mounted that opposition without personal risk was an empty gesture. In July 1966, angered by the rapid Vietnam buildup, a New Haven group endorsed a statement calling for unconditional, preemptive resistance on the part of its signers: "On November 16, we will return our draft cards to our local boards with a notice of our refusal to cooperate. . . ." Simply returning cards was unlikely to bring prosecution, but it risked provoking draft boards into accelerating induction notices, which would force antiwar activists to submit or face prosecution. The rising concern about the war made this provocative new tactic popular, and "We Won't Go" petitions collected thousands of signatures.

By 1967, Muhammad Ali's draft case drew national attention to the Resistance movement. Shortly before Ali's conviction, which was later reversed, *New York Times* columnist Tom Wicker saw broad implications in the case:

A hundred thousand Muhammad Alis, of course, could be jailed. But if the Johnson Administration had to prosecute 100,000 Americans in order to maintain its authority, its real power to pursue the Vietnamese war or any other policy would be crippled if not destroyed. It would then be faced not with dissent but with civil disobedience on a scale amounting to revolt.

Staughton Lynd, a Yale historian and a central figure in the resistance, made the same point in *Liberation* magazine, and 100,000 acts of defiance became the goal of the movement—"an immense and provocative thought," in the words of one resister. This goal spurred the circulation of new petitions and led to the formation of a national resistance organization in October 1967. Scores of educators and religious leaders, among them Dr. Benjamin Spock and Rev. William Sloane Coffin, issued "A Call to Resist Illegitimate Authority." The movement wanted students to abandon their deferments, inductees to stay home rather than flee to Canada, and all resisters to go on strike against the draft. Many would end up in jail, it was thought, but this would serve an important purpose: "The existence of hundreds and perhaps thousands of young men in prison over a matter of conscience would exert a steady moral pressure on . . . every American whose patriotism demanded he think well of his country's place in the world." Immediately, Attorney General Ramsey Clark came under pressure to stem the growing resistance through prompt and vigorous prosecution. Rather than try hundreds of thousands of young people, he chose to prosecute Dr. Spock, Rev. Coffin, and other leaders of the movement. Although their convictions were later reversed, the Justice Department succeeded in conveying a public image of stern enforcement of the draft law.

The leaders of the Resistance soon learned that few were willing to join forces in this battle against the draft system. David Zimmerman, a graduate student at the University of Michigan, abandoned his deferment to express his opposition to being "channeled" by Selective Service while the war was going on, but most students played it safe. A survey taken by the New England Resistance in 1967–68 discovered that four-fifths of its members had deferments.

A number of antiwar organizations were reluctant to ask their members to adopt tactics that involved personal risk. At a national SDS conference, only about one-fifth of the mostly college-age delegates supported a plan to renounce their deferments. "I'm frankly appalled at the fear of alienating students by raising the II-S issue," a leader of the Berkeley Free Speech Movement explained.

The plan that won greater support was one that encouraged all students to keep their deferments, but to refuse induction if and when the deferments expired. The Progressive Labor Party took a similar position:

> While we must . . . oppose II-S as a divisive and class-racial-discriminatory system, we have to do this on the basis of collective struggle against the administration and the government, not by individual sacrifice.

Later, antiwar groups explained their acceptance of deferments by reasoning, as Michael Ferber did, that "the deferred student was oppressed by the system along with the inducted soldier." According to this line of thought, the draft system's channeling policies made the middle-class white student "a legitimate revolutionary protagonist."

To counteract the widespread reluctance of white middle-class students to assume personal risks, the movement began circulating "snowballing" petitions which committed signers to acts of resistance only if similar pledges exceeded a specified number, ranging from one to fifteen thousand. But snowballing petitions never got enough signatures to make the pledges binding.

By mid-1968, the national movement counted fewer than three thousand committed draft resisters. A Boston Resistance newsletter reported that local attorneys "have expressed astonishment at our success so far in tying up the process," but movement strategists knew that they had fallen far short of the number needed to bring the draft to a halt.

Draft-card burning captured more attention from the press and the public. More than any other gesture of defiance, it reflected the widespread and growing willingness of draft-age men to break the law. The first known incident of this kind occurred in 1964; a year later, forty demonstrators protested the Dominican Republic intervention by burning their cards in front of a Berkeley draft board. Congress responded by making the act punishable by five years in prison, and Resistance activists immediately defied the new law. The first one was promptly convicted and sentenced to thirty months in prison. Draft-card burnings by other small groups in late 1965 and early 1966 similarly led to long prison terms.

Once the Resistance movement gained momentum, draft-card burnings became more popular, and the Justice Department began to be more selective about prosecutions. Technically, it could have prosecuted everyone who returned draft cards, burned or not, because the law required each registrant to have one in his possession. However, many of those who were burning their cards were deferred or exempt from the draft—one group of ten consisted of two veterans, two with physical exemptions, and six with student deferments—and the Justice Department was reluctant to prosecute cases of this kind. William Sessions, the department's chief draft prosecutor, refused to be party to what he called "a continuing, open, obvious expressed intent by many groups to absolutely swamp the system." The Justice Department prosecuted fewer than fifty draft-card burners—about forty of whom were convicted—but it never brought action against hundreds of other individuals who burned their cards during the height of the 1967–68 resistance.

The legal community expected the Supreme Court to overturn the convictions—especially in light of the strong trend developing against Selective Service prosecutions—but in the 1968 O'Brien case, the Court dealt the lawyers and the Resistance a harsh surprise. The law against draft-card burning was upheld, and the convicted activists who had been free on bond had to go to jail. The O'Brien case seemed to be an example of the liberal Warren court's reaching, possibly even over-reaching, to help the Justice Department control the antiwar movement. The decision ran counter to other freedom-of-speech cases in which the Supreme Court upheld protesters' rights to wear black arm-bands in school, Army uniforms as civilians, jackets reading "fuck the draft," flags on the seat of their pants, or flags as peace symbols. The effect of the O'Brien decision, and possibly its purpose, was to curtail the most spectacular means of resisting the draft.

By mid-1968, the Resistance movement was frustrated. The war was still escalating, and the draft seemed invulnerable to nonviolent resistance. More daring and violent means were tried. In a well-publicized raid on a suburban Baltimore County draft board, the "Catonsville Nine," led by the Berrigan brothers, destroyed 378 draft files "with napalm manufactured by ourselves from a recipe in the Special Forces handbook published by the U.S. government." Through 1970, hundreds of similar raids on draft boards resulted in damage to hundreds of thousands of draft files. Patterned after the Catonsville Nine, the perpetrators bore names like the Milwaukee Fourteen, the Akron Two, and the Pasadena Three. One group called itself the Beaver Fifty-five, although it numbered eight, not fifty-five, and staged a Halloween night raid in Indianapolis, not Beaver. Some of the incidents were bizarre. The Big Lake (Minnesota) One dumped two large buckets of his own and his family's excrement onto the I-A files of his draft board. The Women Against Daddy Warbucks stole the "I" and the "A" from the typewriter of a New York board to keep it from reclassifying anyone I-A. In the most devastating attack, the Chicago Fifteen destroyed the records of twelve local boards; four months, forty government workers, and $60,000 were required to undo the damage.

In these cases, government reaction was decisive and severe. The Berrigans were caught, convicted, and sentenced to prison. An activist who burned an upstate New York draft board in 1970 was sent to prison for four years. Ten members of the Chicago Fifteen were sentenced to ten-year prison terms.

Some draft resisters went to prison for less violent acts. In August 1966, twelve black demonstrators were arrested for a sit-in at the Atlanta induction center. All but one were convicted, and most were sentenced to prison for three years. John Wilson was convicted of "insurrection" and had to serve his time on a Georgia chain gang. Hundreds of others suffered misdemeanor convictions for sit-ins, unlawful demonstrations, or other forms of civil disobedience directed at draft boards and induction stations.

The activities of Staughton Lynd, Michael Ferber, Benjamin Spock, the Berrigans, and others failed to produce 100,000 signatures on Resistance petitions, and they did not bring the war machine to a halt. But they did draw public attention to draft resistance, and heavy media exposure contributed to the grass-roots, unorganized movement by more than a half million young men who broke the law and defied their draft boards. Enormous numbers of draft-age men were refusing induction, forcing local boards to refer their cases to federal prosecutors. The courts may not have been jammed, but the prosecutor's offices were. The draft did not collapse but it did lose much of its ability to enforce induction orders. For the most part, the movement's draft resistance goal was accomplished, but by members of the legal profession working within, not outside, the "system."

The leaders of this other movement were not national figures; most were local attorneys, prosecutors, and judges. Many were keenly anti-war, but the war usually was not their immediate concern. What they had in common was an abiding respect for the American system of law and a growing contempt for the Selective Service System's disregard of due process. After two decades of General Hershey's leadership, Selective Service had lost the capacity to make local boards operate fairly, consistently, and with proper regard for legal standards. When it tried to enforce the law against those who disobeyed, Selective Service had few friends and thousands of enemies throughout the legal system.

These lawyers, prosecutors, and judges did not draw public attention to the war in the manner of the draft-card burners and the Berrigans, but they did achieve the "immense and provocative" results that activists found beyond their reach. Working alone or in small groups, one case at a time, lawyers developed an astonishing record of preventing the conviction of draft violators. As the legal attacks on the draft system gathered momentum, the criminal justice system became swamped to the point where Selective Service prosecutions became almost impossible. By 1971, the enforcement of the draft law was in shambles. As shown in Figure 4, the vast majority of those accused of a draft offense escaped conviction.

The first sign of this breakdown came in late 1966, when one hundred student leaders from universities across the country sent an open letter to President Johnson, warning that many of their peers would refuse induction if his Vietnam policy did not change. In 1967, columnist James Reston visited campuses and talked with student government leaders. He estimated that as many as 25 percent of all college students might refuse their induction orders. A 1968 *Harvard Crimson* poll found that 22 percent would refuse the draft rather than serve in Vietnam, and a Harris poll taken later in 1968 discovered that 20–30 percent of all college students would "seriously contemplate" refusing induction. In 1969, the student body presidents of 253 universities informed the White House that they personally planned to refuse military service. Throughout the course of the war, more than a half million draft-age men did exactly that.

One of the first to say no was Daniel Seeger of New York, a pacifist

FIGURE 4: EVADERS

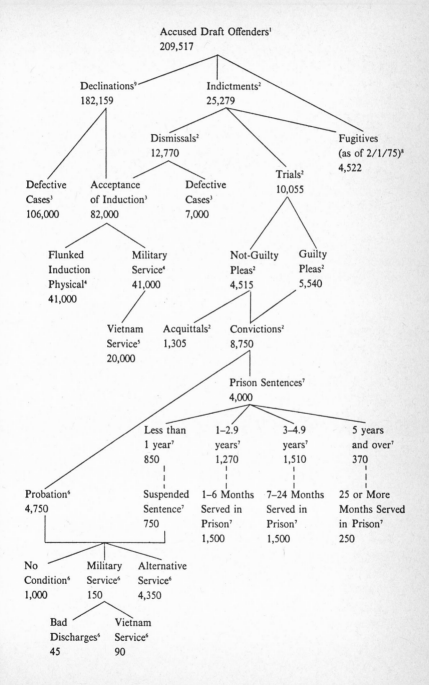

whose case began the unraveling of draft enforcement. In March 1965, when President Johnson had just begun his Vietnam escalation and war protesters were still at the political fringe, Seeger's Selective Service conviction was overturned by the Supreme Court in a ground-breaking case. Seeger had asked for an exemption as a conscientious objector, but his draft board, like most others, granted CO status only to Quakers, Mennonites, and other pacifist sects that believed in God. Seeger did not belong to any of these sects, nor did he believe in God, but the Supreme Court held that he nonetheless qualified for a CO exemption. In doing so, the Court left the clear implication that anyone with a deep-seated personal "religion" opposed to war could be a conscientious objector.

Until *Seeger,* the Supreme Court had not issued a major Selective Service decision since World War II, and the draft system was ill prepared to adjust to new legal requirements. Selective Service headquarters had no mechanism for supervising the implementation of new case law, and local boards were not eager to suffer an intrusion upon their discretion. After the *Seeger* case, many local boards still required CO's to be Jehovah's Witnesses, Quakers, or Mennonites, and many would-be conscientious objectors were wrongfully denied CO status without realizing it. The legal community discovered that draft boards were deviating not just from the *Seeger* holding, but from the procedural standards imposed upon all other federal administrative agencies. Judges were shocked by the incapacity or unwillingness of draft boards to conform to the law. "Selective Service decided not to change its procedures and decided instead to take its chances with the courts," according to one federal judge.

Increasingly, attorneys urged clients to challenge the legality of draft board decisions. However, this could only be done at great risk. No matter how egregious the draft board error, courts refused to intervene unless the individual refused induction and stood trial on criminal charges, or accepted induction and sought release from the military through a writ of habeas corpus.

Regardless of the risk, thousands of draft resisters began pressing their cases in the courts. By 1967, enough were winning acquittals and reversals to provide good case law for future challenges. Where federal judges once might have been willing to let Selective Service get by with procedural shortcuts, they now entertained arguments that probed into every last detail of draft operations.

The Selective Service System could not meet these challenges. Its headquarters kept no current account of rapidly evolving case law. It was not until 1970 that Selective Service strengthened its legal staff to help local boards avoid procedural errors, and it was not until 1972 that it prepared its own manual of draft law.

But by then, the draft system was outgunned. In 1968, a small group of Washington lawyers—Thomas Alder, Charles Halperin, Brian Paddock, and Michael Tigar—established the *Selective Service Law Reporter.* Over a six-year period, the *Reporter* published almost six thousand pages of decisions, regulations, and legal analysis—fifty times the material in Selective Service's 1972 manual. Draft law became a true industry. According to one United States Attorney who prosecuted draft cases, "We were facing a sustained, organized, and pretty well-informed bar. Young lawyers were building careers around these cases." At the height of the war, one draft attorney's handbook listed more than four hundred separate defenses that had been used successfully at least once. A Justice Department official admitted that "it would be rare, after going through [a case] with a fine-tooth comb, not to find some procedural defect."

Most defenses involved variations of the five legal arguments listed below. A few years earlier, they had been just wild ideas; by 1970, they were the law.

1. A draft board had to review an individual's draft file whenever he made an apparently valid (prima facie) claim for a new deferment or exemption. If the board did not, the subsequent induction order was invalid. Draft boards fell victim to this defense when they lost patience with well-counseled registrants who made repeated requests for deferments.

2. A draft board had to approve a request for CO status if an individual made a sincere claim that he opposed all wars, regardless of his religious background. Defense attorneys challenged any induction order that followed a denial of CO status. If a draft board claimed that a registrant was not a true conscientious objector, his attorney could

produce documents or call witnesses at trial to show that, in light of *Seeger,* the board had asked the wrong questions or drawn the wrong conclusions from the facts.

3. When a draft board turned down a request for a deferment or exemption, it had to state its reasons. Draft boards reviewed cases quickly, and many of the claims they reviewed were denied for obvious reasons. But unless they left written records, their induction orders were defective. Even if draft boards stated reasons, they could be challenged as vague, insufficient, or inappropriate.

4. A draft board could not revoke a deferment or exemption, or accelerate an order for induction, as punishment. Long before this issue reached the Supreme Court, Attorney General Ramsey Clark pressured General Hershey into rescinding his delinquency policies in late 1967. However, Hershey restated his personal view that war protestors should be inducted, and a number of local boards followed his lead. Thousands of registrants were reclassified and ordered for induction out of turn. A San Jose draft board clerk testified in court that her board had classified as "delinquents" two hundred registrants who had returned their draft cards. After the Supreme Court outlawed punitive induction orders, draft counselors advised people to pepper their local boards with antiwar leaflets and personal statements, hoping to incite punitive induction orders which were invalid.

5. The "order-of-call" defense was the most extraordinary of all. Draft boards had to issue induction orders in the right order. If a person had been ordered for induction in January when he should have been called in February, he could lawfully refuse induction. To establish this defense, the attorney had to find other registrants of the same board who were older and who should have been drafted before his client. If his client's name was at the bottom of the monthly call list, only one mistake had to be found to prove he was drafted out of order. If his client's name was next-to-last, two mistakes were needed, and so forth.

Skilled investigators scrutinized draft board records and scoured the countryside in search of someone who should have been drafted but was not. Mathematics experts were the best at substantiating this defense. A group of Los Angeles mathematicians sold cassettes explaining the order-of-call defense to draft attorneys, and a Berkeley math major formed his own corporation, Draft Research Associates, charging each defendant a fee of around $250.

Order-of-call mistakes were almost impossible for draft boards to avoid. According to one draft counselor, "You could knock five names off the bottom of any list, and some lists had only five names." The defense was often a godsend for attorneys with clients who seemed hopelessly destined for jail. Leroy Thompson was a prominent black militant and college football star who fled to Canada to avoid the draft. He was arrested on an informer's tip during a visit home, and the FBI and federal prosecutors prepared a careful case against him. However, Thompson's attorney was able to dismiss the case with an order-of-call defense one day before the trial was to start. The FBI was furious, and the U.S. Attorney who prosecuted the case later admitted that "we got blown out of the water."

Late in the war, the order-of-call defense began to be applied to cases in which draft boards had accidentally or intentionally destroyed records of registrants who had passed the age of twenty-six. A fire in the District of Columbia draft headquarters forced the dismissal of several cases. A firebombing in Santa Clara, California, destroyed so many irreplaceable records that counselors put out a call to draft fugitives from the area, urging them to stand trial and raise order-of-call as a defense.

These defense tactics were increasingly successful as the war escalated, but many judges were still reluctant to accept them. When knowledgeable defense attorneys realized that the judge assigned to their client's case was unsympathetic to technical defenses, they delayed the prosecution as long as possible, hoping for a more favorable legal or political environment. Over time, their hopes were answered.

Breakdown

At the start of the Vietnam war, there were scattered federal judges who were willing to dismiss draft cases for procedural irregularities. But in San Francisco, all eight judges dismissed cases for reasons that, in those early days, were not accepted elsewhere. One attorney tried and won a San Francisco case "with defenses that got me laughed out of court in New York." For example, four of the judges ruled that draft board members had to live within the board's geographic area. No San Francisco board met the test, and hundreds of San Francisco draft resisters went free before an appeals court reversed the rule.

One San Francisco judge privately acknowledged that the turmoil and bitter feelings about the Vietnam war affected the way he and his colleagues handled Selective Service cases. Had the war been more popular, he might have been less receptive to technical defenses. Yet like most judges, he couched his dismissals in legal terms, with no mention of the war or the social turbulence it created.

Standing behind the judges were their law clerks, who were often very sympathetic to draft resisters. "We were not that different from people who came before our judges," commented one. These young lawyers, fresh out of law school, spent much of their time looking for procedural irregularities, helping to bolster judges who were inclined to accept far-reaching defenses. Paul Harris, law clerk for a San Francisco judge, was invited to a local bar association's Law Day seminar at a nearby high school, where he found himself on the same platform with a Selective Service official: "He only told them about their obligations—so I had to tell them about their rights." Harris alerted the students that "if you refuse induction, there is a good chance you will not be found guilty because the Selective Service has violated its own regulations when it tried to draft you."

In the years before 1969, all San Francisco federal judges were reluctant to sentence convicted draft offenders to jail. Their typical sentence was two years probation, with a condition of alternative service. Alternative service was administered more leniently by probation officers than was the equivalent CO program run by Selective Service. A convicted draft offender could work nearer his home for more pay, and could select from among a greater variety of jobs.

The judges adopted a liberal sentencing policy partly because they "didn't think it would do any good" to send conscientious offenders to prison. After hearing a number of draft cases, they became convinced that heavy jail sentences did little to deter others from resisting the draft. "These people were not criminals," one commented. "I saw no point in punishing them."

When they sentenced a resister to jail, it was usually because of his defiant attitude. "Even then," one judge recalled, "I was usually reversed on appeal." The defendants were often radical activists who viewed liberal judicial attitudes as barriers to their challenge to the war and the "system." David Harris, a former Stanford student body president, refused to let his attorney argue technical defenses in his behalf. He was sent to prison, as was another defendant who challenged the "imperialist" quality of the law.

The San Francisco judges often encountered hostile reactions from defendants. One young mother spanked her child in the courtroom for giving a bouquet of daffodils to the judge instead of to the defendant, the child's father. But when the judges' lenient attitudes became apparent, the reaction changed. At the start of one draft trial, the defendant's friends contemptuously refused to stand for the judge. After the first recess, they stood.

The leniency of the San Francisco courts encouraged forum-shopping. Before 1970, a registrant could voluntarily change the site of his induction, and if he later refused induction, he would be prosecuted in the new area. One draft resister flew to the Bay Area from Washington, D.C., to refuse induction. The judge gave him probation, exactly what he wanted.

San Francisco prosecutor Cecil Poole, the nation's first black U.S. Attorney, was no more enthusiastic than the judges about Selective Service cases. Poole was convinced that he could not prosecute the cases "in the abstract." He handled them the way he did other victimless crimes, by giving due consideration to community standards. In light of the attitude of young people in the Bay Area, Poole did not believe that draft offenders should be vigorously prosecuted.

Instead of obtaining indictments that federal judges would dismiss, Poole's assistant, Paul Sloan, "began dumping cases on a wholesale basis." Although the San Francisco prosecutors pursued hundreds of cases—Sloan once personally tried thirteen in a single day—these represented a small percentage of the thousands that were referred for prosecution. In 1967 and 1968, more than 90 percent of all cases referred to the San Francisco U.S. Attorney's Office were dropped before indictment.

In 1968, Carlos Ogden, the California director of Selective Service, became concerned that too few draft violators were being prosecuted in the Bay area. Feeling that there was "a breakdown" in the enforcement of the draft law, Ogden complained to Selective Service headquarters, which complained to the Justice Department.

If a prosecutor refused to indict, Selective Service had the right to demand an explanation and special review by the Justice Department. Ogden filed a number of protests, rarely with any success. Although Justice Department officials had views on draft enforcement that Cecil Poole described as "very different" from his own, they rarely failed to support him. According to Sloan, one top official who came out to San Francisco to review his caseload "glanced at the poor quality of the cases, threw up his hands, and said 'no more.' "

Nevertheless, Selective Service officials considered federal prosecutors, not draft board procedures, to be the problem. Sloan complained that "you couldn't talk sense to them. They thought that all that we had to do was to slog away with vigorous prosecution, and our problems would go away." Selective Service officials tried to pressure Sloan to prosecute law clerk Paul Harris for giving his Law Day speech, they tried to pressure Poole to fire Sloan, and—through Republican Senator George Murphy of California—they succeeded in blocking Cecil Poole's appointment as a federal judge for eight years.

In 1969, President Nixon replaced Poole with James Browning, who promised more vigorous enforcement. Sloan resigned soon thereafter to enter private practice, frequently appearing as defense attorney in Selective Service cases. He was replaced by a specially assembled group of former military attorneys. A full-time legal aide was appointed for Carlos Ogden, the state Selective Service director, and President Nixon appointed two new judges who were not as critical of Selective Service.

During Browning's first forty-five days, more than three hundred cases were reviewed. In a marked departure from the past, over half were presented to the grand jury for indictment, and Nixon's new judges began sentencing draft offenders to prison. Gradually, however, Browning found the nation's draft law a "procedural morass," with many cases defective "because of the mistakes the local draft boards have made while processing files." Once again, Ogden complained that "many cases were not reviewed in the depth I would have liked." Despite the new regime, nothing changed very much.

The reluctance of San Francisco prosecutors and judges to convict and imprison draft offenders had a nationwide effect on the enforcement of the draft laws. Judges and law clerks stayed abreast of developments in other jurisdictions. By 1969, Selective Service cases had become the fourth largest category on the criminal docket, and they were a common topic of discussion at judicial conferences and sentencing institutes. In light of the huge numbers of Selective Service cases San Francisco judges had reviewed, their observations and attitudes could not be easily discounted. Judges and prosecutors in other parts of the country realized that many draft offenders were shifting their induction orders to the Bay Area. The ones who did not forum-shop were less affluent, more conscientious, or more poorly counseled. Some officials began to question the fairness of the arrangement.

Case backlogs were beginning to confront dozens of U.S. Attorneys, who found themselves in the same situation Cecil Poole had faced earlier. While judges elsewhere in the country were usually not as liberal as those in San Francisco, almost every judicial circuit began to expand registrant rights and draft board responsibilities. According to a federal prosecutor in Virginia, "judicially fashioned loopholes" made the draft law harder to enforce everywhere.

During the latter years of the Johnson administration, top officials at the Justice Department were concerned about the mounting confrontation between Selective Service and the courts. William Sessions of the Justice Department's Criminal Division blamed Selective Service for "referring draft violations to the U.S. attorneys without weeding out, in a majority of instances, those with fatal procedural defects." He insisted that the best way to enhance the enforcement of the draft law would be to have local boards obey the law and their own regulations. Attorney General Ramsey Clark kept a discreet distance from the dispute; General Hershey recalled that "whenever I tried to call Ramsey for help, he just wasn't around."

In 1969, Clark was replaced by the "law-and-order"-minded John Mitchell; the next year, General Hershey was replaced as Selective Service director by Dr. Curtis Tarr. Shortly after taking office, Tarr testified to Congress that the draft system was enjoying "splendid support" from the criminal justice system. Yet he soon learned of the strength of the legal challenges against the draft. Tarr was barely able to keep the draft system from completely disintegrating under heavy pressure from the courts, an expanding network of draft counselors, and a growing number of cases for prosecution. After a year, he acknowledged that enforcement was "one of the most difficult problems at the time of my appointment."

Tarr drastically expanded his legal staff to cut the backlog of unresolved cases, which by then numbered about 27,000. In 1971, at the behest of Selective Service, Congress directed the Justice Department and the courts to give draft cases precedence over other federal cases in docketing, trial, and appeal. Tarr also tried to improve the operations of local boards by training members better and supervising them more closely. In late 1971, changes in the draft law mandated a major turnover in local board personnel. Thereafter, draft counselors and defense attorneys noticed a marked improvement in local board procedures.

Tarr's efforts received a serious setback from events that were set in motion long before he replaced General Hershey. In 1970, the Supreme Court issued three landmark decisions—*Gutknecht, Welsh,* and *Mulloy.* The cases had been moving up through the lower courts since mid-1966; when they were decided, they marked the watershed in the enforcement of the draft law. Coming at a time when the war and the draft were beginning to wind down, the decisions destroyed much of whatever enthusiasm remained for enforcing the law.

David Gutknecht was a radical pacifist from Minnesota who, like thousands of others, was punitively reclassified and ordered for induction. The Supreme Court declared his local board's action "blatantly lawless," and reversed his conviction for refusing induction. Ironically, Gutknecht himself was not one of the thousands who benefited from the decision; his local board started afresh, inducted him according to proper procedures, and saw him go to Sandstone prison for his subsequent refusal to report for induction.

Elliot Welsh applied to his Santa Barbara, California, draft board for a CO exemption, and he seemed to qualify as a nonreligious objector under *Seeger.* However, his claim was denied. In reversing his conviction for refusing induction, the Supreme Court held that one need not possess specific religious beliefs to qualify as a conscientious objector.

This and the 1971 Clay (Muhammad Ali) case confirmed what many had argued—that Selective Service had misread or ignored *Seeger*, and that many accused draft offenders had been wrongfully denied CO exemptions in the late 1960s. Welsh himself reapplied to his local board and was granted CO status.

On the same day as its *Welsh* decision, the Supreme Court found that Joe Mulloy's Kentucky draft board had unlawfully failed to reopen his case after he had presented a prima facie claim for a CO classification. After the Court's decision, Mulloy's draft board issued him a physical exemption and gave up trying to draft him.

Most judges applied the new case law retroactively, dismissing old cases that did not meet the latest standards. As a result, local board actions that were ostensibly legal in 1968 were often grounds for dismissal in 1970. In effect, this placed the burden on Selective Service to set procedures in Year 1 that would meet the as-yet-unknown judicial standards of Year 2. In a sense, the retroactive application of new case law was the price Selective Service had to pay for not implementing the *Seeger* decision correctly in 1965.

The *Gutknecht, Welsh*, and *Mulloy* cases alerted federal prosecutors across the country that their pending cases needed a second look. Many cases had sat on the shelf for years because of defense counsels' delaying tactics, fugitive defendants (many of whom were in Canada), and the pressing demands of other criminal trials. Most old cases, and a lot of new ones, now could not withstand scrutiny.

The impact of the three cases went far beyond their specific holdings. Defense attorneys, prosecutors, and judges understood that the Supreme Court stood behind the Cecil Pooles and against the Carlos Ogdens. As one federal judge recalled, "we could sense the spirit of those decisions." Emboldened by this mandate from the Supreme Court, they dismissed cases for even the most technical of reasons.

After the *Gutknecht, Welsh*, and *Mulloy* decisions, federal judges also began to alter their sentencing practices. In 1968–69, the average prison sentence for draft offenders had been more than three years— more severe than the penalties for draft resistance during World War II or the Korean War. That quickly changed. Judges who once routinely gave five years were now giving two or three, judges who had imposed shorter terms now imposed probation, and probation no longer necessarily meant alternative service. During 1970, the three Milwaukee federal judges sentenced forty-six of fifty-four convicted draft offenders to prison. Thereafter, they sent only one out of twenty-nine to jail. Judges in Utah and northern Iowa stopped sending people to jail altogether, and judges elsewhere in the country began imposing sentences like a $5 fine or one hour's probation. In Madison, Wisconsin, Judge Samuel Rosenstein flatly refused to convict any draft offenders. Instead, he asked them to do some form of unsupervised alternative service for nine to twelve months, after which he ordered the charges dismissed.

Judge Rosenstein, along with a number of other judges, allowed individuals to do almost anything they wanted, even draft counseling, as their alternative service. A musician from Buffalo, New York, was sentenced to give six rock concerts in Canadian prisons. Chuck Noell, in his book *We Are All POW's,* described his own favorable encounter with a judge:

> His law clerk told me a week later that Judge Broderick had originally planned to sentence me to work in a mental hospital for two years. At the trial, he thought for a couple of minutes about what I said and then essentially sentenced me in his own words to continue the work I was already doing. . . . Both of us came out of the trial with a strong mutual respect. I've paid several social calls on him in the years since the trial, and still do whenever I have the chance.

Faced with stacks of old cases and reluctant judges, prosecutors became less and less interested in enforcing the draft law. The assistant U.S. Attorneys were peers of the accused offenders; their own problems with draft boards cooled their enthusiasm as prosecutors. One U.S. Attorney recalled that "I sometimes had to remind [my assistant] that he was not a defense counsel." In some cities, there developed what one participant called a "cliquelike thing" among draft attorneys, assistant U.S. Attorneys, and law clerks: "Everyone sat around grinning as we worked together to resolve outstanding cases, invariably to the advantage of defendants."

Aside from their personal views about the war or the draft, these were not good cases for young prosecutors to pursue. Especially towards the end of the war, they typically went to the most junior attorney in the office. His superiors screened proposed indictments much more carefully than his dismissal recommendations—perhaps because once indictments were issued, they could be dismissed only with permission of Justice Department headquarters. When cases went to trial, young prosecutors had more to lose than to gain, because their conviction rates often affected prospects for promotions or future job recommendations. They had every incentive to drop cases, and few to prosecute them.

Beginning in the late sixties and accelerating in the early seventies, the number of cases dropped reached epidemic proportions. In Milwaukee, for example, prosecutors trimmed their five-hundred-case backlog to just one hundred immediately following the 1970 Supreme Court decisions. They refused to prosecute any of the roughly fifty accused offenders referred by one local board in Waukesha County.

Other U.S. Attorneys' offices had similar experiences. In the District of Columbia, 99 percent of all 1967–70 cases were never prosecuted. "In the really gross case, if he spat in everyone's face, we would go ahead with prosecution," one D.C. prosecutor commented. A Virginia prosecutor reported that because of the volume of cases, some just "got lost in the shuffle." Prosecutors in New York City, San Diego, El Paso, New Orleans, and Miami dropped more than 95 percent of their cases. The national average was 89 percent.

Only four districts pursued more than 50 percent of their cases. In New Hampshire, which prosecuted 95 percent of its cases, the U.S. Attorney admitted that he had "quite a few acquittals." One tough-minded district's high rate of prosecutions may have resulted from a close kinship with Selective Service; the U.S. Attorney and state Selective Service director drove to work together, discussing cases en route.

In retrospect, San Francisco was not at all unique. It was just early. In 1967–70, the only years for which accurate data is available, Cecil Poole and James Browning prosecuted 11 percent of their cases— exactly the national average, and, in fact, a sterner record than two of the other three California districts.

Until late in the war, juries were the toughest enforcers of the law. Through 1971, juries convicted a higher percentage of cases than trial judges. Defendants who chose jury trials typically tried to maneuver around the prosecution's objections to appeal to the antiwar feelings of the men and women in the jury box, a tactic that usually backfired. The best hope was for a hung jury, as in one Virginia case, where a lone holdout for acquittal later admitted that he would not have voted for conviction under any circumstances. The case was later retried before a judge, who acquitted the defendant on the same facts.

By the 1970s, however, the growing public consensus against the war had reached the jury box. Jurors were instructed by judges not to let their feelings about the war interfere with their role as finders of fact —but that was too much to ask. One juror acknowledged after voting for acquittal that "although we couldn't consider the war itself, we can't ignore it." A Seattle juror admitted after an acquittal that "this war is a nasty situation. If it weren't so nasty, we probably would not have made the decision we did."

Throughout the entire war, draft cases were unusually easy to win. William Smith lost only one case out of hundreds, and that involved a client who had burned his draft card on television. Curry First, who won all thirty of his cases, commented on his shock when he turned to other kinds of law after the war's end: "Losing cases was a new experience to me. I had forgotten that any lawyer, even a very good lawyer, has to lose lots of cases."

Ultimately, of the 210,000 accused offenders, over 200,000 escaped conviction. Only 1,300 were acquitted after trial; almost all the others had their cases dropped before trial—more than half because of defective local board procedures, unenforceable induction orders, or successful technical defenses.

In this respect, Tom Wicker and the Resistance activists proved correct when they set 100,000 as the number of cases necessary to bring turmoil to the legal system and make the draft law unenforceable. There was turmoil in the courts, and for clients of skillful attorneys, the draft law was indeed unenforceable.

The Ones Who Got Away

In 1966, just after draft calls began to rise, John Morton asked his Utah local board to give him a CO exemption. A year later, they turned him down and ordered him to report for induction. Morton refused and, when prosecuted, claimed that his CO application had been mishandled. His trial was postponed while the appellate court considered an interlocutory matter. In 1971, the Tenth Circuit Court recommended dismissal of the case. Over the next year, a federal judge twice denied the government's motion to reopen the prosecution. Morton's case was not finally dismissed until June 1972. By then, it was too late for the local board to reprocess his file before the December 1972 end of the draft.

In retrospect, refusing induction and hiring a good lawyer seems to have been a good strategy for avoiding the draft. Many did engage in elaborate, expensive legal strategies to beat the system. After winning cases because of procedural errors by their draft boards, they reached their twenty-sixth birthdays, got high lottery numbers, or—like Morton—outlasted the war. Even if they were still vulnerable to the draft, the local boards frequently gave them exemptions and forgot about them. It was truly an extraordinary instance when a draft board responded to a successful legal defense by methodically reprocessing the case, taking care not to make any mistakes, and issuing an induction order that was enforceable in court. Especially after 1970, a defendant with a good lawyer had a very remote chance of ever having to enter the Army or go to prison.

But at the height of the war, the results did not seem so assured. The overwhelming majority of draft resisters thought that refusing induction would likely bring long prison terms. Lengthy legal battles involved considerable anxiety, expense, and disruption of personal plans —very real penalties for refusing induction. Tom Blackwell began law school while he was engaged in his legal battle against Selective Service. His prosecutor dropped the case three years later, just a few months before Blackwell graduated. Had he been convicted, he would have been barred from practicing law.

The 210,000 individuals accused of criminal draft offenses were subjected to FBI investigations which left permanent scars on their reputations. Their arrest records are still on file, and they often are viewed by friends and neighbors as having "gotten away" with a crime. Some men accept this as preferable to years in prison or exile, but others are bitter. They endured years of personal upheaval as a consequence of what they believed, and the courts later confirmed, were unfair and illegal actions by their draft boards.

The luckier ones were the roughly 360,000 whose draft offenses were either ignored or never discovered. The findings of the Notre Dame survey suggest that draft boards knew about roughly a third of these crimes, but never reported them to U.S. attorneys. A federal prosecutor in Los Angeles reported in 1970 that "draft boards are just so busy and have such a heavy work load that if it becomes clear they're going to have a lot of trouble with a kid, they just say 'forget it.' "

Isolated cases of unreported draft offenders occurred throughout the war. The mayor's son in a large southern city returned his draft card to his local board. The board mailed it back to him, but he rejected it a second time with a letter promising to refuse induction. He never heard from his draft board again. A young man from Detroit was ordered to take his preinduction physical. When he arrived, he lay down and slept through it. The induction station officials told him he would have to wait several hours for the next group and gave him his Selective Service file. He went home, taking the file with him. He too never heard from his draft board.

Perhaps the most bizarre story of an unreported draft offender involved Albert Jones, a Detroit youth who never really objected to going into the Army. His mother, Sister Lily, was the leader of a small black religious sect, and she wanted him to refuse induction. On the day Jones was to report for induction, his mother held an early morning service, during which he slipped away and reported. When Sister Lily discovered he was gone, she packed her congregation into taxicabs and drove to the induction station. She and her followers stormed in and rescued her son, all the while singing

"When the Saints Go Marching In." She took him home, and he never heard from his draft board again.

The largest category of unreported offenders comprised those who never registered for the draft, and whose existence was unknown to local boards. Of the untold hundreds of thousands who illegally failed to register in the Vietnam era, only a few thousand were ever identified, and just 250 were convicted.

Nonregistration was actively encouraged by some antiwar groups as a means of draft resistance. In 1967, *Peacemaker* magazine circulated a petition to enlist nonregistrants and collected 84 signatures. By the early 1970s, the antiwar movement spread to the high schools, and seventeen-year-olds were advised to resist the draft by not registering. "Check Out the Odds," a manual coauthored by David Gutknecht of Supreme Court fame, tried to persuade eighteen-year-olds that failing to register was the safest means of avoiding the draft:

> For most young men, not registering is the single most effective method of dealing with the draft. At the present time, the Selective Service has no effective method of tracking down 18-year-olds who don't sign up. If you don't register, chances are the draft board won't find out. Most of the tens of thousands of non-registrants are never discovered. And discovery . . . does not always mean that you will be prosecuted. . . . You can always register late.

The characteristics of nonregistrants have always been a matter of speculation. Peter Straub, former Selective Service general counsel, believed them to be jail convicts, patients in mental hospitals, and homosexuals. A 1974 Ford Foundation report conjectured that "they typically lead disjointed lives, moving frequently and hesitant to take permanent jobs lest their delinquent status be discovered and reported." William Walker was an Illinois nonregistrant who fit this image:

> During the first few months after I turned 18, I did confide in some friends and close acquaintances, but the resulting attitude of these peo-

ple was . . . "you'll be sorry." . . . So for the next three and a half years I kept silent. . . . The psychological burden on a non-registrant is great. He knows he has broken a law and that he must shape the rest of his life with this fact always in mind.

Nonregistration was very risky for white, middle-class men. The Minnesota State Selective Service headquarters culled through four Twin Cities high school yearbooks, checking every name from the class of 1969 against its records. Of the 1,082 graduates that year, only 17 had not registered. Letters were sent to them. Nine were found to have joined the service before registering (a lawful act), and the other eight had moved out of town. President Ford's son Jack and many other middle-class whites inadvertently registered late, but few, very few, failed to register at all.

Nonregistration was much more the draft evasion technique of the poor. According to the Notre Dame survey, almost half the nonregistrants were black, and most had low incomes and little education. Homer Singleton, a Louisiana draft counselor, believed that nonregistration was epidemic among migrant workers and bayou dwellers. Nonregistration also may have been common in inner-city neighborhoods, where young people often lead untraceable lives. For many, nonregistration simply reflected their alienation from the American mainstream. Some were so ill informed that they never realized that they had to register. Even if they were aware of their obligations, these underprivileged youths had so few of the benefits of citizenship that they felt no need to assume any of its duties. The war itself may have had a significant impact on nonregistration offenses in the inner city. The Notre Dame survey found that almost all black nonregistration offenses occurred during the latter half of the war. Apparently, rising black consciousness and the plight of black veterans made many inner-city youths reluctant to join the military.

Estimates of the number of nonregistrants vary widely. Comparing registration and census data, some have concluded that as many as two million never registered. But most of these were seventeen-year-old enlistees or aliens with temporary residence permits, who were not legally required to register for the draft. In any event, many of those who never registered are the same people who are never counted by the census. One spokesman for a community organization compared nonregistration for the draft with nonreporting in the census: "It's the same thing. . . . The man with five kids says he has two. We're tired of fools coming to our door talking irrelevant statistics." The Census Bureau believes its 1970 count to have undercounted draft-age men by about 900,000, casting substantial doubt on any effort to measure nonregistrants by comparing census data with Selective Service data.

The findings of the Notre Dame survey indicate that roughly 250,000 young men broke the law by never registering for the draft. Broken down by race, 0.6 percent of all whites, 3.9 percent of all blacks, and 1.7 percent of all other minority (mostly Spanish-speaking) persons were found never to have registered. Most had very low incomes and little education.

Throughout the war, Selective Service maintained a flexible policy toward nonregistration. A young man was required to register within five days of his eighteenth birthday, but he was not subject to the draft until he turned nineteen, and draft boards seldom cared if he waited until then. Before 1973, nonregistrants were reported to prosecutors at the rate of about one thousand per year. Like Greg Hooton of Benton Harbor, Michigan, almost all avoided prosecution by agreeing to register and take their chances with the draft:

> The day after Thanksgiving I got arrested at home and was taken to Grand Rapids to be fingerprinted. There I talked to the U.S. Attorney again, and he gave me what he called "one last chance" to change my mind. When I got home, I spent the weekend talking to people about it, and the total reaction of everyone was that I should register. I don't know what my reasons were, but I did register the following Monday, and the charges were dropped.

This practice ended in 1973, after the draft expired. During that year, almost 3,500 nonregistrants appeared at their local boards, thinking all was safe, but found themselves referred to federal prosecutors. A nonregistration charge was easy to prove and almost impossible to defend, and a number of individuals were convicted. But judges generally dropped charges if the defendant agreed to register, an act which by then carried no risk.

By 1976, nonregistrants were impossible to find. Draft boards no longer existed, police never asked to see draft cards, and neighbors no longer cared. The handful who were inadvertently discovered faced little risk of punishment. In a series of unusual decisions, federal courts interpreted the statute of limitations to mean that a nonregistrant could be prosecuted only if he turned eighteen between September and December of 1971. President Carter later issued blanket pardons to nonregistrants, but none would have been prosecuted anyway.

By the time of Carter's inauguration, just 2 percent of the 570,000 draft offenders stood convicted or still faced criminal charges—a manifestation of what William Sessions of the Justice Department admitted was "selective prosecution." From the prosecutors' standpoint, what happened to draft cases was roughly comparable to what happens to most criminal cases. A great many crimes go unreported, and many criminals remain undiscovered. Even when charges are filed, prosecutors routinely dismiss a majority of the cases. Sometimes the evidence is weak or inadmissible, and other times no public interest is served by strict enforcement of the law. In recent years, only about 33 percent of all accused criminals have been convicted. Yet of the 210,000 accused of draft offenses, just 4 percent were convicted, and only 1.5 percent were sentenced to prison. Had they been prosecuted as vigorously as bank robbers, the federal prison system would have had to double its capacity at the height of the war.

Federal prosecutors realized that extraordinary numbers of draft cases were being dropped, and Selective Service officials knew that the courts were invalidating thousands of induction orders. Yet at the time, no one publicly acknowledged the dimensions of the problem. While the draft was still in force, such an admission might have totally undermined the war effort.

Instead, top officials at the Justice Department and Selective Service denied that more than a small number of cases were defective. Assistant Attorney General Robert Mardian and Selective Service Director Curtis Tarr both suggested that 75–80 percent of the 210,000 accused draft offenders eventually capitulated and reported for induction. This "almost made it seem as if cooperation were the byword of the nation's young," as Stuart Loory commented. Walter Morse, Selective Service's general counsel, further alleged that the 210,000 figure referred only to "initial violations," giving the impression that most of these men were the victims of oversleeping, undelivered letters, or momentary bad judgment. But in 1971, a Selective Service survey was reported by *The New York Times* to show that these 210,000 offenders had ordinarily refused three or four induction orders before their cases were referred to prosecutors, indicating that they were indeed willful violators.

Some men did capitulate, either because their original offenses had not been willful or carefully considered, or because of the strains of being a criminal defendant. Maintaining one's resolve in the face of an FBI investigation, formal charges, and fingerprinting was not always easy. Defense attorney Conrad Lynn described the case of one of his clients who succumbed to these pressures:

> Steve was a bitter black youth who would come to my office with his indictment in his pocket and sit and brood for hours. Several months passed, and finally Steve began to open up. He had little sympathy for the Vietnamese people but a raging hatred of the U.S. Government. . . . After a year had passed the government lawyer placed the case on the calendar for trial. Steve sat in the courtroom during the trial of [another draft refuser]. Suddenly, one day he told me he wished to drop his contest of his case and submit to induction.

Often, however, accused offenders capitulated by agreeing to submit to induction under circumstances that they believed would enable them to fail the physical exam. Accused offenders in San Francisco and Los Angeles sometimes went to Seattle or other induction stations where their chances of failing were very good. Others quickly developed conditions that disqualified them.

Throughout the Vietnam era, neither the Justice Department nor Selective Service kept any statistics on the reasons for case closings. One Justice Department official was publicly quoted as acknowledging that the agency's job was "to prosecute draft dodgers, not keep figures." The only figures they released were those in a twelve-month 1971–72 sample by the Justice Department showing the reasons for case closings after indictment. These data showed that 67 percent were dismissed because of "a bona fide attempt to submit to induction." But the sample did not encompass case closings before indictment, which were usually the weaker cases—and which accounted for 95 percent of the dropped cases; nor did it include cases screened during the nationwide housecleaning of cases following the *Gutknecht, Welsh,* and *Mulloy* decisions.

U.S. Attorney's offices were generally unaware of the official contention that almost all dropped cases resulted from capitulating offenders. Informed about it afterwards, Cecil Poole said, "I can't believe it." Judson Bowles, who supervised the Justice Department's draft prosecutions during the critical 1968–71 period, disputed the official contention, saying, "I don't know where they got their statistics. A great majority of the cases involved procedural errors by the draft board." A high-ranking Justice Department official who had once publicly endorsed the 75–80 percent figure privately admitted that "the problem in prosecution resulted from sloppy preparation by Selective Service," with "a hell of a lot" of cases dismissed for that reason.

To get a reasonable picture of what happened to the 210,000 unconvicted cases, fifteen federal prosecutors were asked to estimate what proportion of their cases were dropped for procedural defects. Eight agreed to give estimates, and their collective judgment was that 58 percent were dropped because of local board errors and that, of the 42 percent who submitted to induction, half failed their physical. The official figure of 75–80 percent inducted was four times too high.

All together, the evidence suggests that roughly 115,000 accused draft offenders had their cases dropped because of procedural errors by their local boards—ten times the number later pardoned by Presidents Ford and Carter.

The Wheels of Justice

With so few draft offenders convicted, one must ask why they, and not the others, paid the penalty demanded by law. In the public mind, the convicted offenders are commonly perceived as either activist radicals who flagrantly resisted the draft, or manipulative "draft dodgers" who tried to lie or finagle their way out of the draft. If the 8,800 convicted offenders were truly "worse" than the hundreds of thousands who were not punished, then selective prosecution was justified.

Neither of these two public perceptions is correct, however. A San Francisco judge complained that "the ones we wanted to convict, we couldn't; the best people who came before us were the ones we had to convict. It was all a terrible game of Russian roulette." Flagrant or manipulative draft evaders regularly availed themselves of technical defenses that set them free. Most successful prosecutions were against those whose religious or political principles, poor counseling, or general misfortune kept them from raising defenses necessary to avoid conviction.

Manipulative "draft dodgers" were rarely caught. Stewart Horn was the exception. He stayed in college for eight years, eventually losing his student deferment because of his slow progress in school. After three unsuccessful appeals to extend his student deferment, he applied for a CO exemption. After that was denied, and after he lost two more appeals, Horn was ordered to report for induction. One day after he was required to appear at the induction station, he applied for a hardship postponement because of his wife's pregnancy. His local board granted him a nine-month extension. After the baby arrived, Horn fled to Canada. He was unhappy with life in exile, so he came home and was convicted. Still, had Horn been properly counseled at trial, his CO application and many appeals almost surely would have given rise to a sound technical defense.

The public's impression of the convicted draft offenders was reinforced by a series of well-publicized cases of fraud or deception, in which the perpetrators were caught and punished. The head of the Young Republican Leadership Conference in Washington, D.C., was sentenced to two years in prison for obtaining fraudulent deferments from his draft board. After an FBI investigation, draft evasion organizations were uncovered in New York City and Cleveland; thirty-eight fathers and sons were arrested for paying up to $5,000 for false papers that would have entitled the sons to draft exemptions. A New York City draft board official was convicted for selling deferments and exemptions for as much as $30,000. In southern California, an orthodontist gave several patients cut-rate braces that had no therapeutic value. One of his patients was convicted for conspiring to avoid the draft, and the orthodontist himself fled to Mexico to escape prosecution.

The publicity generated by these cases, along with the press attention given the more radical exiles in Canada, shifted attention away from the much larger number of persons who quietly accepted conviction as a matter of principle. Willard Gaylin, a Columbia University psychologist, conducted lengthy interviews with dozens of imprisoned draft offenders in 1968, and he was "shocked" at his "naïve assumptions" about the kind of people they were. Expecting political radicals and antiwar activists, he discovered gentle, compassionate people with deep moral and religious principles.

When President Ford's Clemency Board reviewed more than eighteen hundred cases of convicted draft offenders in 1975, the members were startled by the sincerity and decency of the people involved. As a consequence, it virtually abandoned Ford's alternative service requirement and recommended outright pardons for four out of five applicants. These individuals were rarely college-educated, upper-middle-class white radicals. An unexpectedly large percentage came from economically disadvantaged backgrounds. Many were blacks and Spanish-speaking persons. Four of every five were deeply opposed to the war, having committed their offenses as a matter of principle. Of this group, less than 1 percent had ever been convicted of other felony crimes, less than 1 percent had serious drug problems, and few had been fugitives. About a third were Jehovah's Witnesses, Muslims, or Quakers. As Gaylin noted, the persons convicted of draft violations

> . . . were service-oriented individuals who believed that a man must be judged by his actions, not his statements, and that ideals and behavior were not separable phenomena. And assuredly they were not the population at which the Selective Service Act was directed, for under the intention of the act most of these boys were indeed CO's.

These individuals were convicted because they were unwilling or unable to avail themselves of the many easier paths to escape from the draft. Gaylin found that one-third of those he interviewed could have easily qualified for deferments or exemptions, had they wished. One was almost blind, and another had a badly injured leg. Rather than accept easy ways out, they refused to cooperate with the draft system as a matter of principle.

Matt Morris wrote letters to his draft board explaining his antiwar beliefs. "The draft board said that since I was a declared Quaker they were willing to exempt me. . . . I felt that even though I qualified, there were people whose feelings were as sincere as mine who could not. If I were to cop out and take the exemption, I would be leaving them in the lurch. This would have been unethical." Morris went to prison for refusing induction.

Philip Walker's draft board went to great lengths to prevent him from committing a draft offense:

> Shortly after I had applied for I-O [CO] classification, my draft board had written that I would be so classified when my student deferment was up. . . . Three months before I was to graduate, Johnson announced that the military had been bombing North Vietnam for several months. I wrote him a letter of disaffiliation and enclosed my draft cards. An undersecretary sent them to the Iowa state draft board, and some officer returned them to me with a note saying he understood and he would direct my local board to classify me I-O. I re-returned the cards, saying he didn't understand that I no longer cared to be a member of his little organization, and that I definitely wouldn't carry the membership cards. A few months later, my local board sent a I-A classification card, which I duly returned. . . .

Walker then received an induction order, which he refused to obey. His board reopened the case, inviting him to a hearing which he refused to attend. They sent him another draft card, which he returned. Finally, after disobeying a second induction order, Walker was convicted and sentenced to three years in prison.

Clifford Jones was past twenty-five, just six months away from permanent disqualification from the draft. He was working as an aeronautical engineer for the federal government, which qualified him for an occupational deferment. Believing that the draft system was illegal and immoral, Jones refused to apply for a routine extension of his deferment. He then refused induction. When Jones's case reached the Supreme Court, it was denied a hearing. Ultimately, Jones came to regard his efforts as futile and self-destructive:

> The whole fight accomplished nothing. It took me four and a half years and $20,000 in legal fees. I went through eight different jobs and had a total of nine months' unemployment and an intense amount of personal anguish.

Just as some refused deferments and exemptions, so others resisted the temptation to raise technical defenses, preferring instead to challenge the fundamental legality of the war. Richard Lavelle fired his counsel, a nationally renowned draft attorney, who wanted to soften the antiwar character of Lavelle's defense and thereby keep him out of prison. Lavelle insisted on "maintaining my fundamental indictment against U.S. policy as criminal before morality and law," and he refused to raise any technical defenses in his own behalf. Lavelle was convicted and sentenced to five years in prison.

Frank Burton insisted on defending himself. His judge gave him a copy of the procedural rules and coached him about the defenses he could raise in his behalf. Burton ignored the judge's help, telling the jury that the rightness of the war was the issue they should debate. The judge had to overrule him, causing an uproar that left three persons charged with contempt and a cleared courtroom. It took the jury less than an hour to find Burton guilty.

Federal judges, liberal and conservative alike, refused to accept direct legal challenges against the war, and defendants like Lavelle and Burton almost always were convicted. The only exception was when Massachusetts Judge Charles Wyzanski dismissed the case against John Jeffron Sisson, Jr. Sisson was a graduate of the Phillips Exeter Academy and Harvard College whose defense, very simply, was that he refused to participate in an immoral war. Working in 1968 as a reporter for a civil rights newspaper in Alabama, Sisson refused to apply for CO status because he knew he did not qualify as a religious objector. After he failed to report for induction, Judge Wyzanski dismissed his case, declaring that Sisson could not "constitutionally be subjected to military orders . . . which may require him to kill in the

Vietnam conflict." The Supreme Court refused to overrule the dismissal, although it later declared in the *Gillette* case that "selective" objectors like Sisson did not qualify for CO status.

Many others were convicted because they failed to raise good defenses not as a matter of principle, but as a consequence of poor legal representation. Although the network of skilled draft counselors reached almost everywhere, it was most accessible to college students and others with connections to the antiwar movement. Many draft offenders never knew about this network and had to rely on less experienced local attorneys whom they discovered through haphazard means. One federal judge recalled that general practitioners had trouble with draft cases unless he personally advised them about the defenses available to their clients. A prosecutor admitted that most of his convictions "were against lawyers who were not very good." One common ploy of the inexperienced attorney was the insanity defense. An attorney would bring in psychiatrists who claimed his client was temporarily or partially insane, arguing that his affliction prevented him from submitting to induction but did not affect his other behavior. This tactic never worked. Herbert Black was the victim of poor representation. Black's attorney misplaced his CO application while redecorating his office, and forgot to mail it on time. Although Black would have qualified for a CO exemption, he was convicted for refusing to report for induction.

Many people were convicted despite the apparent illegality of their induction orders. One out of ten applicants to President Ford's Clemency Board was convicted after being improperly denied CO claims that were valid under the doctrine of *Seeger* and *Welsh*. Typically, local boards erred by insisting that CO status was reserved to members of specific religious sects. Either the lawyers representing these men failed to raise proper arguments at trial, or judges were ill informed as to the current state of the law.

A great many convicted draft offenders failed to realize that they qualified as CO's under existing law. Raul Ramirez asked his board for a CO application form in 1969, but the religious orientation of the form discouraged him from filling it out. Ramirez heard about the *Welsh* case, and he asked the board to give him another form. When they sent him the identical one, he again failed to complete it. He believed that it was impossible for him to express his beliefs properly on a form designed for members of organized religions. A draft counselor would have told Ramirez to attach his own statement to the form, but without such advice he never got CO status, later refused induction, and was convicted.

Even members of pacifist religious sects did not always receive the CO exemptions to which they were entitled. Peter Wagler was raised in an Amish family. When he came of age, he stopped attending church, although he still subscribed to the group's principles. Although Wagler qualified as a CO even under the old, pre-*Seeger* standards, his local board denied his claim, citing his poor church attendance as its reason.

As in earlier wars, Jehovah's Witnesses went to prison rather than cooperate with the requirements of the Vietnam-era draft. Despite their obvious qualification as conscientious objectors, almost two thousand Jehovah's Witnesses were convicted of draft offenses. The Witnesses were typically working-class people, polite, deeply committed, and not highly educated. They often brought their church leaders, families, and friends with them to court. Their trials were religious experiences, a confirmation of the depth of their beliefs. The teachings of the Watchtower Bible and Tract Society preclude participating in any war except Armageddon. "Actually, you can't call us 'resisters,'" commented Witness Paul Jenkins. "We believe Satan uses the worldwide political system, which the Book of Revelations calls 'a wild beast,' to cause wars, so we don't take political stands or participate in wars." Many Witnesses refused CO status and insisted that they qualified for ministerial exemptions instead. They all had ministerial duties, but rarely as full-time jobs; Selective Service regulations required that they be denied ministerial exemptions for that reason.

Most local boards did give them CO status, with or without their consent. However, many Witnesses then refused to perform alternative service, and that is what led to their convictions. Jenkins called Witnesses who obeyed draft board alternative-service orders "immature" in their beliefs, because their religion required them to refuse the command of any institution whose sole purpose was war. However, as

Jenkins noted, "if a Witness is ordered by a judge to alternative service, he can accept it then." Witnesses who were convicted and sentenced to two years of alternative service had no religious problem in completing it. After 1970, Witnesses were seldom sent to prison. Yet Abner Johnson came to court for refusing to obey his draft board, explained Witness doctrine to the judge, and promised to perform any alternative service ordered by the court. The judge, notwithstanding, sentenced Johnson to prison.

Black Muslims also felt the full force of the law. Members of the Nation of Islam refuse on religious grounds to fight in any war not declared by Allah. According to the Justice Department and many draft boards, they were not conscientious objectors because they objected only "to certain types of war in certain circumstances." The Muhammad Ali case attracted public attention to pacifist Muslims in 1966 when he asked his Kentucky draft board for a CO exemption. The board found his beliefs insincere, to which Ali replied:

> It would be no trouble for me to accept [induction] on the basis that I'll go into the armed services boxing exhibitions in Vietnam, or traveling the country at the expense of the government. . . . If it wasn't against my conscience to do it, I would easily do it. I wouldn't raise all this court stuff and I wouldn't go through all of this and lose and give up the millions that I gave up and my image with the American public, that I would say is completely dead and ruined and so I wouldn't turn down so many millions and jeopardize my life walking the streets of the South and all of America with no bodyguard if I wasn't sincere.

Ali was convicted in June 1967 for refusing induction, sentenced to five years in prison, and stripped of his heavyweight championship. Four years later (throughout which he was free on bond), the Supreme Court reversed his conviction on technical grounds. Ali went free, but about one hundred other Muslims did not.

While four-fifths of those convicted for draft offenses were confirmed war resisters, the rest were prosecuted much as if the draft law were a kind of federal vagrancy statute. Most of these two thousand individuals were hard-luck youngsters who lived at society's fringe. They often came from broken homes, disproportionately from the South. They had below-average IQs and usually were high-school dropouts. Many had serious drug or alcohol problems. Some, as Willard Gaylin found, fit "the stereotype of the self-destructive, unrealized goof-up." Robert Jackson was sent three separate induction orders, and each time he failed to report. The first time, he had gotten into a fight and been hospitalized for stab wounds. The next time, he was in jail for a minor offense. The third time, he was addicted to drugs. Jackson's draft board pressed charges, and he was convicted.

People like Jackson often moved from place to place, never bothering to tell their families or their local boards how to locate them. They used their draft cards for identification, never really understanding what the draft involved. When their turn came for induction, they could not be found. These men probably would have submitted to induction instead of going to prison, yet many were obviously disqualified for the draft. John Blass had an IQ of 49 and a sixth-grade education. Paul Allen's wife was in the midst of a serious kidney operation, which doctors didn't expect her to survive. He was her sole means of support and was qualified for a hardship deferment under any reasonable standard. Luther Wilson's father was dead, and his mother was seriously ill with sickle cell anemia. His draft board denied his request for a hardship deferment. Ernest Eckhart had a disabling physical injury which embarrassed him when he had to undress in front of other persons. He refused to report for his preinduction physical. Even though Eckhart's disability qualified him for a medical exemption, his draft board classified him I-A. But being disqualified for military service was not a valid defense to a draft violation, and each of these men was convicted.

Others committed trivial, even accidental violations of Selective Service regulations—usually for failure to keep draft boards informed of their whereabouts. When Paul Taliaferro moved to a new address, he reported his change of address to the local post office, enabling mail to reach him, but he never reported the change to his draft board. Steven Greene had his mother telephone his new address to the local board. Unfortunately, his mail often failed to reach him because he neglected to put his name on his mailbox. Robert Craig continued to receive mail at home while he was away at college. However, his father had recently died, and his mother was reluctant to see her only son go to Vietnam. Without telling him, she returned all letters from his draft board. Taliaferro, Greene, and Craig were all convicted by overzealous prosecutors.

There were obvious dangers of abuse in a statute that could be applied arbitrarily to individuals whom local officials wanted to punish. In Mississippi and Louisiana, the draft was used as a weapon to intimidate and imprison black civil rights workers. Bennie Tucker, later the mayor of a small Mississippi town, had his CO application denied because, according to his draft board, he "caused nothing but trouble." After his election to the city council, he was issued four induction orders. Hubert Davis filed to run for mayor of another Mississippi town and immediately received his induction order. Robert James was granted CO status by a Mississippi draft board that was unaware of his local civil rights activities. After working for sixteen months in two local hospitals and having his work become better known, his draft board ordered him to report to a new alternative service job in a distant town. He refused the order and was sentenced to five years imprisonment. Mississippi civil rights worker Willie Jordan reported for induction a few minutes late, and induction station officials refused to process him. For that offense, Jordan was sentenced to five years in prison.

An extreme case of harassment involved Mrs. Jeanette Crawford, a New Orleans civil rights leader who refused to testify before the Louisiana House Committee on Un-American Activities. Within a week, all three of her sons were ordered for induction or for preinduction physicals. James, her oldest son, was accused of not having registered for the draft. The fact that he had been in the Army for thirteen years did not deter prosecutors from pursuing him or the FBI from staking out the Crawford house to arrest him. At the time, James was in Germany. When his commanding officer learned of the warrant, James was put in the stockade. While James' problems were resolved in a few days, his brother Warren paid a heavier penalty. Warren refused induction, was convicted, and was given the most severe sentence of any nonviolent draft offender of the Vietnam era—six concurrent five-year sentences.

Civil rights workers and Black Muslims usually paid the heaviest penalties for draft law violations. Throughout the country, the prison sentences imposed on blacks averaged about one year longer than those given to whites. Stiff sentences were also assessed against radical activists who used the courtroom as a forum for directly challenging American involvement in the war.

However, these sentencing inequities were minor compared with the overwhelming differences in punishment from one judicial district to the next. In 1968, while San Francisco judges were offering probation to most offenders, south Texas judges sentenced fourteen of sixteen to five-year prison terms. An individual's sentence rarely depended on the seriousness of his offense; it usually hinged on the judge sitting before him.

Congress had written the law to include prison sentences, but judges still had discretion to decide whether imprisonment served a valid purpose. Refusing the draft did not indicate behavior that was likely to be dangerous to society in the future, but most violations were deliberate and would have been repeated had the occasion arisen. One federal judge observed that draft offenders "don't threaten society in the same sense as do—for example—professional bank robbers. They probably threaten it more, in the long run, by making law violation fashionable, and suggesting that every man is free to obey or disobey the law, as it pleases him." Another judge insisted that he "didn't become a judge to preside over the decline and fall of the American republic."

Some judges believed that, regardless of the moral rightness or wrongness of an individual's action, the government had a responsibility to uphold its duly constituted laws. As one noted, "I am opposed to conscription. I also believe that the war in Vietnam is both immoral and impractical. My sentence policies are based upon the fact that as long as a law exists, it should be imposed to effectuate its intent and purpose." Another judge commented that regardless of his admiration for conscientious draft resisters, "it is their duty legally to comply with the law or accept the penalty as part of their sacrifice to their principles."

A few judges imposed four- or five-year sentences as a means of assuring that individuals would serve about two years before being paroled. As General Hershey once observed,

The young man who assumes a responsibility to answer the call of his country serves a minimum of twenty-four months away from society, work, and family. I see no reason why a Selective Service rejector should be removed from society, work, and family for a lesser period.

Although these arguments made sense in theory, many lawyers and judges who saw these cases were troubled by the fact that the few draft offenders who went to jail did nothing different from the many who did not. One judge spoke with relief about how he sentenced almost everyone to probation: "If I had sentenced these people to jail, I would feel very troubled about it right now."

The moment of sentencing was often a moment of triumph and moral vindication for the draft resister. He had stood his ground in defiance of the institutions of war. One convicted offender even staged a "victory dinner," and his friends sang choruses of "For He's a Jolly Good Felon." Most could easily have left for Canada before starting their prison terms. Border authorities often checked names against an FBI list of criminal defendants, but thousands managed to cross the border without difficulty. Most judges set no bail for draft violators, even after conviction. Others set modest bail of at most a few thousand dollars, which defendants sometimes paid through funds collected by antiwar groups. A few, however, went directly to prison:

> They said that I could be released without bail if I signed a paper saying that I'd appear when my trial came up. I said that I could not honestly say —that I hadn't made up my mind yet. Since I refused to sign, they put $5,000 bail on me. This was beyond anything I could raise. I had to go to jail.

If a convicted offender really wanted to run out his string, he could remain free until all his appeals were lost, after which he would still have ten days to leave the country. However, those who took flight typically did so right after conviction. Andrew Daley of New York City, angry about living in "a nation whose laws and customs did not afford [him] the same opportunities and protection afforded to white citizens," left the country without waiting to see whether his judge would sentence him to probation.

Less than 10 percent of those convicted left the country, and of these most later returned and served their sentences. Some of the other 90 percent might have escaped if they had had more money, but most rejected the idea. Going to Canada meant cutting old ties and making a possibly irreversible change in their lives. Some viewed it as "running away from the fight," a "copout," or worse:

> Up to the very last week [I] considered going to Canada. I checked airlines, thought about the timing of when I'd have to leave, but I just couldn't do it. . . . It's my country and I'm not going to run away from it. Then, in the next few years, after this is all over, if I meet someone who has lost his son in Vietnam, I don't want to have to say that I had run away. There is this thing in me. These guys are getting killed every day, and that's the constant factor of the whole issue. They're Americans, and America is as much a part of me as it is of them. They're being shot at—I don't feel I should run away.

Frequently, the convicted draft refuser faced his prison sentence with optimism. Draft resistance manuals spoke encouragingly of what prison experience could be like for the antiwar martyr: "It can be a source of growth and satisfaction if it comes about as a result of doing what to you is the right thing. . . ." "The noncooperator can find numerous opportunities for creative service with fellow prisoners—in recreational work, education, letter-writing, and fellowship." Willard Gaylin found one new arrival at Allenwood to be full of confidence: "The experience of prison life by itself is a rare one and is a character-building thing. . . . I definitely think it will be."

But a Brooklyn judge, in sentencing Robert Modell to prison, knew better what prison life had in store:

> I take it you look with pride on the possibility of being punished. I think that's foolish. . . . I think you underestimate prison. It is not an experience that should be welcomed. Even in the best of the federal penitentiaries, it is a horrible way to spend a life. It is very damaging and, in some instances, dangerous.

A few draft offenders could not tolerate prison life. A member of the Hare Krishna sect escaped from prison because of physical threats and harassment by inmates and guards. Another developed a heroin addiction while in prison and returned a few years later after an armed robbery he committed to support his habit.

A draft offender's prison experience depended largely on where he was sent. One inmate who served his time in Allenwood, the white-collar prison of the federal system, complained about the antiwar movement's "ridiculous" claims that draft resisters were being mistreated: "I've seen in certain publications where we were dragged nude, a thousand yards, down freezing corridors and things like that. They may mean well, but the exaggerations turn me off."

Instead, abuse came in subtle ways. Prison officials sometimes offered to set up draft offenders as "model prisoners," giving them extra privileges in return for not politicizing other inmates. When they refused to comply, they were sometimes the victims of retaliation by the guards. As a fellow inmate recalled, "These kids [took] a lot of abuse that isn't in the record . . . much more than a typical prisoner." They were often denied participation in work-release or rehabilitation programs, the common explanation being that they did not need rehabilitation.

Even those who adjusted well found the day-to-day routine annoying and degrading. One spoke the mind of many when he complained about things "that sound petty on description: . . . when they distribute the mail they make cracks about your mail . . . the hassles in the clothing room . . . the trying to get the right size . . . the indifference . . . the standing up, always in line, standing for count . . . the patronizing." Above all, they were bored. One wrote, "I'm tired of being in jail. There is no fellowship here—and I am lonely." Another went over in his mind "at least a thousand times" his experiences in high school and college, thinking "who'd ever thought just four years ago. . . ." For most, prison was an unending nightmare. As nonviolent individuals, they had little in common with other inmates. As pacifists, they had little in common with prison guards. It was hard for them just to "do time" and let the months slip away. Their friends and families suffered, too. Marriages and engagements were broken off, and the wives and girl friends who remained faithful sometimes had a very difficult time:

> [Our baby] arrived prematurely, early in May. Having been promised a call to Bob after the baby's birth, I eagerly called the prison. The officials refused to let me speak to Bob, even after I explained that the baby was having difficulty breathing and was in danger of death. "If she dies, call back," the guard told me, and hung up.

Few kept track of their legal situations while behind bars, and lawyers rarely watched for new law that might have overturned convictions. The Justice Department refused to review the files of the four thousand persons whose convictions had been brought into question by the 1970 *Welsh, Gutknecht*, and *Mulloy* decisions. Two years later, having done nothing about the problem, Justice Department official Kevin Maroney wrote Senator Edward Kennedy that a comprehensive review of convicted draft violators' cases would serve no meaningful purpose:

> Since twenty-two months have elapsed following the Supreme Court's decision in *Welsh*, and twenty-six months since the decision in *Gutknecht*, I believe it may safely be assumed that any individuals who were convicted prior to these decisions, and whose conviction would have been affected by them, are no longer imprisoned.

Marvin Karpatkin and the Central Committee for Conscientious Objectors prepared habeas corpus petitions for a few inmates, but nothing was done on a nationwide scale. Many months after the Welsh decision, Paul Davis was transferred from Ashland to Springfield prison, where he first learned that his case could be overturned. He then wrote a letter to a draft attorney and got out of jail. Roger Buford had been punitively reclassified by his local board, making his conviction illegal under *Gutknecht.* By the time he found out about the decision, wrote his own brief, and got out of prison, there were just three days left to his sentence. Buford's draft board then reclassified him I-A. No one knows what happened to him after that.

As a general rule, federal parole boards treated draft resisters well. Most spent six to twelve months in prison, less than half their original terms. There were exceptions: Richard Duvall of New Orleans was imprisoned for four years, most of it in maximum security at Terre Haute.

Like most other inmates, draft offenders wondered what would happen to them when they finally went home. They had spent months or years living among men who spent their lives in and out of prison. Having been warned since childhood about prisons and "ex-cons," they could not be sure how the outside world would react to them or what their own feelings would be:

> What concerns me . . . is whether I will remain bent out of shape after I get out. Having been in an almost constant state of suppressed rage for two years, will I be able to relax, to regain some of the gentleness and tenderness which I was trying to nurture?

A few were just plain angry: "The one thing that has changed is that I'm no longer dedicated to nonviolence." John Peters, the founder of PISS (Prison Information and Support Service), refused to change out of his prison uniform to fill out the necessary forms of release. Guards carried Peters away from Lewisburg prison in the middle of the night and delivered him to Boston, where they left him on the steps of his parents' house. Inmate Vincent McGee admired the draft offenders' personal qualities when they came to prison, and he was saddened by the transformation that so many experienced:

> The assets that they have in education, human concern, and dedication are mostly lost in the prison experience. The horror of that experience for these strong men of gentle conscience and demeanor sets too many of them against the system and cost the nation, on their release, years of dedication to community service and skill.

Back home, one of the ex-convict's first discoveries was that his draft challenge had cost him irretrievable years. Typically, five years had passed between his first induction refusal and his release from prison. The years had involved so much uncertainty and anxiety that they had seldom been used to prepare for the future.

Readjustment was not made easier by hometown receptions that were often antagonistic. One former inmate passed an examination for a post office job, only to learn that his draft conviction made him ineligible. Another entered law school and discovered two years later that his state bar would not let him practice law. In Mississippi, an ex-inmate's parents suffered so much that they had to move away from their hometown.

Others fared better, but only after years of readjustment. Don Kelleher experimented with drugs and joined the Weathermen in New York City; he later enrolled in nursing school, where he performed so well that he earned admission to one of the nation's finest medical schools. Chris Endicott was a onetime Harvard classics major who worked as a roofer in Vermont after getting out of prison; Endicott is now finishing Rutgers Law School and has been assured by local bar officials that his draft conviction will not keep him from practicing law. Paul Jenkins found that putting "Selective Service violator" on his resumé did not keep him from getting several jobs as an accountant: "The phrase was enough to prompt conversations which usually turned out pretty nicely." The legal consequences of a felony conviction—loss of voting rights, licenses, and public employment opportunities—seldom affected their lives significantly.

Some convicted draft offenders do not regret having made sacrifices for the sake of principle. Peter Halsted, who spent thirty-three months in prison, commented that "morals cease to be morals, and beliefs to be beliefs, when they are set to stew in a pot of random concerns about one's personal comfort or the fate of one's skin." Many insist that their personal stands were vindicated when America turned away from the war:

> Friends ask us if we would do the same thing again, and our answer is "yes." . . . The iron bars of prison were temporary, and now we have free minds. When our children ask us what we did to stop the killing, we can answer them.

For most, however, there remains a sense of failure and frustration. The war ended, but only after many years. The time they spent in prison did not seem to affect the public's attitude about the war:

As one is ground between the massive mill wheels of the U.S. Department of Justice, one of the first things to be crushed is the belief that his action had made any difference in the imperial policy. . . . the only problems you have caused, you have caused yourself and those you love.

Some had carried the original high hopes of the resistance movement with them into prison. They expected to be joined by thousands, possibly tens of thousands of others. The prisons were to be turned into concentration camps of antiwar patriots, and the conscience of the world would be shocked. But once they got to prison, they discovered that they were just another casualty in a resistance movement that suddenly had other tactics, other purposes. Lonely and forgotten, they were unable to find any good reason why they, along with so few others, were in prison. Years of struggle against the legal system had been turned into pointless self-sacrifice:

> I think this was a political act—hoping that if enough of us took this course it would create chaos in the draft. It obviously isn't working. If everyone who said he would go to jail rather than serve had gone, the joint would be jammed. It should be at its peak. I'm afraid as a political act it's a disappointment.

Were they to have a chance to relive their lives, many would have accepted deferments, exemptions, and technical defenses as valid means of resisting the war. Others would have gone to Canada. After getting out of prison, one disappointed ex-convict encouraged others to resist the draft, but warned that "one should fight the battle but duck the bullets."

All the while, the public's attention was transfixed either on the POW's in North Vietnam or the exiles in Canada. In prison and out, the draft offenders felt "the same way Antigone did—behind walls and forgotten." In one sense, however, imprisoned draft offenders were very much on the minds of millions of American youngsters. In living rooms across the country, the choice was made clear for nineteen- and twenty-year-olds who might have had second thoughts about obeying their draft boards: Report for induction, or you'll go to prison. Two million complied with induction orders, and two million others were pressured into enlisting by the threat of induction. If nobody had been convicted, if nobody had been sent to prison, then many of these people might have had second thoughts, and the draft system—and the war effort—might well have collapsed.

IV | DESERTERS

Over the Hill

In the lexicon of military crimes, few are more serious than desertion in combat. The Senate Armed Services Committee called it a "crime against one's country," a "crime against citizenship," and a "crime against fellow servicemen." In times of declared war, desertion is punishable by death. In World War II, forty-nine men were sentenced to death for desertion, although only one, Eddie Slovik, was executed. Only wartime espionage, where the death penalty is mandatory, is punished more severely. The Vietnam war was never formally declared by Congress, so no American deserters faced the death penalty. But it was a full-scale war, and battlefield desertion was no less serious a matter.

The unpopularity of the war gave desertion an added dimension. By the late 1960s, the offense began to have political overtones, and desertion came to be seen as the military counterpart of draft resistance. Yet throughout the war, politically motivated deserters were far outnumbered by those whose absences were not direct responses to their feelings about the war. Nor was desertion, despite the attention it has received, the prevailing form of indiscipline within the armed forces. The 100,000 Vietnam-era troops discharged for absence offenses were dwarfed by the 463,000 who received less-than-Honorable discharges for other reasons.

Throughout the war, tens of thousands of soldiers were separated from service each year for a variety of offenses against military authority—AWOL, drugs, insubordination, racially motivated assaults, fragging, and so forth. Much of this was not a direct consequence of the war in Southeast Asia, but the imprint of Vietnam was unmistakable on this generation of soldiers. Most of those who got into trouble were draftees or draft-induced enlistees, and they served in a military undergoing a massive crisis in morale and discipline. In 1971, for example, a random group of 100 Army soldiers would have produced the following disciplinary incidents:

7	Acts of desertion
17	AWOL incidents
20	Frequent marijuana smokers
10	Regular narcotics users
2	Disciplinary discharges
18	Lesser punishments
12	Complaints to congressmen

The crisis was a product of many factors: manpower policies that relied heavily on men whose backgrounds made them only marginally suitable for service and who were, consequently, much more likely to become disciplinary problems; social turmoil in civilian society, manifested by drug abuse, racial strife, and antiauthoritarian attitudes; the strains caused by the war itself; and the failure of military leaders to strike a proper balance between permissiveness and uncompromising discipline. These problems resulted in more than half a million servicemen's receiving General, Undesirable, Bad Conduct, or Dishonorable Discharges.*

---

*Official military terminology regarding the types of discharges is extremely complex and confusing to the uninitiated and, indeed, to many in the armed forces. Here is a short glossary: Honorable—the best and most common discharge, conferring full entitlement to veteran's benefits. General—considered "under honorable conditions" but less meritorious than the fully Honorable, likewise conferring full entitlement to benefits. Undesirable—issued "under other-than-honorable conditions" imposed administratively for substandard behavior of a culpable nature, generally resulting in denial of benefits. (In 1976, the designation "Undesirable" was abolished and replaced by "other than honorable conditions.") Bad Conduct—a "punitive" discharge imposed after conviction by a court-martial for a criminal violation of military law. Dishonorable—a "punitive" discharge adjudged after conviction by a general court-martial for an especially serious offense.

The public's perception of these half million men is dominated by its general attitude toward deserters, and its belief that all such men are simply quitters unwilling to fight. John Saunder abandoned his patrol in Vietnam, and wandered for days in the jungle before encountering some Viet Cong soldiers. They turned down his offer to help them fight, but they had him tape anti-American broadcasts and write propaganda leaflets. Eventually, the twenty-one-year-old Marine sergeant made his way from Vietnam to Stockholm. After about a week in Sweden, he surrendered to the American embassy. Convicted by court-martial for desertion and aiding the enemy, Saunder was sentenced to a long term in military prison.

John Mason was ordered to participate in a parachute drop on a hill, but he asked to be left behind. Turned down, he walked away from camp. When Mason was caught several weeks later, he was on a truck, without his rifle, heading for Saigon. His clothes torn and his face badly bruised, he claimed that he had been kidnapped by the Viet Cong. He, too, was court-martialed and sent to prison.

Every war has its Saunders and Masons, but Vietnam produced another kind of battlefield deserter—the conscientious war resister. Mark Gilman deserted from a search-and-destroy mission after his platoon was ambushed. "I saw my buddy shot beside me," he recalled. "That's what made me desert. I could think of no good reason why he should die, why I should die, why any GIs should die in Vietnam." Gilman made his way to Sweden and settled into a life in exile.

Originally discharged from the Marines as unfit, Terry Samuels worked hard to get his draft status changed so he could join the Army. "I was red, white, and blue all the way," he recalled. Trained as an infantryman, Samuels resisted his father's urgings to desert rather than go to Vietnam. But once there, his experiences scarred him deeply. "I went to mental hygiene at Cu Chi about six months after I got there and told them my head was getting pretty messed up. . . . I only kept track of the innocent people I killed, the civilians, prisoners, a lot of NVA and VC who we'd captured and who I'd been told to 'take care

---

Both punitive discharges preclude benefits. In the eyes of the veteran, anything worse than a General is considered a "bad" discharge.

of.' It came to thirty-seven." Refusing to participate in the war any longer, Samuels left his unit and found passage to Canada.

Ernest Gruening, one of only two senators to vote against the Tonkin Gulf Resolution, believed that soldiers who deserted under fire were committing principled, even heroic acts:

> It is clear that when they got into Southeast Asia and saw the innocent noncombatants, the burning of women and children with napalm, the saturation bombing which destroyed homes, hospitals, and whole families, making homeless refugees of those that were not killed, turned loose in a defoliated and craterized wasteland—these nonresisting draftees could no longer participate in this massive butchery, and deserted.

Hawks and doves alike used the image of battlefield desertion to make political and moral arguments that advanced their own points of view. This led to an "either-or" stereotype of deserters, with the public assuming that most deserters left because they refused to participate in combat. The only thing in doubt was the rightness or wrongness of what they did.

Yet, by historical standards, combat-related desertion was rare in Vietnam. More than 100,000 self-absented soldiers were still at large when the Civil War ended in 1865, almost all of them front-line troops. As recently as World War II, more than 20,000 soldiers were convicted for desertion in combat. But throughout the Vietnam war, only a few thousand men were court-martialed for unauthorized absence in Vietnam or for disobeying orders to go to the combat zone, and just twenty-four were in fact convicted of deserting with intent to avoid hazardous duty. In the Army, for example, fourteen soldiers were tried for this offense between 1968 and 1972, the peak years of the war. In only six cases did the court find the defendant guilty as charged. All but one of those convicted were sentenced to one-to-five-year prison terms.

Although there were several incidents in which entire units refused to go into combat, there was little battlefield desertion in Vietnam. Commander after commander can recite instances of short-term absences, but few can recall cases like Saunder's or Mason's. A military judge who served in Vietnam for two years at the height of the war could recall only one case of bona fide desertion, and that involved a soldier who escaped from the stockade while facing charges for a violent crime.

The simple fact was that in Vietnam there was no place to go. Almost all lengthy AWOLs involved noncombat troops stationed in Saigon, Da Nang, or other rear areas. Except for brief visits to the local hooch— and even that was risky—troops in the field were in no position to desert. "What are you going to do?" asked one. "Walk through Cambodia?" The Viet Cong were not interested in giving shelter to American deserters. As one of their spokesmen warned, "If GIs desert and go over and live with our forces, they will have a difficult life to lead." With no access to funds and no orders home, only the most enterprising of soldiers could falsify orders or stow away on commercial flights out of the country. Some did make their way to Saigon's "AWOL alley," where they sometimes hid from authorities for months. About one hundred were apparently left behind after the last American combat soldiers left the country, all of whom were eventually picked up by local police before the collapse of South Vietnam.

The easiest way to desert from Vietnam was to take advantage of a mid-tour leave. After five or six months in Southeast Asia, servicemen were allowed to take a week-long "R and R" (rest and recreation) break in places like Hong Kong, Japan, or Hawaii. Once out of Vietnam, they could travel to the United States or, with help from the local antiwar underground, head for Canada or Sweden. Throughout the war, only five thousand servicemen were discharged for deserting in the midst of a Vietnam tour. About half failed to return from R and R, and many of the rest went AWOL from noncombat situations.

Another seven thousand deserted in the United States after receiving orders to report to Vietnam. Some of these men were late-blooming conscientious objectors who did not realize how much they opposed the Vietnam war until confronted with orders to go. But most sincere war resisters chose other times and other ways to take their stands. More than any other single category of deserter, those who refused to report to Vietnam were motivated by fear, not conscience or any other mitigating circumstance. "I hate to admit it, but most of these guys went over the hill to save their necks, not because they opposed the war," said Frank Paquin, who was strongly antiwar while in the service. "The war became an issue only when they were scheduled for Vietnam, and then it was a matter of avoiding being killed." Bill Hansen, an exile in Canada, said that his reason for not going to Vietnam "was initially a fear for my life. That was my first flash. Like, man, I might be killed." Another exile recalled that "I wasn't exactly conscious of the fact that I was a deserter, I was only conscious of the fact that I wasn't going to Vietnam—it's called survival."

Sometimes, the threat of Vietnam was used as punishment, making it easier for men to choose desertion over duty. Jim McAllen described how "the sergeant in charge of my platoon told me that since I had a young wife and child, I should do extra favors for him to be kept off the West Pac quota list. I refused to bow down to his subpar intelligence, and within two weeks I had orders to go to Vietnam. I went home on leave, and I refused to return."

One exile told how his experience at a California missile base made him less reluctant to desert to avoid Vietnam:

> We had a red alert, which meant war to us—there was an attack coming. After we found out the control center made a mistake, and that it was only a practice alert, we discovered that some warrant officers and noncommissioned officers and a couple of other people in prominent positions on the base had gotten into their cars and just flat left—which as far as I was concerned was desertion in the face of the enemy, since we believed we were going to be attacked. When it was realized that "x" number of personnel had fled, we were told not to say anything to anyone, or else they would "get our asses."

In all, twelve thousand individuals either deserted during a Vietnam tour or deserted when they received orders to report to the war zone. They account for a small proportion of the hundred thousand servicemen punished for absence offenses and a tiny fraction of the nearly half million who were stigmatized with less-than-Honorable discharges* for violations of military discipline (see Figure 5). Yet the image of the

---

* The confusion over discharge terminology is compounded by the fact that a "less-than-Honorable" discharge means a General, Undesirable, or worse, while a discharge "under other-than-honorable conditions" means an Undesirable Discharge or worse.

FIGURE 5: MILITARY OFFENDERS

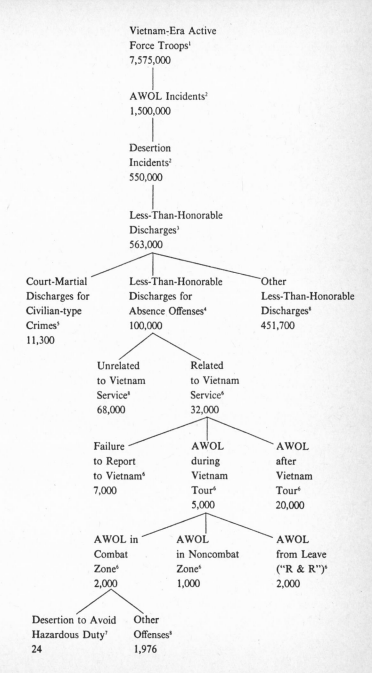

Vietnam-Era Active
Force Troops[1]
7,575,000

AWOL Incidents[2]
1,500,000

Desertion
Incidents[2]
550,000

Less-Than-Honorable
Discharges[3]
563,000

Court-Martial
Discharges for
Civilian-type
Crimes[5]
11,300

Less-Than-Honorable
Discharges for
Absence Offenses[4]
100,000

Other
Less-Than-Honorable
Discharges[8]
451,700

Unrelated
to Vietnam
Service[8]
68,000

Related
to Vietnam
Service[6]
32,000

Failure
to Report
to Vietnam[6]
7,000

AWOL
during
Vietnam
Tour[6]
5,000

AWOL
after
Vietnam
Tour[6]
20,000

AWOL in
Combat
Zone[6]
2,000

AWOL
in Noncombat
Zone[6]
1,000

AWOL
from Leave
("R & R")[6]
2,000

Desertion to Avoid
Hazardous Duty[7]
24

Other
Offenses[8]
1,976

deserter as a man who fled rather than fight persists in the public mind. The Defense Department has acknowledged that this image is grossly inaccurate. As it commented in an official AWOL study:

> Since the beginning of military forces, the urge to go "over the hill" has been more than some could resist. The reasons are as old as man—financial or family troubles, romantic involvements, earlier misconduct that led to disciplinary action, inability to adjust to military life, or family pressure before going overseas.

Every official analysis of Vietnam-era deserters has found the same thing—that the overwhelming majority were neither conscientious nor cowardly. They were men who decided simply to put their own interests over the day-to-day needs of the military.

Personal and family problems accounted for almost half of all absence offenses. For most enlisted men, military life was their first experience away from home. When their grandmothers died, their mothers fell ill, or their girl friends dropped them, they often wanted to go home as quickly as they could. Frequently, the problem was financial. The military pay scales were so low—starting at $115 per month—that married soldiers sometimes had to go home just to keep their families off welfare. At the height of the war, a Defense Department survey found that roughly seventy thousand military families were living below the poverty level. In 1971, Republican Congressman William A. Steiger of Wisconsin complained of a "definite poverty cycle" for soldiers at some military bases. At Fort Gordon, Georgia, a community services officer told Steiger of the "bleak subsistence existence" of new recruits:

> If you take the typical married first-termer, add his base pay allowance, and subtract his taxes and savings bond payments, he has about $240 a month. You can rent a lousy place for $100 including utilities and roaches, but then you've got to add transportation and carfare because he's living off base—about $50 a month in payments for his car and another $30 for gas and repairs. If you are very frugal, and do all your shopping at the commissary, you can get by on $50 a month. So $230 is taken up, which leaves you $10

for recreation—providing everything else is perfect. Of course, if the kids need dental care or glasses, forget it.

Money problems often exacerbated a soldier's family problems. Gilly Meaks' father committed suicide after suffering from cancer for three years. His mother was partially disabled, unable to work, and his family had no money. Meaks tried to get a hardship discharge, but after a long wait he learned that his papers had gotten lost. Tired of waiting, he went AWOL to support his mother, and was later given a bad discharge.

Peter Clarke had been married for seven months and was the father of a newborn baby girl. A high school dropout, he was working in a local A&P as a stock boy. His father told him the Army would give him an education, pay him well, and help him take care of his family, so he enlisted. After finishing basic training, Clarke was shipped to Fort Ord, California, but his pay was so low that he could not bring his family with him. Upset about their three-thousand-mile separation, his wife stopped answering his letters. Clarke tried, without success, to get leave to go home. Finally, he went AWOL and caught a plane back to New Jersey. Within a week, he was picked up and brought back to Fort Ord. He was reduced in rank, lost pay, and had to pay the plane fare of the two military policemen who arrested him in New Jersey. With his financial situation worse than ever, Clarke's marriage collapsed. His wife met someone close to home who had a good steady job. When she asked him for a divorce, Clarke went AWOL again, and was eventually given a bad discharge.

The military offered a variety of measures to help solve these personal problems—Red Cross counseling, home leave, compassionate reassignments, even hardship discharges—but the mechanisms were seldom administered effectively. Complaints to Congress reached totals as high as 250,000 per year, prompting congressmen to criticize the military's inability to solve the serviceman's problems.

Many soldiers were too impatient or uninformed to ask for help, and others had commanding officers who were insufficiently responsive to their problems. John Morehead went home on leave to get married. The day after his wedding ceremony, a hurricane flooded his mother-in-law's house where he and his bride were living. They lost everything. He got an extension of leave to try to repair the house, but it could not be restored to livable condition. His wife had a nervous breakdown. Morehead asked for a hardship discharge or a six-month emergency leave, but he got neither. He stayed home anyway, in AWOL status, and was later given a bad discharge.

Many deserters complained that military officials added to their problems more than they helped: "The GI has to go to his platoon sarge, and then his first sarge, and then his CO, and the sarge has been around twenty years and knows all the answers. . . . You can't leave without permission, and if you leave anyway, or you leave to complain, you can be AWOL." A Defense Department review board, part of President Ford's 1974–75 clemency program, found many a deserter who insisted that

> the noncommissioned officers over him not only did not help but in some cases intentionally or unintentionally blocked his way from going to higher authority to obtain help. In other cases, alleged indifference on the part of unit officers to listen to or be aware of his problems frustrated the individual. Often, a promise to look into the matter or to help resolve a problem apparently was not followed through. . . .

Similarly, the Presidential Clemency Board found that 14 percent of all absence offenses were attributable to "procedural unfairness" on the part of the military.

Hugh Nolan was waiting at Fort Dix for pending orders to report to Europe. His records were inadvertently shipped ahead, and he was not paid for forty-five days. His family was evicted and forced to live in an automobile. They had no money to buy food. Nolan asked for emergency leave and a short-term loan from the Red Cross, but he got neither. He even traveled to the Pentagon to ask for help, but to no avail. Finally, he found a civilian job, and his family's financial situation began to improve. When his orders for Europe finally came through, Nolan decided to stay home. He was later arrested as a deserter and given a bad discharge.

Sometimes, however, stories of family problems or complaints about military mistreatment were mere alibis for deserters who simply did not like the service. They went home to solve minor personal problems, but stayed away permanently. One Camp Pendleton Marine told his court-martial judge that he had gone AWOL to help his invalid grandmother, but admitted on cross-examination that she lived in Boston and that he never left California while he was AWOL.

These were men whom the military called "bad apples"—immature, undisciplined, and unable to adjust to the constraints of military life. Usually, they came from broken homes and had records of juvenile misconduct. One deserter said he enlisted "because I was getting into trouble all the time, and I felt that service life might settle me down." They coped with the military no better than they coped with anything else. Robert Sherrill described two such individuals who, predictably, got into immediate trouble in the Army:

> Private Johnny Dee Smith's . . . record began with a burglary in the first grade; as he said later, "I've been pulling burglaries ever since." He dropped out of school when the school psychologist said there was no point in his trying to go beyond the ninth grade. He served eight months in jail for burglarizing a safe. The year before he joined the Army, he got into a knife fight with his father and attacked a friend with a pair of scissors. At fifteen he was arrested for carrying a pistol and a machete. He had taken potshots at cows and children. At sixteen he had been arrested for shooting up a house with a twelve-gauge shotgun. At eighteen he was picked up in Las Vegas for possessing drugs and carrying a loaded revolver. He often used narcotics—LSD, amphetamines, codeine, cocaine, morphine, opium, everything. At least once he posed nude for a homosexual photographer. Before joining the Army, he attempted suicide by slashing his wrists. But the Army took Smith in without a question. . . . He had just been released from the Modesto, California, State Hospital; he went into the Army as an alternative to becoming a permanent resident in the insane asylum. . . . After one day of basic training, he later recounted, "my nerves were about to blow." And since nothing was done for him at sick call, he went AWOL. . . .

> Peter Watson . . . said he never knew his real father and that his stepfather was "drunk all the time" and beat Watson's mother as well as Watson and his two brothers. Sometimes the stepfather threatened the family with a gun. The longest period Watson lived in one place was one and a half years, with

an aunt and uncle to whom the court had awarded him because his mother and stepfather had by that time abandoned him. Later he lived with older brothers. He quit school in the ninth grade. The years he recalled most fondly were those between the ages of fifteen and eighteen, when he left home and roamed the country, working here as a bus boy, somewhere else as a farm hand, on down the road in a factory—"I was free, and no one was telling me what to do or yowling at me all the time." Then he joined the Army, and everybody began yowling at him again. He couldn't take it, couldn't take the senseless punishment, the senseless restrictions. Four times he fled the Army, four times he was captured and brought back. . . .

If there is such a thing as a "prototype" Army deserter of the Vietnam era, he lived in a small town and grew up in the South. He came from a low-income family, often with only one parent in the home. He had an IQ of 90, and dropped out of high school in the tenth grade. He enlisted to get away from problems back home, to learn a skill, or just to find something to do. He finished advanced training and had almost two years "good time," which often included a full tour in Vietnam. However, he rarely progressed beyond the lowest ranks. He was arrested at least once by civilian police, and he frequently committed other minor infractions against military discipline. After going AWOL once or twice, he went home to stay, usually because of family problems. Two years later, he was arrested and given an undesirable discharge in lieu of court-martial. He entered the service at age eighteen, committed his first serious offense at nineteen, and was discharged at twenty-one. About 75 percent of all deserters were white, but a nonwhite serviceman was twice as likely as a white serviceman to become a deserter. Only about one hundred were women.

Marine deserters were younger and more poorly educated than their Army counterparts. They were more likely to desert because they could not tolerate military life and were punished more severely for their AWOL offenses. Navy deserters were overwhelmingly white, with long histories of petty misconduct and minor punishments. Air Force deserters tended to be black, better educated, and discouraged about the menial tasks to which they had been assigned. They were also more likely to go AWOL at least partly out of opposition to the Vietnam war.

Vietnam-era deserters were typically teenagers who, had they been in civilian employment, probably would have quit or been fired. Had they been in school, they probably would have dropped out or flunked out. In either case, their failure would have set them back a few years, making it harder for them to get training or find a good job. But eventually they would overcome their early mistakes, and no one would care what they had done at age eighteen or nineteen.

In the military, however, quitting is desertion, and may be punished by a long prison term and a bad discharge, a stigma that attaches for life. Questions about the discharge keep appearing on employment forms and keep coming up in conversation. The veteran continually has to pay a price for his youthful mistake.

When the Vietnam-era recruits came to basic training, they saw wall posters describing the consequences of going AWOL. One had the caption "FAMILY DISGRACE" under a picture of a forlorn mother sobbing, her face hidden in her hands. Recruits also saw a thirty-minute color film, *The Smart Way Out*, telling the story of Good Joe and AWOL Johnny. Joe followed the rules, got an Honorable Discharge, and had "years of happiness" as a result. But Johnny "couldn't take his mind off a little girl back home," got an Undesirable Discharge for going AWOL, and led a life of "bitterness, loneliness, and poverty." He ended up as an unemployed drunk, arrested by the police for vagrancy.

Pentagon officials claim that this combination of punishment and warnings was in fact successful, that the rate of Vietnam-era AWOLs was no higher than that of World War II or the Korean War. They claim that there was nothing unique or extraordinary about these offenses; only about 10 percent were motivated by opposition to the war, and the rest were no different from the AWOLs that the military has always experienced.

The statistics are correct, but they vastly understate the impact of Vietnam. Only the rate of short-term AWOL (less than thirty days) was comparable to that of earlier wars, and short-term AWOL almost always involved petty misbehavior that bore little relationship to the war. The statistics for long-term absence offenses tell a much different story. Absences of more than thirty days, administratively called "desertion,"* increased to an unprecedented level. In 1966, the Army and Marines reported about fifteen desertion cases per thousand troops. The rates climbed to more than fifty per thousand in 1969, and about seventy per thousand in 1972. By contrast, long-term absence rates during the Korean War were only about twenty-five per thousand troops.

During the entire period of the Vietnam war, there were approximately 1,500,000 AWOL incidents and 500,000 desertion incidents. At the peak of the war, an American soldier was going AWOL every two minutes, and deserting every six minutes. This had an enormous impact on the ability of the armed forces to function. Absence offenses caused a total loss of roughly one million man-years of military service, almost half the total number of man-years American troops spent in Vietnam. The Senate Armed Services Committee estimated that in 1968 alone, well before AWOL and desertion reached their peak, absenteeism was costing the military the equivalent of ten combat divisions of fifteen thousand men each. While few of these young men were consciously voting against the war with their feet, their behavior was unmistakably connected with the unusual stress which they and the armed forces experienced during the Vietnam era.

The Bottom Third

Gus Peters came from a broken home, dropped out of school after the eighth grade, and was unemployed for most of his teenage years. His IQ was only 62, and he scored around the tenth percentile in his preenlistment aptitude test. His physical condition was no better. Peters was poor military material, and before Vietnam he would have been rejected. But throughout the war, Peters and hundreds of thousands of other men like him were brought into the military via "Project 100,000" or similar manpower programs. Pet-

---

*Administrative desertion is easily confused with the crime of desertion, which requires the military to prove beyond a reasonable doubt, in a general court-martial, that the soldier intended to remain away permanently, regardless of the length of his absence.

ers was, as a career sergeant called him, "one of McNamara's boys."

These men represented the Defense Department's contribution to the Johnson Great Society. The ostensible purpose of the manpower programs of the 1960s was to apply military training and discipline to the rehabilitation of America's disadvantaged youth. Yet instead of reducing the effect of social and economic inequities, they had the opposite effect. The burden of the war shifted even more to society's less privileged. While these men were volunteering and filling draft quotas, their more favored peers were staying in college, joining the reserves, or figuring out other ways to stay away from Vietnam.

Project 100,000 also had important political advantages for President Johnson, whose foreign policy increasingly began to intrude on domestic concerns. By expanding the pool of potential manpower at the lower end of the scale, his administration could fight the war in Vietnam without resorting to the dramatic and politically undesirable alternatives of mobilizing the reserves or ending college and other popular deferments. The war, despite its increasing call on the nation's manpower resources, did not have to disrupt the daily lives of more affluent and politically vocal citizens.

The enlistment of men like Peters represented a dramatic shift from earlier manpower policies. Following World War II, the armed forces began studying the connection between the background characteristics of recruits and the quality of their military service. *The Ineffective Soldier,* a major postwar study by Eli Ginzburg, examined the causes of poor performance among World War II servicemen. Ginzburg stressed the need to examine carefully the intelligence and education of prospective recruits. He found, for example, that high-school dropouts were five times as likely to perform poorly as those with some college, and three times as likely as those with a high-school education.

Building on Ginzburg's analysis, the armed forces developed a series of tests designed to measure the qualifications of young men for military service. The Armed Forces Qualification Tests were designed to screen out men who could not acquire military skills and to classify those who could in accordance with their mental ability. They divided potential soldiers into five categories, with the lowest, Category V, disqualified from service and the upper three clearly acceptable. It was within Category IV, the marginal group, scoring between the tenth and thirtieth percentiles on the AFQT, that the standards could be altered in response to changing needs.

In the late 1950s and early 1960s, the military took steps to raise the quality of men accepted into service. In 1958, additional tests were developed to limit the number of persons accepted from Category IV. All persons at this level had to score 90 percent or better in at least two aptitude areas to qualify for service. The Pentagon hoped that about half of the Category IV people—who in 1957 were almost 40 percent of the total then being drafted—would be excluded. This would have reduced the total number of Category IV servicemen to about 19 percent of total strength, roughly matching the proportion of volunteers.

High standards proved to be a luxury of peacetime. As the requirements of the Vietnam war began to be felt, enlistment standards were progressively lowered. First, high-school graduates scoring in the top half of Category IV were declared acceptable. Later, Category IV high-school dropouts were allowed to join if they passed an extra battery of tests. These and other changes had an immediate impact on the preinduction rejection rate, which fell from 50 percent in 1965 to 34 percent in 1966.

This easing of enlistment standards was originally meant to be accompanied by an experimental program, the Special Training and Enlistment Program (STEP), offering special remedial programs designed to bring the men up to par with ordinary recruits. However, Congress refused even to test the STEP idea and, in 1965, rejected a $10-million Pentagon request for training, education, and social service programs. Nonetheless, the armed forces continued to accept ever-mounting numbers of recruits with marginal aptitudes and minimal education.

Once the Johnson administration drafted the armed forces to help fight the War on Poverty, military manpower policies focused on the underprivileged in earnest. The Task Force on Manpower Conservation, chaired by Daniel P. Moynihan, discovered in its 1964 report that each year the military rejected 600,000 disadvantaged young men as unfit. Eighty percent of them were high-school dropouts, and about 25 percent had not completed grade school. Almost half came from families with annual incomes under $4,000. The Task Force report, entitled "One-Third of a Nation," proposed a sweeping program of rehabilitation, a program that formed much of the basis for the Johnson administration's War on Poverty that was to come.

President Johnson immediately enlisted the Selective Service System in what Labor Secretary Willard Wirtz called "the most important human salvage program in the history of our country." Selective Service's job was to steer preinduction rejects into federally sponsored assistance programs. Local draft boards sent out 134,000 letters urging people to contact local employment offices for job training and placement. About 20 percent responded, but less than 4 percent were ever referred to jobs. Eventually, only 2,200 got jobs of any kind, and just 189 were enrolled in job training programs.

Selective Service was clearly not equipped to run employment or rehabilitation programs, so attention then turned to the armed forces. Ever since the debate on universal military training in the early 1950s, the idea of using the armed forces to educate, train, and invigorate the youth of America had attracted substantial support. Disadvantaged black youths became special objects of concern. The Pentagon noted that if black representation in the military were increased to its proportion of the population, the unemployment rate among black male teenagers would have been reduced to as little as 7 percent.

The armed forces had traditionally offered blacks more upward mobility than almost any other public or private institution. Nearly 40 percent of young blacks questioned in a 1965 survey gave self-advancement as the reason for enlisting—close to twice the proportion of whites, who were mostly motivated by the draft. Moynihan saw particular benefits for blacks in expanding the military's role. "Very possibly our best hope is seriously to use the armed forces as a socializing experience for the poor—particularly the Southern poor—until somehow their environment begins turning out equal citizens." Moynihan, who was also the author of a controversial report on black family structure, saw the military as

an utterly masculine world. Given the strains of disorganized and matrifocal family life in which so many Negro youth come of age, the armed forces are a dramatic and desperately needed change; a world away from women, a world run by strong men and unquestioned authority, where discipline, if harsh, is nonetheless orderly and predictable, and where rewards, if limited, are granted on the basis of performance.

With 40 percent of all blacks scoring in Category IV of the AFQT, the only way to accomplish these goals was to relax standards for enlistment. The result was Project 100,000. Unlike the earlier Project STEP, it was made applicable to draftees as well as volunteers.

Billing it as a Great Society program when he announced it on August 23, 1966, Defense Secretary Robert McNamara promised that Project 100,000 would rehabilitate the nation's "subterranean poor." These youths, said McNamara, "have not had the opportunity to earn their fair share of this nation's abundance, but they can be given an opportunity to return to civilian life with skills and aptitudes which for them and their families will reverse the downward spiral of decay." After serving in the military, they would return to civilian life with an earning capacity "two or three times what it would have been had there been no such program." The Department of Defense, he added, was "the world's largest educator of skilled men." McNamara's words were echoed by General Herman Nickerson, Jr., Deputy Chief of Manpower for the Marines: "Those of our youth who lack education, those who live in ghet-tos, combine the ills of idleness, ignorance, and apathy. Our task is to help cure these ills with education, training, and incentives."

Yet many career officers were skeptical about relaxing standards, especially for draftees who were often not as motivated as volunteers. As the *Army Times* editorialized:

Are the services likely to get any reasonable mileage from such people? Past performance indicates not. . . . Is this any time to require the services to take on a large scale "poverty-war" training mission? We would think not. The services more than have their hands full with the fighting war.

Despite congressional resistance to STEP just one year earlier, the Pentagon revived plans for special in-service programs to help low-IQ troops pass muster. Secretary McNamara suggested the use of personalized training tapes utilizing closed-circuit television, permitting each man to progress at his own pace. But the war was already a heavy drain on the nation's resources, and once again Congress rejected the funding requests. Rehabilitation programs became but a shadow of what McNamara originally had in mind. About 17,000 recruits took courses designed to improve their reading skills to fifth- and sixth-grade levels, and a little more than 6 percent took advantage of a transition program that offered education and vocational training.

Lacking remedial programs, the military included Project 100,000 recruits in the regular training cycle. Secretary McNamara rationalized this fundamental omission by insisting that "these men should never be singled out or stigmatized as a special group." Classifying them as potential problems, he argued, might make that prediction self-fulfilling. Recruits who failed remedial reading courses were sent on to basic training anyway, and those who did poorly were "recycled" or sent to motivational platoons for extra discipline.

Because low-quality recruits were rarely offered special help, they often performed as poorly as manpower experts predicted. Gus Peters failed basic training, largely because of his reading and writing difficulties. When he tried to learn to be a tank driver, he continued to have problems. Ridiculed by other soldiers and unable to cope with military life, Peters went AWOL and was later given an Undesirable Discharge. After six months in the service, Peters was worse off than before. He still had no skills and no useful job experience, and he now was officially branded a misfit.

Commanding officers generally had little difficulty identifying Project 100,000 men, if only by their poor performance. At least one Army post had a policy of not promoting them beyond the rank of buck sergeant, no matter how good they were. Called the "moron corps" by fellow soldiers, they were commonly abused and disparaged: "They were pretty damn bad. Somebody had to help them get dressed in the morning," explained one officer at Fort Polk. "You had to take more time to explain everything to them. Since they couldn't understand what was going on, they were greater disciplinary problems." Said another, "Lots of these guys just weren't fit to do a job. I had to help one buy a toothbrush and pack his bags so he could report to another duty station."

John Grant had an IQ of 66. He married his wife when she was fifteen and pregnant. Grant could not do even the simplest arithmetic; according to a military psychiatrist, "one couldn't tell whether he was attempting to subtract, add, or was merely stating numbers at random." In one year, Grant went AWOL fifteen times, usually by bribing guards with drugs.

Another Project 100,000 soldier, Kenny Matts, was mentally retarded as the result of a childhood brain injury. He flunked a medic training course and went AWOL. "It was hard to learn in the Army," he said. "I had to take notes, and I couldn't spell."

Grant and Matts were drawn into military service by recruiting campaigns consciously directed at disadvantaged teenagers. Centers were set up in ghettos, and black recruiters were used to "rap with the brothers" on street corners. In *Pawns,* Peter Barnes quoted white Marine recruiters in Oakland, California: "We use their language . . . we say 'man' . . . we even call the cops 'pigs.' " At that office, 120 of the 125 men recruited in one year were from lower-class neighborhoods; of the 120, 90 percent were Category IV or lower, generally with police records, and most were black or Chicano. "President Johnson wanted these guys off the streets," said the colonel heading the Army's San Francisco recruiting office. "The Defense Department gave us an objective. We never had any problem. We got more than one hundred percent every time."

Rarely did Army and Marine advertisements suggest that their main business was fighting. Instead, they stressed the glamour, training, and excitement of military service. The Army advertised the modern technological "Action Army" of helicopters, electronics, and missiles. Murray Polner wrote of an eighteen-year-old he met in basic training who volunteered as a helicopter gunner, one of the most dangerous of combat jobs, "because his recruiter said it was like riding shotgun on a stagecoach in the old west." An ad in *Hot Rod* magazine read: "Vietnam, Hot, Wet and Muddy—Here's the place to make a man."

From 1966 to 1968, Project 100,000 brought in 240,000 recruits, usually to the Army and Marines. Many more Category IV troops were signed up through relaxed standards not officially part of Project 100,000. These were indeed the people whom Moynihan and others had targeted for military service. Forty-one percent were black, and almost 50 percent came from the South. This contrasted with a military-wide black representation of 12 percent, and a southern share of 28 percent. Almost 60 percent of the Category IV recruits came from broken homes, three-quarters were from low-income backgrounds, over 80 percent were high-school dropouts, and half had IQs of less than 85. More than 40 percent had a reading ability at less than a sixth-grade level, and almost 15 percent read below fourth-grade.

Not many qualified for advanced military specialties, and they rarely were offered military jobs helpful to them in civilian life. Over 40 percent of the Project 100,000 men were given combat-related assignments in armor, infantry, or artillery, and half the Army and Marine contingent went to Vietnam. This should have come as no surprise. A study conducted in 1964, before the institution of the special programs, showed that enlisted men with poor educational backgrounds had a very high likelihood of serving in combat specialties. But this was not seen as a problem, perhaps because low-IQ troops were considered good fighting men. One officer commented that he would "prefer a company of riflemen with fifth-grade educations over a company of college men anytime."

However, marginally qualified troops also posed serious disciplinary problems. A Category IV soldier was three times as likely to go AWOL during basic training as the average soldier. He was twice as likely to be given an early discharge, and two and a half times as likely to be court-martialed. Of all those discharged for absence-related or other disciplinary offenses during the Vietnam era, about one-third had AFQT scores in Category IV. Approximately eighty thousand Category IV recruits were sent home with Undesirable, Bad Conduct, or Dishonorable Discharges, and another 100,000 with General Discharges. They may have been mustered in through special standards, but that was not the way they were mustered out.

Ultimately, the War on Poverty proved to be a casualty of the war in Vietnam. By 1970, troop ceilings began to fall, and the notion of using the armed forces as a part of the Great Society passed with the coming of the Nixon administration. Project 100,000 quotas fell to 75,000 that year, and 50,000 the following year. The proportion of Category IV troops recruited outside Project 100,000 fell at the same rate. The military became more exacting about the performance of marginal recruits. In 1968, for example, the Marine Corps dropped less than 7 percent of Category IV soldiers during basic training; by 1971, they were discharging almost half. In 1972, Project 100,000 was officially terminated, and replaced by "New Standards," an equivalent program geared to the upcoming All-Volunteer Force.

The Defense Department still considered Category IV troops to be useful soldiers, as long as they were assigned to the 20 percent of all military jobs for which they had sufficient aptitude. In an era of voluntary enlistment, the Pentagon thought lower-aptitude soldiers would fill lower-skill jobs with more enthusiasm than higher-aptitude men who usually wanted something better. As Roger Kelley, then assistant secretary of defense for manpower, commented:

> There are two kinds of quality mismatches in military jobs. One occurs when people are assigned work that is over their heads. The other occurs when people are underchallenged in their work assignments. Recruiting bright young high school graduates for the bottom fifth of jobs in the Army and Marine Corps is a classic example of the latter kind of mismatch.

With this in mind, Defense Secretary Melvin Laird directed the armed forces to accept additional Category IV troops. But senior military leaders, disillusioned by their experience with Project 100,000, persuaded Congress to block Laird's initiative. By 1975, the proportion of Category IV recruits had fallen to 6 percent, and by 1977, to just 4 percent.

The armed forces have now returned to their pre-Vietnam belief that the military is not the institution for rehabilitating disadvantaged teenagers. "There is an inordinate amount of administrative and training effort involved in handling marginal personnel," said Colonel Samuel Hays, director of West Point's Office of Military Psychology and Leadership:

They have more disciplinary offenses, more vehicle accidents, go AWOL more often, have more personal problems and more mental breakdowns. They take longer to train for the same degree of skill. They are less flexible in their utilization. Their effect on the social solidarity and *esprit* of units to which assigned tends to be negative and destructive. In significant numbers, their ways of thought and habits of life make their barracks a less desirable place to live, thereby tending to drive out the better qualified.

In the opinion of many military leaders, social planners, and liberal critics, Project 100,000 proved a failure. While it expanded the wartime manpower pool, it also required additional resources which the services could ill afford. But above all, it was a failure for the recruits themselves. They never got the training that military service seemed to promise. They were the last to be promoted and the first to be sent to Vietnam. They saw more than their share of combat and got more than their share of bad discharges. Many ended up with greater difficulties in civilian society than when they started. For them, it was an ironic and tragic conclusion to a program that promised special treatment and a brighter future, and denied both.

Kooks, Heads, Brothers

"The young soldier just does things to irritate us," said one veteran sergeant. "I obey because it's the Army. They don't, often because of no reason other than they're supposed to."

"There's a guy sitting on top of a half-truck with twenty-five people around, he's smoking a big joint, and nobody says anything about it," commented another. "They question you, they ask why. We say because we're soldiers. But that's not reason enough for them."

The attitudes and characteristics of the Vietnam generation of soldiers were unique in American military history. Even had there not been a difficult war, these young men would have severely tried the patience and resources of the armed forces, just as they did the other institutions in America they confronted. "Kooks," one general called them, "men who are coming in undisciplined, the product of a society that trains them to resist authority."

They were, in spirit, like the legendary "Kool-Aid Kid" of Fort Polk, Louisiana. The Kid balked when his commander tried to get him to buy U.S. savings bonds, and he tried to persuade his comrades to join him in refusing. In retaliation, the commander had him court-martialed for failing to salute a chaplain and for not keeping an orderly bunk. Angry at getting a six-month sentence, the Kid reached for the only thing handy—a pitcher of cherry fruit drink—and threw it at the court-martial officers. He was then charged with "assault with Kool Aid" and given a Bad Conduct Discharge.

The young men of this generation spoke a different language, affected different life-styles, and had a different view of themselves, their country, and the Army. In line with the so-called permissiveness of the times, they did not take willingly to the authoritarian nature of military society, a mode of behavior directly contrary to the casual attitudes and questioning rebelliousness they brought from civilian life.

New recruits were "like foreigners," said one colonel. Appeals to their patriotism, selflessness, and sense of duty made no impression. There was indeed a generation gap in the armed forces, a gap of more than age alone. As David Cortright, author of *Soldiers in Revolt,* explained:

> Many young people today simply do not find the military relevant to their basic needs. There is something in the nature of contemporary society that weakens the warrior ethic, some characteristic of our affluent, technological civilization that seems incompatible with the military.

These soldiers were the product of a turbulent, disorienting, conflict-ridden period. Whether or not they themselves were socially or politically conscious, they were deeply affected by the unrest in the society from which they came. It was a society in trauma—racial conflicts, riots, drugs, crime, political assassinations, a "new morality," and above all, a growing public disenchantment with the war. "I think you'd be naïve if you didn't say yes, the Army does have these problems," said Army Secretary Robert Froehlke. "It has serious problems because society has these problems. And there is no way for the Army to avoid the problems of society."

Unable to comprehend the radically different attitudes of young troops, senior officers tried, often vainly, to cajole, persuade, or order men to respond to discipline. "The Brass realize something's wrong, and they ask what it is," complained one young officer. "But they won't listen when you tell them to change the whole thing." Ward Just, a persistent critic of the Vietnam-era military, observed that "all the Army has to counter [antiauthoritarian behavior] is its traditions and its discipline, command and obedience." It could have responded to grievances by loosening its more rigid requirements, like haircuts and drill instruction. It could have improved communications between officers and men. But the military was not a flexible institution; it was slow to change, slow to respond to the changes in civilian society.

When the military did try to change, it often found that its problems ran too deep to be solved. Recruits remained unappreciative and unappeased, and senior officers grew frustrated by what they perceived as the failure of the younger generation to meet them halfway. Whatever officers did often seemed to be too little or too late.

Even under the best of circumstances, morale would have been a serious problem because of the disappointing progress of the war, scandals in the upper ranks, and atrocities at My Lai and elsewhere. But the clash between the generations made morale not a problem, but a crisis. This was, in the words of the Washington *Post,* an "Army in anguish."

Two barometers of this crisis were drugs and racial conflict, problems that the military shared with civilian society, and which grew to epidemic proportions during the war. A study of soldiers entering Vietnam in 1967 showed that 20 percent were already using marijuana. By 1970, this figure had risen to 50 percent. An employee in a drug rehabilitation center in Vietnam estimated that of the seven hundred heroin addicts there in mid-1971, 60 percent had been users before they entered the Army.

Yet Vietnam seriously aggravated the drug problem. A Harris survey of veterans found that such factors as "the pressures of war, fear of being killed, the courage to kill, coping with Vietnam, and homesickness" accounted for more than half of all drug cases. The watch-and-wait boredom of combat service accounted for another 22 percent. As one drug counselor put it, "Many GIs find the war so confusing they feel they are in a dream. Life is unreal. Values are crazy. Heroin use and fragging officers are acceptable. Everybody does it. Vietnam is a bad place, and most people want to get through as quickly and painlessly as possible. Marijuana slows time down; heroin speeds it up. The days go bip, bip, bip." The combat soldier's problem, it seemed to him, was to get through an unpleasant experience as painlessly as possible, and drugs were one solution.

In the early years of the war, drug use generally involved marijuana, not heroin. Marijuana could be obtained from bars, shops, hotels, and pedi-cab drivers in Saigon. Joints sold for 20 cents each. Yet marijuana use in Vietnam was then estimated at about twenty-five soldiers per thousand, lower than the overall Army rate of thirty per thousand. Between 1966 and 1967, however, the number of soldiers under criminal investigation for marijuana use climbed from fewer than one hundred to more than thirteen hundred. By contrast, only twenty-nine people were under investigation for possession, use, or sale of opium or morphine. Heroin was not yet in evidence.

The Army reacted to the marijuana problem, as one officer recalled, "by handling drug cases just like we handled sticking up a gas station." By 1969–70, military police in Vietnam were making more than eleven thousand drug arrests per year, 90 percent involving marijuana. Under Operation Intercept, Vietnamese troops and aircraft spotting teams located and destroyed marijuana crops. Yet despite this crackdown, the proportion of pot-smoking soldiers in Vietnam rose from 29 percent in 1967 to almost 60 percent in 1971. More than half were heavy smokers.

Heroin first attracted official attention in 1970. As late as 1969, only 2 percent of all troops returning from Vietnam were known to use heroin or morphine. But by 1971, the total exceeded 22 percent. Nearly 10 percent used heroin or other hard drugs on a daily basis, and thousands of combat troops began to be arrested for heroin abuse.

The heroin epidemic was considered especially frightening because of the type of person involved. The military expected most addicts to be blacks or Chicanos from disadvantaged backgrounds, groups that comprised roughly 70 percent of civilian addicts, according to one study. Yet, by contrast, more than 70 percent of all military addicts were white. They typically came from small midwestern or southern towns, had no history of hard drug use, and lacked any obvious character disorders. As one drug counselor in Vietnam said:

> The thing that is really eye-opening about it is that those kids, and they were kids, nineteen and twenty years old as a median age, looked like an exact cross-section of the young men coming into the Army. This business about ghetto kids and high-school dropouts—that's myth. . . . These kids are a cross-section of what the Selective Service was picking up throughout America. And this is what really shatters you.

The use of drugs was peculiarly a generational problem, and it was treated differently from alcohol abuse. In 1971, the Government Accounting Office estimated that there were 150,000 alcoholics in the armed forces. But alcohol was primarily the drug of career sergeants and officers, and it was cheap and plentiful at all military bases. Alcoholism was either ignored or seen as a medical problem. By contrast, drug abuse often brought stiff punishment. Until 1971, soldiers with drug habits often got Undesirable Discharges for unfitness. If their drug problems caused them to go AWOL, that was considered an aggravating factor which resulted in harsher penalties.

As the true dimensions of the drug problem became known, however, the military began trying less punitive approaches. In late 1970, the military initiated a limited "amnesty" program—later renamed "exemption," perhaps because of the political connotations of the original term. Drug rehabilitation centers were established throughout the Army, eleven of them in Vietnam; Navy and Air Force programs were started the following year. The Veterans Administration opened more than two dozen specialized treatment centers in the United States. Yet these efforts had little success. Many soldiers were reluctant to identify themselves as drug users, suspicious of the treatment they would get if they did.

By late 1971, with estimates of Vietnam drug use higher than ever, the military stopped relying on voluntary programs. Urinalysis was made mandatory for all soldiers leaving Vietnam, and later was extended worldwide. Those who failed the test were detoxified in quarantine centers until their habit was broken, which usually involved a long, unpleasant delay before going home. But even this did not keep the heroin epidemic out of America. Drug users learned how to bypass the test, and detoxification did not mean cure.

In line with the new, nonpunitive approach toward drug abuse, Defense Secretary Melvin Laird announced that addicts were to be treated as medical problems, given General Discharges, and made eligible for veterans' benefits and postservice medical assistance through the Veterans Administration. Individuals previously given discharges under other-than-honorable conditions exclusively for drug use were made eligible for automatic upgrades.

The new policy was generous in theory, but worked poorly in practice. The Pentagon could not accurately identify which discharges were in fact attributable to drug use. Many heavy users had been given "unfitness" discharges, yet their records gave no indication of drugs. Others went AWOL to support a habit and were punished for unauthorized absence. Under considerable pressure from Congress and the American Civil Liberties Union, the Defense Department tried to contact recently discharged veterans whose records showed drugs as a reason for separation. But the files were so incomplete that it managed to locate just a tiny percentage. As a result, the drug upgrade program reached very few of the people eligible for it.

The military was more successful with its efforts to stop the drug problem in Vietnam in the early 1970s, if only because troop levels were falling and combat engagements were becoming rare. In 1972, the Defense Department announced that it had "reversed a heroin epidemic in Vietnam" and that only 4.5 percent of the men tested were diagnosed as drug users. Yet, by the admission of the Army's legal command in Vietnam, drugs remained a problem until a few months before the last troops were withdrawn. The military solved the problem only by leaving Vietnam.

For thousands of men, leaving Vietnam did not solve anything. Their habits came home with them, causing incalculable tragedies. In Vietnam, a heroin habit could be sustained for perhaps $2 to $6 a day. In the United States, an equivalent daily supply of lower-grade heroin might cost as much as $200. General Walter Kerwin, deputy chief of staff for Army personnel, suspected that "some of the people who were volunteering to go back to Vietnam for maybe the second or third time did that for the specific purpose of drugs." When users came home, they helped spread the drug culture and drug supply at military bases, on the streets, and on the campuses of America. The inevitable results were crime and imprisonment for thousands of Vietnam veterans. Heroin became a symbol of the Vietnam war, both to veterans and to the American people.

Racial tension, like drugs, was a problem the armed forces inherited from civilian society. The authoritarian nature of military society, which placed a white and heavily southern command structure over a young and substantially black enlisted population, aggravated racial hostilities and hindered official efforts to overcome discrimination.

Before Vietnam, the military had been regarded as one of the best opportunities in American society for blacks to achieve upward mobility. Partly because of relaxed enlistment standards, large numbers of black youths joined the service during the early Vietnam escalation. Unlike their fathers, who may have been content to hide their hostility toward a white-dominated military, the black soldiers of the 1960s were openly resentful, aggressive, and conscious of their alienation. The Kerner Commission saw American society dividing along racial lines, and this was especially true in the armed forces.

Blacks found community not in the service, but among themselves. The intense racial consciousness of young blacks was hard for white officers to understand. "What defeats me," said a battalion commander, "is the attitude among the blacks that 'black is right' no matter who is right or wrong." At an official "rap" session in Germany, a general was told that all whites were pigs and he, being white, was also a pig. "I burned buildings in Chicago and shot whitey, and it doesn't bother me one bit," added the black soldier. "I'd just as soon shoot at whitey as the VC."

Black consciousness fed white racism. One soldier recalled hearing blacks called "reindeer," "Mau Mau," "jig," "spook," "brownie," "warrior," "coon," "spade," and "nigger." There was an atmosphere of mutual fear and distrust. As a white Green Beret recalled, "Blacks pretty much stuck to themselves and hated everyone else. I turned into a bigot in the military when I was on a bus with mostly black GIs, and they harassed and accosted me. You were told not to walk around the barracks at night, especially alone." A black GI responded that "whites think every time colored guys get together, well, he's a Panther, he's a militant."

Racial conflict was especially troublesome in Vietnam. By 1970, black unrest had begun to hinder the fighting effort. There was fear among white officers that black soldiers would turn their guns around and, as the soldier had said, "shoot at whitey" instead of the Viet Cong. Some, in fact, did. In one incident, two white majors were shot trying to get some black soldiers to turn down a noisy tape recorder.

Racial problems did not often translate into specific grievances that could be redressed through normal channels. A 1971 Defense Department survey of Air Force units in Southeast Asia found minority group frustration so high that many men found it difficult or impossible to articulate their complaints. When grievances were aired, they commonly pertained to offensive language, prejudice in assignments, harassment by military police, inability to buy black-oriented products in military PXs, and, especially in Germany, housing discrimination and a hostile social climate.

The resentment black soldiers had toward their white commanders often provoked harsh and shortsighted responses which aggravated the conflict. Many commanders tried to enforce discipline by banning such symbolic acts of racial identity as "dapping"—the complex handshake between "brothers"—and the clenched fist salute. Prison terms were sometimes imposed on blacks who tried to persuade others that they were being used to fight a "white man's war."

The military justice system was a major source of tension. Many blacks saw it as the embodiment of white racist justice: "If some brothers jump on a white guy, he's going to go to the authorities because all his life he's been used to going there. But if a brother goes to the police, he knows he isn't going to do anything for you, no way. So what's the use? The brothers don't even bother with the police."

Blacks filled more than their share of stockade cells. A 1971 study by the congressional Black Caucus discovered that half of all soldiers in confinement were black, a finding matched by an NAACP study in

Europe during the same year. The NAACP also learned that a white first offender was twice as likely to be released without punishment as a black first offender. At Camp Casey, an Army base in Korea, blacks accounted for 17 percent of all troops, yet they comprised 62 percent of all prisoners.

A 1972 Defense Department Task Force on Military Justice reported that blacks of comparable education and aptitude who committed offenses of comparable seriousness were receiving much harsher punishments than whites. At Camp Casey, blacks accounted for 26 percent of all nonjudicial punishment, 57 percent of all special courts-martial, and 83 percent of all general courts-martial. The NAACP study found that 45 percent of all less-than-Honorable discharges went to blacks. An Urban League study showed that blacks in the Air Force received Dishonorable Discharges at more than three and one-half times the rate of all airmen.

In part, the disproportionate impact of military justice was a direct consequence of Great Society initiatives to make military service available to the large segment of the marginally qualified who were black. In 1971, 60 percent of all blacks who were administratively discharged were in Category IV, as compared to 17 percent of the whites. The NAACP study found that many young blacks were ignorant of their rights and accepted administrative discharges even when charges against them were very weak. It noted that legal counseling was of little help because of the deep distrust blacks had for white military lawyers.

Whatever the reasons, blacks received a disproportionate share of the less-than-Honorable discharges awarded during the Vietnam-era. In 1973, this fact led the Equal Employment Opportunity Commission to hold that requiring job applicants to have an Honorable Discharge in and of itself constituted racial discrimination in employment.

Vietnam and Back

Beyond everything else, the war itself "tore the fabric of the Army," as a top-ranking general conceded. Not many soldiers deserted on their way to Southeast Asia or in the midst of combat, but every Vietnam-era deserter was, in a sense, making a judgment on the war. He chose self and family over the cause for which he was asked to fight. Had the war made more sense to him, his decision might have been different.

Enlisted men's views about the war split about evenly between hawks and doves. In 1971, a survey of men on their way to Vietnam found that 47 percent thought the war was a mistake, and another 40 percent thought America was not fighting hard enough to win. Both groups questioned the wisdom of what they were doing. Murray Polner interviewed hundreds of servicemen for his book *When Can I Come Home,* finding that "not one of them—hawk, dove, or haunted—was entirely free of doubt about the nature of the war and the American role in it."

A relatively small number of soldiers bore deliberate witness to their political or moral views by deserting, refusing to obey orders, or engaging in antiwar politics in defiance of the military. In the early days of the war, resisters often stood their ground, hoping that their commanders or courts-martial would show compassion, if not understanding, toward their beliefs. Michael Pacek, a Czech refugee, had lived through the Nazi occupation and Soviet takeover of his country, and his family later escaped to America. Pacek enlisted in the Marines in 1958, reenlisted in 1961, and was sent to Vietnam as a "military adviser" in 1963. After two combat missions, he had flashbacks of Czechoslovakia and refused to participate in any more fighting. Pacek was court-martialed, sentenced to five years in military prison, and given a Dishonorable Discharge.

In 1966, three Army privates (the "Fort Hood Three") refused to board a troopship for Vietnam, claiming that the war was "immoral, illegal, and unjust." All were given three-year sentences. In 1967, two officers refused to train Vietnam-bound troops in cases that received nationwide publicity. They, too, were court-martialed, sentenced to military prison, and dismissed from service.

Antiwar soldiers were often willing to try for a CO discharge, which was especially difficult to obtain (see Part II). Many CO applications were rejected because the law was not properly applied. Gilbert Owen almost applied for a CO draft exemption, but decided against it. After two weeks in basic training, he discovered he had made a mistake.

Owen applied for a CO discharge, but the chaplain who interviewed him found his beliefs based on contacts with "pacifistic organizations and individuals rather than on religious convictions." In the earlier *Seeger* case, the Supreme Court had declared this distinction invalid, but Owen's CO claim was rejected anyway. He then refused to accept combat equipment or to wear his uniform. A general court-martial sentenced him to eighteen months in prison and a Bad Conduct Discharge.

The hostile attitude of commanding officers and other military officials sometimes discouraged sincere war resisters from applying for CO discharges, leaving them little apparent recourse but to go AWOL. "The chaplains played a disgraceful role in the whole business," in the opinion of Maury Maverick, a Texas attorney who counseled dozens of soldiers through the CO process:

> More than anyone else, they should have understood how a man's conscience could forbid him from fighting. But instead, in the tradition of old war movies, they gave man-to-man talks about how soldiers have to do what they're told. For those who went ahead and applied for CO anyway, these chaplains invariably wrote negative reports—and that was hard for soldiers to overcome. I saw it happen again and again.

After three years in the Navy, Curt Chadwick was in no danger of going to Southeast Asia, but decided to take a principled stand against the war. He tried to apply for a CO discharge, but admitted to a Navy psychiatrist that he had experimented with drugs. The psychiatrist threw Chadwick's records in his face, telling him to get out of the office and forget about being a CO. Chadwick then went AWOL.

Alfonso Martinez decided in the fall of 1965 that he was a conscientious objector, and he refused to obey orders to train for combat. He was court-martialed and sentenced to six months imprisonment. After getting out of jail, he applied for a CO discharge. While it was pending, he again was court-martialed for refusing to obey orders, and was sent to prison for another six months. Martinez disobeyed orders a third time and finally was discharged—but not before serving yet another term in prison.

A high-school dropout with an IQ of 80, Ron Hodgkins never realized his pacifist feelings until after he was drafted. For eighteen months, he repeatedly inquired about becoming a CO. Hodgkins was not very articulate, and no one who talked with him thought he was sincere. "All I could tell them was that even if someone was trying to kill me, I couldn't kill in return. They just didn't believe me." After Hodgkins was ordered to Vietnam, he went AWOL.

Any act of defiance was regarded as a direct and dangerous threat to military authority. Commanding officers had difficulty finding the proper accommodation between the needs of military discipline and the increasingly visible efforts of servicemen to assert civilian notions of free speech and other constitutional rights while in uniform. "Resistance in the Army," labeled "RITA" by the Pentagon, led to widespread military surveillance of servicemen and civilians. In 1970, a major national scandal erupted when the public discovered the existence of hundreds of thousands of military dossiers on Americans who publicly opposed the war.

Military action against in-service dissent focused on GI coffee houses, underground newspapers, and leafletting. In Japan, six Marine members of the Vietnam Veterans against the War were arrested for leafletting. When their handouts were confiscated, military policy gave them receipts for "pamphlets contain[ing] propaganda. . . . Title: July 4th. Subtitle: Declaration of Independence." The six Marines were charged with "conduct of a nature to bring discredit upon the armed forces." Prosecutions were brought against other servicemen for failing to stand for the national anthem, picketing against the war during off-duty hours, making "disloyal statements" in servicemen's newspapers, presenting a petition to a United States embassy, and distributing Congressional Record excerpts of speeches by antiwar senators. Many were given less-than-Honorable discharges, and some were sent to prison. One soldier even got a less-than-Honorable discharge for sending home a Christmas card sharply critical of the war.

Opposition to the war accounted for perhaps 10–15 percent of all absence offenses, but the influence of antiwar servicemen far exceeded their numbers. They tended to be brighter and better educated than other troops, and they were able to draw public attention to their activities. They made indiscipline a political act and made resistance to military authority more respectable.

Yet despite strong feelings about the war, this generation of soldiers, like others before it, almost always obeyed orders to go overseas. Once in Vietnam, fighting was a matter of survival, regardless of a soldier's opinions. It was hard for him to sympathize with the Viet Cong when they were trying to kill him and his buddies. Combat troops broke rules all the time, especially with drugs and short-term AWOLs, but their superiors had a tolerant attitude. "If I caught a guy with marijuana and docked him half a month's pay, it wouldn't matter to him," commented a master sergeant who spent several tours in Vietnam. "They all had money to burn, so there was nothing you could do to stop petty drug or AWOL problems. If I had booted them out, I wouldn't have had any company left."

The most serious symptom of the crisis in discipline in Vietnam was "fragging," real or threatened assaults on officers and high-ranking sergeants. The practice got its name from the fragmentation grenade, which could be rolled under the quarters of sleeping officers. Any premeditated assault against a superior was, in effect, a "fragging." From 1969 to 1971, the Army reported more than 600 such incidents, resulting in 82 deaths and 651 injuries. One soldier recalled a planned parade for a general whom the troops disliked: "We broke into the demolition room and stole some grenades and blew up the reviewing stand." In one incident outside Hué, two dozen soldiers threw stones and gas pellets at an officers' club. The plan was to kill the escaping officers with grenades, a step the attackers did not carry out. Stories like this had a telling effect on junior officers. As one commented, "All it takes is a 'How are you, Joe,' and bang, someone will shoot you."

Toward the end of the war, the threat of fragging was accompanied by another challenge—the increasing refusal of enlisted men to go into combat. In March 1971, a reconnaissance company was ambushed by a North Vietnamese unit of much greater strength. After an intense firefight, the survivors made their way to safety only to discover that some classified documents had been left behind. The brigade commander ordered the company to retrieve the documents, but fifty-three men refused to go. Orders issued from progressively higher levels of command were also refused. The brigade commander considered pressing court-martial charges against all fifty-three, but he was overruled by the commanding general. The men were found to have had "extenuating circumstances" for refusing to obey a lawful order. During his year of legal defense work in Vietnam, David Addlestone encountered dozens of combat refusals and hundreds of minor acts of insubordination, almost always ending in little or no punishment.

The simple fact was that courts-martial were not practical in the field. The paperwork, time, and trouble they required could not be afforded. Sending a man to the rear to stand trial operated much like a reward, freeing him from the dangers of combat. As a consequence, courts-martial were generally reserved for those who committed violent crimes or desertion under the most aggravated circumstances.

Despite the attention it received, deliberate antiwar activity was not prevalent in Vietnam. Resistance usually did not occur until after the soldier returned home and had time to reflect on what he had seen and done. As Paul Starr commented, "Even for those who detested the war, refusing orders and deserting were simply not very feasible options halfway across the globe from home." Doing research for *War Resisters in Canada,* Kenneth Emerick discovered five combat veterans in Canada, each of whom had deserted only after coming back from Vietnam. He described them as having "rationalized and postponed their deeper perception of events until after they returned home."

Ron Cannille served a full tour in Vietnam as a machine-gunner. Back home, just eighty-four days before the end of his three-year enlistment, he went AWOL for eight hours to take part in a peace demonstration. He was thrown in the stockade, where he became one of the "Presidio 27" soldiers court-martialed for mutiny after a sit-down strike.

Jerry Rathbone accidentally killed his best buddy during a combat assault, an incident that turned him strongly against the war and ultimately caused him to desert when he returned:

Most GIs get back from Vietnam and they forget; they don't say anything; they say well, it's over, I can forget about it. And that's one of the reasons I deserted, right there, I didn't want to be part of that. I had to make my commitment. I had to make people stop and think, "Well, why the hell did he desert with only 137 days left?" This isn't one of those cases where people could say, "Oh, he deserted 'cause he couldn't get along with the army, or he deserted 'cause he's a coward."

But far overshadowing the after-the-fact antiwar sentiment among returning veterans was the problem of psychological readjustment from combat, commonly called the "post-Vietnam syndrome." Bob Dantlee earned a Bronze Star and a Purple Heart, but he deserted after coming home from Vietnam:

> I didn't notice much mental strain, but it was an entirely different story when I returned. I got depressed very easily, was very moody, and felt that no one really cared that I served their country for them. And this was very hard to cope with, mainly because while I was in Vietnam I gave it 100%. I saw enough action for this life and possibly two or three more. I hope somebody understands what I was going through when I returned.

Often, drugs were part of the post-Vietnam syndrome. Sergeant John Cutter arrived in Vietnam without combat experience. His leadership qualities were so strong that his company commander promoted him to platoon leader, a job normally held by a commissioned officer. Cutter led a number of combat missions, during which he took Methedrine to stay awake. The Methedrine made him jumpy, and one of his troops persuaded him to take opium to help him relax. Over time, he developed an opium habit which he kept secret from his superiors. After his Vietnam tour, Cutter was assigned to Germany, and then reassigned to a base near his home. Rather than let his family see him as a drug addict, he stayed in Germany in AWOL status and tried to enroll in a local drug clinic. After a few weeks, Cutter was arrested. The Army sent him home with his drug habit and an Undesirable Discharge for AWOL.

The military was poorly equipped to help men like Dantlee and Cutter with their physical and psychological problems. Combat veterans could qualify for disability ratings which increased their entitlement to veterans' benefits, and military doctors were sometimes suspicious that men were faking conditions to improve their ratings. As a result, many who thought they had serious injuries complained that they were poorly attended. If they wanted to see their own doctors, they had to go AWOL.

John Rainwater, an American Indian, received a Bronze Star for heroism when he moved through a minefield under heavy fire to save wounded comrades. Later, he became squad leader of nine men, seven of whom (including himself) were wounded in action. When Rainwater came back to the United States, he was refused permission to see a military psychiatrist. Frustrated, he went AWOL several times to visit his hometown doctor. An Army psychiatrist later confirmed his combat-induced psychological trauma, but Rainwater was nonetheless given an Undesirable Discharge for his AWOLs.

Many returning veterans found it hard to take pride in their sacrifices, regardless of their views about Vietnam. Bill McKuen was "shocked by what everyone was saying about the war, and I got the feeling that I'd been wasting my time over there. That's partly why I went AWOL." Grant Johnson returned from Vietnam to an Army base near Birmingham, Alabama. As a child and teenager, he had never paid much attention to white racism; as a Vietnam veteran, he refused to tolerate it. "My first thought was how great it was to be back home, and then I began to notice the hate stares. After all I had been through, I had returned to racist America, and I was keenly aware of it." Johnson left his base, left Alabama, and eventually went to Canada.

Most of the returning veteran's day-to-day contacts were with other soldiers, the bulk of whom had never been to Vietnam, and they were no more sympathetic than the general public. Sam Jollio served in six combat campaigns, received numerous decorations, and rose to the rank of staff sergeant. He was wounded in combat, and he saw his fellow soldiers killed. After two Vietnam tours and one serious injury, Jollio came back to the United States. To the soldiers and sergeants back home, he was only a "rice paddy NCO" who owed his rank to the war. Tired of being harassed and ridiculed for his war record, Jollio went AWOL.

Garrison officers sometimes had little patience with combat veterans.

Jimmy Lee objected to the training of new men for Vietnam: "They were playing games. Half the kids were only seventeen, and if they went over to Nam with what they were teaching, they wouldn't have lasted two days." Lee told the officers what he thought about the training: "I had three courts-martial and three Article 15's in my first two months back and got busted to private. So I just walked away." When he walked back a year later, Lee was handed a bad discharge.

Men who had been through Vietnam knew what did and did not matter in the war zone. When they came home, they continued the "distinctly nonmilitary style" that Haynes Johnson and George Wilson described in *Army in Anguish:* "a floppy 'Boonie' hat, a slouching and slow-moving walk, hair parted crookedly in the middle, and perhaps a sparse mustache." But their stateside commanding officers, many of whom were young and had never been in Vietnam, told them to "act like soldiers," and they had to go through the same daily regimen of inspections, formations, and petty harassment they had experienced as recruits.

The military had no readjustment programs for men who returned from Vietnam with only a few months left on their enlistments. Short-timers were of little use. There was no point in retraining them or giving them positions of responsibility. The Pentagon knew about the problem, but never addressed it satisfactorily. In 1971, an early release plan was initiated for returning soldiers with less than five months remaining, which often meant a soldier had to extend his tour in Vietnam beyond the normal twelve months if he wanted an early discharge.

Typically, combat veterans just sat around bases in the United States with little to do, waiting for their enlistments to end. They were often assigned to casual duty—KP, picking up cigarette butts, and the like. One Vietnam veteran was given the job of "assistant runner." He ran errands only when the Colonel's chief messenger was busy, but he had to stay at the ready just in case. He went AWOL in disgust.

After processing more than five thousand Vietnam-era deserters, military officials in charge of President Ford's clemency program reported that combat veterans "were not always gainfully employed, but seemed to be assigned make-work tasks to occupy their last few months of obligated service. Some were of the opinion, upon being assigned to training units, that they were being recycled through basic training, and this was the reason they offered for leaving." As Peter Barnes wrote in *Pawns*, "The final months in a soldier's career can be almost as miserable as the days in Vietnam. He fought and bled for Uncle Sam. He now expects to be treated like a hero, or at least a man. Instead, however, the Army demands that he revert to his precombat role of nigger."

Many of these men also suffered the consequences of long separations from their families, wives, and girl friends. As with the Kentucky teenager who left an Army hospital bed the day he got a "Dear John" letter, AWOL was sometimes the only answer.

When returning veterans went AWOL, they were often given bad discharges. "If we'd let people go home just because they wanted to, no one would have been left," explained a battalion commander at Fort Meade. "Without a stigma, everyone would have vanished." "Deserter" was the stigma. To the public, these veterans were indistinguishable from those who fled to avoid Vietnam.

About twenty thousand servicemen completed full tours in the war zone and received Undesirable, Bad Conduct, or Dishonorable Discharges for absence offenses that occurred after they returned to the United States. Although no official statistics are available, the evidence suggests that another thirty thousand received bad discharges for other kinds of post-Vietnam misconduct. Eighty percent of these men had served in combat. As a consequence, they lost all rights to veterans' benefits. Jim Stokes served in Vietnam for a year, earning a Purple Heart when he let an enemy grenade explode in his hands to protect his platoon. He was later discharged for AWOL. Jim Barajian suffered a detached retina during his Vietnam tour and is now nearly blind in one eye. After his court-martial conviction for desertion, he developed a disabling back injury from sleeping without a mattress in his prison cell. Like five thousand other Vietnam veterans with combat wounds or other service-incurred injuries, Stokes and Barajian were deprived of government-sponsored medical benefits.

One senior Pentagon official described the military's treatment of the returning Vietnam veteran as "our most shameful episode of the war."

Canceling Them Out

When General David Shoup became commander of a Marine Corps division at Camp Pendleton in 1957, he opened the brig and released everyone but the felons. "Go back to work," he told them. "That's what you're here for, not to sit around going stir-crazy. If you cut out again, we'll find you and put you back to work. And we'll keep doing it until you finish your time. So settle down and serve it now." Shoup straightened out the division and cut down on AWOLs. He did so without courts-martial, prison sentences, and bad discharges. Shoup's hidden ingredient was leadership. As a 1971 Army report stated, "positive leadership is the key to low AWOL rates."

But during Vietnam, the armed forces had difficulty in applying "positive leadership." The corps of lieutenants, captains, and low-ranking sergeants—the men who had day-to-day responsibility for enlisted troops—was badly strained by the wartime escalation. General William Westmoreland, then Army chief of staff, commented that

> six years of war—and this has been the longest war in our history other than our War of Independence—has truly stretched the Army almost to its elastic limit. It has been a very traumatic experience for us. We had to lower our standards to provide the officers and noncommissioned officers to man this Army because the reserves were not called up. . . . We had to lower our standards to meet the requirements in numbers.

As a result, the responsibility for dealing with the intense morale and disciplinary crisis in the ranks fell upon young and inexperienced leaders. Captains and lieutenants were trained and given commands just eighteen to twenty-four months after joining the service. Many were not college graduates, and few, if any, had ever been in leadership positions. Yet, at age twenty or twenty-one, they were put in charge of 40-man platoons or 150-man companies. The sergeants who assisted them were often just as inexperienced. Enlisted men who showed promise of leadership ability were sent quickly through noncommissioned officers' school, made buck sergeants, and promptly put in charge of eight- to ten-man squads. Barely out of high school, these "shake and bake" sergeants lacked the military savvy and experience so vital to their roles.

The inexperience of the junior command was aggravated by rotation policies. Commissioned officers, sergeants, and enlisted men did not stay together long enough to establish the relationship of trust so necessary for effective leadership. "Whenever I am asked, 'What is the basic problem of the Army?'" General Walter Kerwin said in 1971,

> I do not respond that it is drugs or race or discipline; it is the fact that we have so much turbulence, mainly driven by Vietnam, that leadership and discipline have gone down because everybody has developed what I call the "look the other way" syndrome. The man is not there sufficiently long to get a handle on his unit. For instance, not too long ago at Fort Carson, we found a unit that had five first sergeants in one year. I think it goes without saying, no matter what the business is, if you change the leadership five times, you are going to have a certain instability in the unit . . . because there is not that feeling of belonging and pride.

The problem was especially acute in Vietnam. The rotation policy may have been humane, but it had a devastating effect on group esprit. As psychologist Dr. Peter Bourne observed,

> With each soldier concerned primarily with his own personal survival until his rotation date, at which point his own involvement with the war would be over, the conflict [took] on a uniquely individualized character. The man feels no continuity with those who precede him or follow him; he even feels apart from those who are with him but rotating on a different schedule.

In the early part of the war, officers and sergeants were shifted from unit to unit every few months. Career officers saw service in Vietnam as a way of "getting their ticket punched," earning the credentials necessary for future advancement. The military later stabilized command assignments, but senior Pentagon officials acknowledged that twelve months was still too short a time for an inexperienced officer to mold an effective unit. Some volunteered to stay in the combat zone, but many were no less eager to go home than the men they led.

Rapid turnover aggravated morale problems. Officers who inherited bad units often saw their mission as just trying to keep problems from getting worse. An inexperienced company commander, coming to a unit with men who had already seen combat, had understandable difficulty asserting his authority. By the time he had overcome that handicap, his rotation date was near. His interest then lay in suppressing the outward manifestations of resistance and resentment—just getting by until the problems could be left to his replacement.

Part of the same generation as the men they were commanding, young officers were often unwilling or unable to deal with the antimilitary attitudes of their men. "I'd say at least seventy-five percent of the people I know, young soldiers, lieutenants, and captains, have told me privately they agree with what I've said," recalled one officer publicly active in opposing the war. "Either they don't have guts to say it publicly, or they don't feel it was their place to speak up." These officers tolerated the eccentricities of their troops—the sloppy dress, the love beads, the pot smoking—which were symptoms of an undisciplined force. More significantly, they failed to deal with incipient personnel problems until they became serious.

Sometimes, young officers overreacted. Although there are detailed regulations governing discipline and punishment, military justice relies heavily on the judgment of individual commanders, each of whom has wide discretion to punish offenders as he sees fit. Company-grade punishments—loss of rank, small fines, confinement to quarters, assignment to unpleasant duties—are the responsibility of captains, lieutenants, and sergeants. Their recommendations also carry considerable weight with the field-grade officers who decide whether to press court-martial charges or begin administrative discharge proceedings.

During the Vietnam period, the result was often fickle, unpredictable justice. David Segal, a University of Maryland sociologist who coordinated a Pentagon AWOL study, found "no systematic difference" between AWOL offenders who were punished and those who were not. When enlisted men felt victimized by arbitrary treatment, there was little they could do. Each military base had an inspector general to hear grievances, but he was usually a high-ranking officer with other duties and close ties to commanders. Enlisted men could file complaints, but they took months to be processed.

Whether an inexperienced officer was too lenient or too harsh, his incapacity for leadership produced the same outcome—disciplinary problems that eventually became untenable. As one career sergeant recalled, "We spent 95 percent of our time handling the 5 percent who were troublemakers." Ultimately, when all else failed, the only recourse was to discharge poor performers. In the words of Army General William Berg, former deputy assistant secretary of defense for manpower:

> You bring somebody into the service and hope he is fully productive. Some of them, for reasons of immaturity or inexperience, cannot measure up. . . . But after you have exhausted every possible remedy that you have to make this man productive, and he has already cost you a lot of lost time and everything else, you finally reach a point at which the only thing to do is cancel this guy out.

When men were "canceled out," they were given discharges that indicated the quality of their military service.

Discharge characterizations have been part of the military system since the Revolutionary War. By the 1840s, the standard discharge certificate described a man's service as "honest and faithful." If it had not been, these words were lined out in ink. After the Civil War, each soldier's service was described in longhand at the bottom of his discharge. In 1893, a plain, uncharacterized certificate was instituted by the Army as an alternative to what by then was called the "Honorable Discharge." This new discharge was not exactly neutral, however, because it included a character description on the back. These less-than-honorable certificates were later printed on blue paper, and court-martial discharges on yellow, so veterans of the two world wars came to think of bad discharges as "blue" and "yellow" discharges.

In 1947, a joint Armed Services Committee recommended shifting to the five-tiered system still in use today. The change was thought necessary to help in the adjudication of veterans' benefits claims, because the blue and yellow discharges "did not clearly provide a characterization for those whose service was neither honorable nor less than honorable within the time-honored meanings of these terms." Five types of discharge were created: Honorable, General, Undesirable, Bad Conduct, and Dishonorable.

The purpose of the discharge system was to reward faithful service and to punish, and thereby deter, unsatisfactory performance. "Anything else," in the words of a Defense Department spokesman, "would diminish the value of the discharge to the man who has given honorable service. You need a way to characterize the service for what it truly is." Yet this theory did not work well in practice. Many officers had little understanding of the military justice system. "Many people got Honorable Discharges because company commanders didn't know their jobs," recalled one career Army attorney. "They didn't know how to do all the paperwork for bad discharges."

Nor did the threat of a bad discharge have much deterrent effect. In examining the reasons why men might be discouraged from going AWOL, an Army study found that the desire for an Honorable Discharge "might" have a significant effect, but was not a particularly important factor in deterring AWOL. Most poor performers were only interested in getting out of the service as fast as possible, without going to prison. The concept of a lifelong stigma was too abstract to have any real meaning for them. "They were told what the implications were, as plain as day, but they didn't give a damn," recalled a battalion commander at Fort Meade:

> Those with a modicum of intelligence, who thought ahead about the consequences of bad discharges, were probably deterred—but the guy who had troubles usually had less intelligence and didn't think ahead. Most of these kids weren't bad. They were just dumb.

Only after the serviceman left the armed forces and had to cope with civilian life did he begin to appreciate the far-reaching impact of his bad discharge. By then, he was a civilian, and it was too late for his punishment to have a deterrent effect on him or anyone else. As a Defense Department report on military justice commented, bad discharges "became, in reality, a punitive sanction for the individual involved, but with little positive benefit accruing to the services."

Although the Honorable Discharge is officially viewed as a reward for achievement, 93 percent of all Vietnam-era servicemen received one (see Figure 6). It did not distinguish truly honorable from merely satisfactory service. According to an Army staff sergeant at Fort

Meade, "the only thing an Honorable Discharge proves is that a guy hasn't committed murder, rape, arson, or something like that. It was given to so many people who didn't deserve it that it really doesn't mean much. I wish they had given a break to the guy who really served well."

The Honorable Discharge sometimes contained a hidden qualification which undercut its value in civilian life, especially in the job market. Before 1952, the military stated the underlying reason for each separation plainly on the discharge certificate. However, the military then began using three-digit Separation Program Numbers ("spins"). These numbers corresponded to 446 capsule reasons for discharge. According to General Leo Benade, former deputy assistant secretary of defense for military personnel policy, this system of coded numbers was intended to "mitigate any adverse effect to people who were being discharged for less than honorable service." However, the numbers were inserted in every serviceman's record, including the 93 percent who got Honorable Discharges.

The clerks who made the entries sometimes followed the instruction of discharging authorities and other times merely acted on their own. There was no precise system for determining the appropriate spin number, and the choices were not subject to review. Servicemen were not told which number they were getting: because the spin was camouflaged as the first three digits of a much longer separation number, they were often unaware that the code existed at all.

Very few of the spin codes reflected well on a man's military record, such as by describing meritorious service, honors and awards, or special skills acquired during service. About half of the 446 spin codes were neutral—"expiration of term of service," "early release for Christmas," and so forth. The remainder—more than two hundred separate codes —contained descriptions that ranged from derogatory to damning, including one—"withdrawal of ecclesiastical endorsement of chaplain (5IN)"—that may have been the military equivalent of "go to Hell."

Some spin codes were phrased in generalities:

28C Unsatisfactory handling of personal affairs
46A Unsuitability, apathy, defective attitudes, and inability to expend effort constructively

FIGURE 6: MILITARY PUNISHMENTS

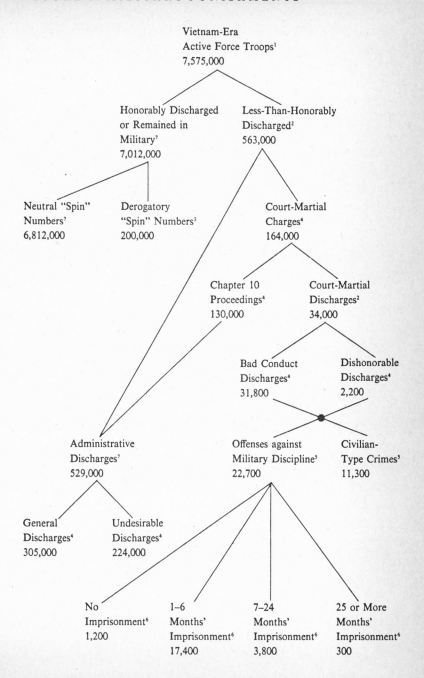

Vietnam-Era
Active Force Troops[1]
7,575,000

Honorably Discharged
or Remained in
Military[7]
7,012,000

Less-Than-Honorably
Discharged[2]
563,000

Neutral "Spin"
Numbers[7]
6,812,000

Derogatory
"Spin" Numbers[3]
200,000

Court-Martial
Charges[4]
164,000

Chapter 10
Proceedings[4]
130,000

Court-Martial
Discharges[2]
34,000

Bad Conduct
Discharges[4]
31,800

Dishonorable
Discharges[4]
2,200

Administrative
Discharges[7]
529,000

Offenses against
Military Discipline[5]
22,700

Civilian-
Type Crimes[5]
11,300

General
Discharges[4]
305,000

Undesirable
Discharges[4]
224,000

No
Imprisonment[6]
1,200

1–6
Months'
Imprisonment[6]
17,400

7–24
Months'
Imprisonment[6]
3,800

25 or More
Months'
Imprisonment[6]
300

288   Habits and traits of character manifested by antisocial or amoral trend

382   Demonstrates behavior, participates in activities, or belongs to associations which tend to show that the individual is not reliable or trustworthy

461   Inadequate personality

Others used clinical terms, but were no less imprecise:

36C   Maladjustment, situational, acute
36D   Passive-aggressive reaction
36F   Primary childhood behavior reaction
369   Cyclothymic personality*

A few described specific objectionable characteristics:

36A   Immaturity with symptomatic habit reaction (somnambulism)†
36B   Immaturity with symptomatic habit reaction (stammering)
41E   Obesity
262   Unsuitability—Enuresis‡

Some referred to sexual behavior:

362   Unsuitability—homosexual tendencies, desires, or interest, but without overt homosexual acts in service
512   Homosexuality (Class I)
513   Homosexuality (Class II)
514   Homosexuality (Class III)

Originally, spin codes were intended only for internal use in evaluating applications for reenlistment and were kept confidential. However, copies of the codebook were given to the Veterans Administration, which used them in deciding veterans' benefits claims. Sal Horley volunteered for two tours in Vietnam before being wounded seriously enough to get an early Honorable Discharge. But he had also picked up a heroin habit during his second tour and was given spin number

*Alternate periods of elation and depression.
†Sleepwalking.
‡Bed-wetting.

384—"unfitness—drug addiction or the unauthorized use or possession of habit-forming narcotic drugs or marijuana." Horley kept trying to get medical attention for his leg wounds from his local Veterans Administration hospital. Each time, he was turned down and accused of faking his injury. Eventually, a VA official told Horley that his discharge form indicated that he had been discharged not for combat wounds, but for drug addiction.

Copies of the codebook soon made their way to large employers, who discreetly used them to evaluate job applicants. One Marine veteran applied for jobs with the California state government and a number of other places. He proudly showed them his Honorable Discharge, only to encounter strange reactions and unexplained rejections. Finally, someone asked him why he was a homosexual—and he learned about his spin number for the first time.

By the early 1970s, word about spin numbers began to spread among veterans' counselors. At first, the Pentagon reacted by "classifying" the codebooks. But faced with growing criticism, it acknowledged the unfairness of the practice. On May 1, 1974, the Pentagon prohibited future use of spin numbers and invited veterans discharged between 1952 and 1974 to exchange their discharge papers for clean, "spin-free" certificates. The National Student Association obtained and published a copy of the codebook, prompting a nationwide campaign to find veterans with bad numbers. The Defense Department refused to notify all veterans directly, however, and only a few thousand asked for new certificates. Some of those who did learned to their dismay that they will never be free of their spins. A Louisiana veterans' counselor observed that "if you ever gave your discharge form to a personnel office, chances are it's still on file. If you go back with a clean discharge to apply for a job, they'll still look at your old spin number. After all, it tells them something they want to know. I'm afraid that some vets will never shake their numbers." No official tally has ever been made of bad spin numbers, but one Defense Department sampling suggests that about 200,000 Vietnam-era veterans may have black marks on what they think are fully Honorable Discharges.

The spin code, despite its adverse effects on so many ex-servicemen, was not an integral part of the discharge system and was not a substitute for the four other discharges that characterized the service of veterans who did not receive honorable certificates. Of these, the General, next in rank to the Honorable, is perhaps the most anomalous. Roughly 300,000 Vietnam-era servicemen received a General Discharge, which the military considers "under honorable conditions," yet "less-than-Honorable." Although it ordinarily qualifies an individual for veterans' benefits, it characterizes his service as "not sufficiently meritorious" to warrant the fully Honorable Discharge.

The General Discharge was not intended to be a form of punishment. Yet its categorization of recipients as among the bottom 7 percent has an inescapable impact upon employers and others in civilian society. Macy's department store, for example, had a policy (at least during the Vietnam era) "not to hire anybody who received anything other than an Honorable Discharge." A spokesman for Macy's added that "this practice was followed by every major corporation I knew of in the City of New York that hired people in the retail field—including positions for sweepers, scrubbers, and cleaners." Recent surveys have found that while very few employers flatly reject veterans with General Discharges, roughly one-third do discriminate against them. As one veteran recalled:

> I was busted for having two joints and given a General Discharge after three years and nine months of my four-year enlistment. Adjusting back into society wasn't easy. I couldn't find a job because I had "bad paper." This caused financial problems for my family and later resulted in my getting divorced. I have two children to support.

In practice, there was no precise distinction between soldiers who received General Discharges and those who received better or worse discharges. In the Army, for example, General Discharges were given in 90 percent of all separations for personality or behavior disorders, whereas the Navy gave three-fourths of these cases Honorable Discharges. In the Army and Marines, separations in lieu of court-martial were almost invariably Undesirable, whereas in the Navy and Air Force, many of these separations resulted in General or Honorable Discharges.

Many soldiers who received General Discharges either had a history of minor infractions or else committed major offenses but were given light punishment because of extenuating circumstances. But General Discharges were also given for reasons wholly unrelated to discipline; they were used to "fire" servicemen who were incapable of performing satisfactorily because of physical, mental, or psychological disabilities and who were thus deemed unsuitable.

General Discharges for unsuitability were awarded for a great variety of reasons: inaptitude, character or behavior disorders, apathy, defective attitudes, "inability to expend effort constructively," alcohol or other drug abuse, homosexual or "other aberrant tendencies," financial irresponsibility, excessive bed-wetting, or other factors.

General Discharges could also result from unfitness proceedings, through which servicemen could also receive the more severe Undesirable Discharge. Unlike the General, the Undesirable is considered "under other-than-honorable conditions" and does not bestow veterans' benefits. An individual could be discharged as unfit for any of the following reasons: sexual misconduct, drug abuse, "shirking," failure to pay debts, failure to support his family, "unsanitary habits," conviction for a criminal offense by civil authorities, and absence for one year or more. But by far the most common ground was "discreditable involvement" with military or civilian authorities—in other words, a determination that the individual was a general troublemaker.

A comparison between the reasons for unsuitability and unfitness shows how subtle and arbitrary the distinctions were. "Apathy" to one commander might have been "shirking" to another; "financial irresponsibility" to one might have been "failure to pay debts" to another. Marijuana possession to one might have been abuse of drugs to another. These distinctions were ultimately a matter of judgment, bias, or even whim. In military shorthand, General Discharges for unsuitability were given for aptitude problems—"soldiers who would if they could, but they can't." Undesirable Discharges for unfitness were for attitude problems—"soldiers who could if they would, but they won't." To make this distinction properly, a discharging officer had to make a determination difficult even for a skilled psychologist.

Often, events beyond the control of the soldier determined which discharge he got. Bobby Banks qualified for a medical discharge after an Army psychiatrist interpreted his problem as a character disorder due to "impulsive, escape-type behavior, and unresolved emotional needs marked by an evasion of responsibility." He was processed for a General Discharge, but just before his papers came through, a race riot occurred in the unit. Although Banks was not personally involved, his commander cracked down on discipline, and he got an Undesirable Discharge.

Although the Pentagon officially defines the Undesirable Discharge as "nonpunitive," it has a serious adverse effect in civilian life. About one-third of all employers refuse to consider job applications from veterans with Undesirable Discharges, and two-thirds discriminate against them. State and local laws often bar them from employment rights, occupational licenses, and welfare benefits. As a consequence, the Undesirable Discharge has led many a veteran into a hopeless downward spiral. Paul Dodson could not afford to go to school because of his ineligibility for GI Bill benefits, so he tried to get a job as a trucker. Large firms refused to hire him because of his discharge, so he had to work intermittently for small companies. At most, he made $70 per week, but he often was laid off. In between jobs, his bad discharge barred him from unemployment benefits. James Duke, a sailor stationed in Guam, experimented with LSD one night. Afraid that his "trip" would give him continuing nightmares, he told his commander what he had done. The next day, the sailor was on his way home with an Undesirable Discharge. For the next five years, Duke drifted from place to place, unable to find a job and too poor to go to college without GI Bill benefits.

As the war approached its end, administrative discharge determinations became more and more lenient. Many of the same soldiers who once would have gotten Undesirable Discharges received General Discharges instead. The Army increased its General Discharge rate from 1.7 percent in 1969 to 8.2 percent in 1975, curtailing sharply its practice of giving Undesirable Discharges for unfitness.

The Undesirable Discharge, because it is given "under other-than-honorable conditions," was also used as a sanction in place of discharges imposed by court-martial. In the early years of the war, AWOL and comparable offenses very often meant a court-martial and a Bad Conduct or Dishonorable Discharge after a prison term. But in 1968, new legislation increased the legal protections available to servicemen facing a special court-martial and a possible Bad Conduct Discharge. Each defendant was normally guaranteed the right to a legally qualified defense attorney, a certified military judge, and a verbatim trial record. This made special courts-martial an added drain on scarce resources.

The technicalities of a criminal trial, with a heavy burden of proof and complex rules of evidence, made the court-martial a cumbersome instrument for all but the most serious of cases. One old-time sergeant griped that

> the NCO's word isn't taken at face value anymore. The other day it took four witnesses just for me to get disciplinary proceedings under way. The JAGs won't go to court if you're the only witness. The Army's got to find a better way to get rid of people faster who don't want to be here.

What made recourse to court-martial even more unattractive was the uncertainty of the result. A commander could be fairly certain that an uncomplicated AWOL case would result in conviction. But whether the sentence would include a discharge was another question. A pretrial agreement, appeal, or clemency action might result in the imposition of a lesser penalty.

"It became increasingly clear," said the chief Army legal officer in Vietnam, "that trial by court-martial was an awkward, ineffective, and expensive means of attempting to cope with a large-scale problem. . . . Soldiers whose behavior indicated that they lacked the desire or ability to rehabilitate themselves [had to be] eliminated through administrative channels."

At about the same time, Congress and the Nixon administration began cutting back on manpower levels. A congressional ceiling set in 1971 required the armed forces to separate 65,000 soldiers almost immediately. All branches of service, but especially the Army and Marines, began relying on a relatively uncomplicated, reliable means of ridding themselves of troublemakers. Criminal charges were filed and court-martial actions initiated, but defendants were then given the chance to request Undesirable Discharges "for the good of the service," popularly called "Chapter 10 discharges." This was, in effect, a plea bargain. The accused soldier waived his right to trial in return for a guarantee that he would not be convicted or sent to prison. However, he usually got an Undesirable Discharge, and the charges, which were never legally proved, remained on his record.

Commanders began resorting to this technique with gusto in the latter half of the war. In 1969, the Army issued only 532 Chapter 10 discharges, but it gave out 7,000, 12,000, and 26,000 in the next three years. The Marine Corps showed a comparable increase, from just one case in 1967 to almost 5,000 in 1971. The vast majority of these discharges—over 90 percent—were Undesirable, and this method of separating soldiers quickly came to dominate the military justice system. In fact, Chapter 10's became so prevalent that in mid-1972, the Department of the Army had to caution its commanders against using it to circumvent efforts at rehabilitation of marginal soldiers. Altogether, about 130,000 Vietnam-era servicemen received Chapter 10 discharges, more than half of the 224,000 Undesirable certificates imposed during the period.

Accepting an Undesirable Discharge in lieu of court-martial was voluntary, but there was little incentive for the average soldier to resist. Most succumbed after a little persuasion: "They started putting pressure on us to take a fast discharge," one veteran recalled. "We could be out of the stockade in ten minutes, and out of the Army in a day and a half. One Army lawyer said that the only way to avoid five to nine years in prison was to sign. It was real strong pressure, and one of my buddies took it because he had personal problems and had to get home." Some units had regular "UD days," especially when stockades got overcrowded. An Army lawyer recalled making weekly trips to the stockade, offering an Undesirable Discharge to anyone willing to sign the forms: "They were so eager to get out of jail and out of the Army, we could clean the place out in a day." But many soldiers did not realize that the evidence against them was weak, and they wrongly assumed they would be convicted.

Some soldiers never realized what they were signing. Tommy Sanders wanted to be court-martialed because he thought he was innocent, but he did not know his rights. He just signed some papers and found himself out with an Undesirable Discharge. But most soldiers who accepted Chapter 10 Undesirable Discharges did not know or care what it would mean to them later on. As one veteran described it:

> The UD is like the tattoo a young sailor gets on leave in some exotic port. It remains on him forever, and there's little chance that he can ever get it removed. It helped to believe that the UD was only temporary. There is a rumor, probably as old as the Army itself, that after six months, it automatically is changed to an Honorable or General Discharge. It doesn't.

Nonetheless, the Chapter 10 discharge was sometimes called the "golden loophole" by soldiers who were tired of the military and wanted to go home. Anyone AWOL for more than thirty days became the responsibility of the base closest to his place of arrest, so servicemen could engineer more lenient treatment by choosing where to return to military control. Counselors often recommended good places to surrender, and some bases were overwhelmed with returning deserters.

The rule of thumb was that an AWOL under three months would keep you in the service, an AWOL over nine months would risk court-martial, but three to nine months brought a quick ticket out of the service. Sam Barnes "looked around for ways to get out, and finally decided to go AWOL." He spent a few months living in a commune, surrendered at the appropriate time and place, got an Undesirable Discharge, and went home for good. So did Phil Cook, although he had a little more trouble. He went AWOL three times and then asked for his Undesirable Discharge. He was unsuccessful at first, so he left three more times. "I just decided to go AWOL as often as I had to until I got my discharge." A Fort Meade sergeant recalled how civilian employers of AWOL soldiers intervened on their behalf, asking the military to "get Jimmy Jones his Undesirable Discharge expeditiously, because we need him on the job."

However, the golden loophole was no absolute guarantee that a deserter would stay out of prison. Late in 1972, two deserters surrendered to Army authorities after having spent four years in Sweden, both expecting to get quick Undesirable Discharges. One spent a couple of months in the stockade before getting his. The other deserter, with an almost identical case, spent six months awaiting trial. His court-martial gave him two more years and a Bad Conduct Discharge.

The decision whether to court-martial was made by field-grade commanders, usually upon the advice of military lawyers. Offenses considered less serious were tried by special courts-martial, the military equivalent of misdemeanor courts, which could impose Bad Conduct Discharges and up to six months in prison. General courts-martial could impose Dishonorable Discharges and up to life in prison, but severe sentences were usually reserved for those convicted of murder, rape, or robbery. Of all soldiers punished and given other-than-honorable discharges for AWOL or other violations of discipline, just 8 percent were sent to prison, and only 2 percent served more than six months in confinement.

Military defendants who stood trial were almost always convicted, fined, and reduced in rank. Rarely, however, did they receive punitive discharges. The 450,000 special and general courts-martial of the Vietnam era produced only 31,800 Bad Conduct and 2,200 Dishonorable Discharges. About a third of the punitive discharges were for crimes against person or property that would have been punished severely by civilian courts. The other two-thirds were for violations of military discipline, usually AWOL, which were essentially indistinguishable from the type of misconduct that resulted in the 130,000 Chapter 10 Undesirable Discharges. Oddly enough, offenses committed in Vietnam or on the way to Vietnam were not punished more harshly than those that had no direct relationship with the war. Nor did the length of the AWOL have much effect on the degree of punishment. The only significant differences between deserters with Undesirable Discharges and those with punitive discharges were that the latter were more likely to be Marines, onetime exiles, or servicemen discharged early in the war.

Most Americans care little and know less about the different discharges. Personnel officers of large companies may understand the system, but the rest of the public is confused about the differences between "Honorable" and "honorable conditions," "less-than-Honorable" and "other-than-honorable conditions," "unsuitability" and "unfitness," "Undesirable" and "Dishonorable," and so forth. A Louisiana judge once concluded that General Discharges were given by general courts-martial; to him they were the worst of all possible discharges. To most people, any veteran with less than an unblemished, fully Honorable Discharge is suspect. For more than half a million men of the Vietnam generation, this means lifelong stigmas on their records.

During President Ford's clemency program, veterans of other eras wrote by the dozens, asking that their bad discharges be changed. "It's ruined my whole life," complained a World War I veteran who had gone AWOL more than fifty years ago. Father Theodore Hesburgh, a member of President Ford's Clemency Board, received the following letter from a World War II veteran with a Dishonorable Discharge:

Dear Father Hesburgh,

I am writing you simply because I understand your feelings on amnesty for the men that just wouldn't serve in an undeclared war.

I was in the Second World War. I went in the infantry in the beginning of 1942. I returned home in 1947. Why so long, you may ask. I'll tell you.

After training, we were shipped to Africa. We went in through Kasserine Pass with the First Armored Division. We were almost wiped out. . . . We were sent back for seconds, and we made it this time against the desert fox. I also went on the invasion of Sicily and the invasion of Italy and the invasion of Anzio Beach. When the Army got ready for D-Day, quite a few of the four-invasion assault troops were sent to England to join that invasion. . . . We jumped out of the landing craft on Omaha Beach (Red Beach One). . . . There were a lot of dead men there. We got off the beach, though, and something else—the men at Omaha and the 101st Airborne were the only troops to use bayonets in that war. The 29th was called the "Purple Heart" Division. No trooper got off clean. I ended my soldiering at Aachen in a mine field. Someone fell off the tape line, and the whole place blew. I went with it, but I'm alive. A lot of guys aren't.

Well, in 1945, the Germans quit. I asked for some leave, which I hadn't had for a real long time. I was refused, so I went AWOL. I went about thirty days and came back to the outfit. I was told they needed an example to scare the new occupation troops coming in, so I ended up in an Army court charged with everything they still had hanging around that had to be cleaned up. There are no lawyers in Army court, just officers who read books. I was given a general court-martial when they got finished charging me. I was sent up for ten years in a federal penitentiary. . . . They then sent me home with other prisoners, chained in the hold of a liberty ship. . . .

I tried for a long time to get justice, but who cared? Only my family. When I got out with a great combat record and a dishonorable discharge, the employers only saw my jail sentence. I finally got past that after a few years, but I never got any veterans' benefits or my insurance, back pay, or anything. As the court-martial says, "to forfeit all pay and allotments, due and to become due." Anyway, that's what I got, and I got a gang of medals, too. A five invasion man. One out of some four hundred soldiers with that ribbon for the European Theater of Operations.

I know what a jail term can do for you in the job market, education, etc. I wouldn't want these guys to get it my way. I think they need a break. Keep fighting for them, reverend. I wish to God someone would have fought a little for me so long ago.

Sincerely,
An Old Soldier

V | EXILES

On the Run

A few minutes after his ship left harbor, Keith Considine left his quarters, donned a life jacket, and jumped into the ocean. On cue, a group of Vietnam Veterans Against the War rescued him in rented canoes, taking him away to the sanctuary of the antiwar underground. Considine was one of at least fifty thousand Americans who became political fugitives during the Vietnam era, most of whom fled to another country. Not since eighty thousand Tories fled to Canada during the Revolution had America witnessed such an exodus of people fleeing its borders. Perhaps more than any other single aspect of the Vietnam war, the exiled draft resisters and deserters symbolized the conflict over the morality of the war and the values of those who refused to fight it.

While other groups of offenders were largely overlooked, the exiles captured the attention of the public and the press. Over time, they became the stuff of political mythology. Their supporters believed them to be bright, principled antiwarriors; to their detractors, they were overeducated cowards. Most people thought the law was at their heels, that arrest or surrender meant long prison terms, and that what exiles hoped for most was vindication through an amnesty that would bring them home in triumph.

Little of this was true. Exiles and other fugitives were neither the best nor the worst of their generation. They were a cross-section of young men who, for a variety of reasons, refused to submit to the draft or the dictates of the armed forces. They were rich and poor, black and white, college graduates and high school dropouts. Some were related to influential people; both Morris Udall and Spiro Agnew had nephews living in exile. Some adjusted very well to life as immigrants, but most did not. While the American public hotly debated the amnesty issue, most exiles quietly came home and seldom went to prison.

Just one-sixth of all draft resisters and deserters ever hid from the law (see Figure 7). Most of the 210,000 accused draft resisters remained home to face charges. Those who took flight generally did so long before formal charges were brought against them. Although a number were later indicted and declared fugitives from justice, most never were the subject of legal proceedings. But they all lived with the constant fear that discovery meant certain arrest, trial, and imprisonment.

By definition, all deserters were fugitives from military control, but few concealed their identities, hid in the underground, or took exile in a foreign country. For most, desertion was like walking off a job—no phony ID, no stolen jeeps, no jumping over fences, and no rescues in rented canoes. Cunning or careful planning was necessary only for deserters in the combat zone.

Four of every five deserters went home, resumed their civilian lives, and followed normal routines. They worked steadily, often at their old jobs. They were, as some described themselves, "self-retired veterans." They believed that punishment was inevitable and that it would be worse the longer they failed to report. But surrender was best left to another day. As the time began to stretch into years, many married and raised families. Some filled highly reputable jobs, acquired their own businesses, or worked for federal, state, or local agencies. A few held positions of public trust: sheriff, police chief, juvenile probation officer, narcotics agent. At times, they worked and prospered even though many people in their communities knew they were deserters.

They expected to be caught eventually. Anyone absent for more than thirty days was supposed to have a "Deserter Wanted by the Armed Forces" notice sent to the FBI and his hometown police department. After 1971, the Army offered a bounty of $25 to any police officer who arrested an AWOL soldier. But many local police never received the notices, or else just ignored them. In Berkeley, California, the city council passed a resolution barring the local police from tracking or arresting deserters.

FIGURE 7: EXILES

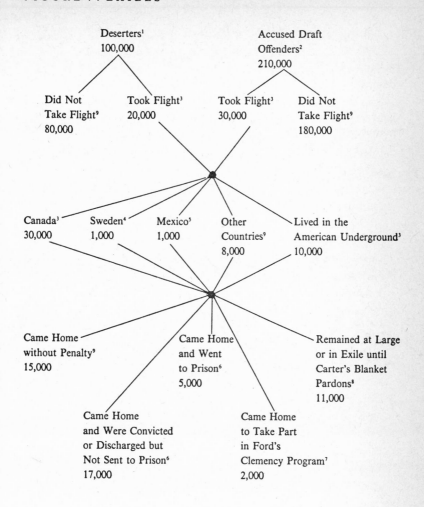

Deserters[1]
100,000

Accused Draft
Offenders[2]
210,000

Did Not
Take Flight[9]
80,000

Took Flight[3]
20,000

Took Flight[3]
30,000

Did Not
Take Flight[9]
180,000

Canada[3]
30,000

Sweden[4]
1,000

Mexico[5]
1,000

Other
Countries[9]
8,000

Lived in the
American Underground[3]
10,000

Came Home
without Penalty[9]
15,000

Came Home
and Went
to Prison[6]
5,000

Remained at Large
or in Exile until
Carter's Blanket
Pardons[8]
11,000

Came Home
and Were Convicted
or Discharged but
Not Sent to Prison[6]
17,000

Came Home
to Take Part
in Ford's
Clemency Program[7]
2,000

A Seattle steelworker quit the Army, went home, and nothing happened: "I worked under my real name all the time, filed my income taxes under my real name, and got my refund checks. If the FBI had wanted me in all those years, it would have taken them about ten seconds to find me." A wildcatter from the Texas oil fields admitted he was a fugitive when stopped for speeding by his hometown deputy sheriff, but he just got a traffic ticket. A Santa Barbara deserter was visited by the FBI and admitted he was a fugitive. He asked the FBI man, "What do you want me to do?" The agent said that since the man was living at home he was not really "at large." The agent closed the case file and went away. A military attorney observed that "from month to month, you could see how much time and energy the FBI was putting in its enforcement effort. Every so often, we would get shipments from a particular place, and we always knew where the local FBI was trying to improve its statistics."

No sweep would have caught Joe Browning, even though he lived at home under his real name. His house was at the end of a cul-de-sac, and every time an unfamiliar car came down his street, he jumped out a window and ran off to the local pool hall. But fifty thousand other draft and military fugitives were not prepared to live with the fear Browning endured for years. Not willing to wait for the official-looking stranger at the door, they left their hometowns, often refusing to tell friends and family where they were going, so that no one would have to lie to the FBI. They assumed false identities, sometimes aided by documents stolen by activists from draft boards. Another tactic was to watch the obituaries until a man the proper age died. The fugitive then wrote for a copy of the decedent's birth certificate, which could be used to get a driver's license, social security card, and other identification. Sometimes fugitives were given complete sets of identification by friends, who then reported them lost or stolen. Passports were more of a problem, expert forgeries costing as much as $1,500.

Roughly ten thousand fugitives stayed in the United States, living as political outcasts—"the way our grandfathers did in Europe"—avoiding personal entanglements and suspicious of every chance meeting. It was hard to build employment records that could help them find good jobs. A young man who always thought of himself as a "termite" admitted spending virtually "every moment living in fear. . . . I worry that the longer I stay [with a job], the worse my chances are. I make up a social security number, but by the time it hasn't checked out, I've left. I can't make any lasting friends. I have to keep it all inside unless someone else volunteers he's a deserter, too. I'm lonely, but I can't get too involved with girls. They always want to know about your past, and you have to lie."

Driven by fear and suspicion, many fugitives rearranged their entire lives to avoid arrest, often eluding the FBI for years. One person changed his name, moved to a new community, raised a family, and became prosperous and locally prominent. Another moved to the mountains, where he built a tree house and lived for six years as a hunter and trapper. Other fugitives changed their routine very little. They had already been part of the youth subculture in cities and college communities, good sanctuaries for someone with draft or military problems.

Fugitives were afraid that being stopped for hitchhiking or jaywalking could mean the end of freedom. A young man from Washington, D.C., had been a draft fugitive for five years before he was arrested for shoplifting in Virginia. A Minnesota resister was arrested in Eureka, California, dressed as a department store Santa Claus. Some fugitives were caught by the FBI at antiwar rallies and conferences.

For help and comfort, many turned to the organized "underground" —a network of priests, radicals, and ordinary citizens who helped them move from place to place or settle down in a new community. Trusted counselors offered entry to the network by putting a fugitive in touch with one person, who passed him on to another. One man traveled from Chicago to New York, being handed from person to person, and he was astonished to learn who was involved: "I traveled from small town to small town, chauffeured by well-to-do young housewives who often kept small children in the car to avoid suspicion. I spent nights at wealthy farms and large houses that must have belonged to professional people. Sometimes I was taken to religious retreats and orphanages. They never showed me maps or told me where I was, and it took several days and many different trips to go from one city to the next. Frequently, I encountered other underground people going in different directions." The network was especially active in rural New England, dubbed "little Canada" because of the many farms, communes, and college campuses that hid fugitives from the FBI. These New Englanders were merely emulating their ancestors, who a hundred years earlier had run the underground railroad for fugitive slaves.

The farmers, professionals, and housewives in the underground committed felonies by harboring draft fugitives and aiding their interstate flight. "Enticing and procuring a soldier to desert" was also a federal offense. The network was never penetrated, however, and official pressure was directed only at the counselors who served as points of entry. Two prosecutions were brought against counselors in Boston and Bloomington, Illinois. One was acquitted, and the other had his conviction overturned on appeal. Both individuals had been accused of encouraging fugitives to go to Canada, rather than "enticing" the act of desertion itself.

Dozens of counseling organizations did much the same thing. The San Francisco "GI Help" program offered military fugitives "places to crash" and "information about the alternatives of exile to Canada or Sweden, open resistance to the military, going underground, or seeking various kinds of discharges." Local police once raided its headquarters and discovered a dozen AWOL soldiers sleeping on the floor, but no charges were brought against the program. The Defense Department furnished Congress with the names of twenty-three organizations, representing hundreds of antiwar counselors, "that have definitely been linked with deserter inducement programs." Although these counselors were subjected to political surveillance, they never became the targets of a major Justice Department criminal investigation.

In low-income and minority neighborhoods, there was an unorganized, spontaneous underground protecting people known to be wanted for draft or military offenses. Ed Sowders, a Vietnam veteran deserter who lived in the "poor people's underground" for three years, recalled how

this community-based network of relatives, neighbors, and friends helped me remain in my own home, safe in the knowledge that they would inform me or my family of anything out of the ordinary. My mother received several phone calls from neighbors and friends, informing her that they had just received visits by agents. Of course, no one provided information about me. One man said, "For christsake, if you see Eddie, tell him to get out of town, they're looking hard this time."

The network twice saved Sowders from certain arrest. Trapped in his house by FBI agents, he escaped amidst a specially choreographed pack of teenagers with baseball bats and gloves, ostensibly heading for the neighborhood park. Later, he was arrested for a minor traffic offense; with no valid identification, he was held awaiting a fingerprint check which was certain to mark him as a deserter. A number of neighbors came to the station, accused the police of breaking up a local party, and convinced them to release Sowders before the fingerprint check came through. He eventually surrendered to the FBI, but on his own terms —in a public antiwar ceremony in Washington, D.C.

Sowders was an unusually resourceful fugitive. Not many others were able to use the underground as more than a temporary shelter as they moved from place to place, making plans to take exile in a foreign country.

Taking Exile

Tens of thousands of draft and military fugitives went into exile during the war. A few nations, notably West Germany and Japan, actively pursued American deserters and returned them to military custody. But most countries left them alone if they caused no trouble. Drifters moved from border to border without difficulty, and small colonies survived for years without work permits or social benefits in Holland, France, and England. But there were few real choices for fugitives who wanted to establish roots. An antiwar guidebook rated all the countries in the world for exile, giving poor recommendations to most:

Living in the Amazon might sound romantic, but the prospect of life in a Brazilian jail brings one back to reality and away from Brazil.

The applicant must give proof of a minimum deposit of $10,000 in a bank established in Haiti. Political exiles aren't rich. To hell with Haiti.

The letter which we received from [Venezuela] was rather hostile, and we would suggest forgetting it. The embassy also sent us one entire pamphlet of speeches made by Nixon praising Venezuela.

Early in the war, Mexico was a common choice of deserters from military bases in the Southwest. The border was easy to cross and living costs were low, but finding a job was difficult for a "gringo" without a work permit. Except for a few entrepreneurs who risked severe criminal penalties for drug dealing, almost all of the roughly one thousand exiles in Mexico eventually returned to the United States or left for a more hospitable country.

There were only two real choices for exiles who wanted to settle down—Canada and Sweden. Canada was an attractive refuge. It had no draft and did not consider AWOL a criminal offense, so exiles did not fear extradition to the United States. Canada offered not only sanctuary, but work permits, welfare benefits, full legal status as immigrants, and eventual citizenship. In the face of economic and cultural domination by the colossus of the south, official Canadian sympathy toward the exiles enhanced the country's international prestige and self-esteem. Many Canadians were quietly elated that America was getting its comeuppance in Vietnam. They had long worried about the exodus of talented young artists and professionals to the United States, and the flow of war resisters was helping to reverse the trend. In 1970, the northward exodus exceeded southward migration for the first time in memory. Furthermore, according to External Affairs Minister Mitchell Sharp, Canada "looked back to see what the United States had done during the period 1939–1941 when we were at war and they were not. We found that Americans had accepted deserters from the Canadian army without question. So we said, 'Well, that's fine. The Americans are in a war that we're not in, so we will apply the same policy in Canada that they applied to us.'"

Many exiles were drawn to Canada by its beauty, robust life-style, and freedom from American social pressures. The independence and the romance of the last frontier were just what some fugitives were looking for:

It isn't just in terms of geography and economy that Canada is a frontier country; it's the men and their experience. Hitchhiking in Canada, one is picked up by men who have worked in, and who talk of, the mines, the railroad, the sawmills, the oil fields, and the forest. As for me, it is a time to try new ways of living, to try new faces, to think, to remember.

Young Americans could follow the example of Jim Grady, a pacifist who fled the World War I draft, spent the rest of his life in Canada, and was an eighty-year-old prospector in British Columbia at the start of the Vietnam war. It was easy for exiles to develop an attachment for Canada: "If this is jail, it sure is a big, beautiful one."

Yet the most important attractions of Canada were its familiarity to Americans and its openness to immigrants. Throughout its history, Canada has greeted foreigners warmly, and Montreal, Toronto, and Vancouver have large, tightly knit communities of first-generation immigrants from all over the world. Americans could easily blend into Canadian life, or they could stay within their own indigenous communities.

Getting there was easy. America and Canada have the longest friendly border in the world. At more than a hundred separate border stations, guards usually wave travelers through after a few perfunctory questions. American border officials looked with suspicion on the draft-age traveler with a lot of luggage and checked the National Crime Information Center (NCIC) list before letting him pass. But most draft fugitives chose exile long before they faced formal charges, and even those who were indicted had a week to cross the border before appearing on the NCIC list. Deserters had at least a month before their names were listed.

For some, crossing the border had an element of suspense. Ron Danielson, an Army deserter, was detained for questioning at the American border station at Blaine, Washington. He raced away on foot, but was captured by American immigration officials fifty feet inside Canadian territory. The event was recorded on film by a Vancouver *Sun* reporter who happened to be standing nearby. This violation of Canadian territorial integrity prompted official demands for the return of Danielson. After spending a week in an American jail, he was delivered to the border, where Canadian officials set him free.

George Csikor, a Hungarian refugee and Canadian citizen, was awaiting trial for refusing induction into the American army. Csikor was living in the San Francisco Bay area at the time, and the president of the University of Victoria Student Union smuggled him out of the country on a flight to Vancouver, using tactics that prompted *Amex-Canada* magazine to call the episode "a veritable spy thriller escape story." Scott Peters was less successful. Peters was one of sixty-six inductees aboard a Boeing 737 en route to basic training at Fort Lewis, Washington, when he hijacked the plane and forced it to land in Vancouver, British Columbia. Within a week, Peters was deported from Canada and delivered to a Seattle jail. (The one other exile hijacking during the war involved a deserter who demanded to be flown back to the United States. He kept a knife at a Swedish girl's throat, but three fellow exiles came aboard the SAS plane and talked him out of it.)

A little pocket money was all that was necessary to enter Canada as a temporary visitor. Those who were better prepared tried to establish permanent status as "landed immigrants" right at the border. They had to score fifty out of a possible ninety points on a rating system that gave credit for education, skills, fluency in English, and other assets. An American high-school graduate with a Canadian job offer had thirty-seven automatic points, and an immigration officer could give him as many as fifteen more based upon a subjective evaluation of his character. The neatly dressed, polite fugitive had a good chance to earn the fifty points on the spot. Others entered Canada as visitors, slipping back across the border when they thought they could qualify as immigrants. Only a handful were said to have had difficulty, usually "because they were not calm and did not use common sense." For the draft fugitive with a college degree, "it was like checking into a hotel."

Canada refused to accept the less-educated, lower-skilled military fugitives until 1969. Deserters could enter Canada as visitors without work permits, but they were subject to arrest and immediate return to American military police. Even after 1969, military fugitives were sometimes turned back under Canadian immigration law, which excluded "criminals," "mentally defective persons," and "persons who are likely to become public charges." If an immigration officer suspected that an individual used marijuana, he could refuse entry. Military fugitives found it more difficult to get the fifty points necessary to become legal immigrants. Marriage to a Canadian citizen was one way to sidestep the requirement, and some deserters advertised in Canadian newspapers and paid as much as $2,000 to make the necessary arrangements.

Those who could not qualify as landed immigrants often lived for years as illegal aliens, facing the constant threat of deportation. In 1972, the Canadian government declared a ninety-day amnesty for illegal immigrants, and twelve hundred Americans signed up for landed status. Soon afterwards, a severe recession resulted in a more selective immigration policy, but by then the Vietnam war was almost over.

Sweden was almost as attractive a place to take exile. Like Canada, it offered a wide-open outdoors; it also provided perhaps the world's most generous social services and welfare benefits. Furthermore, Sweden considered the exiles more than mere immigrants; they were political refugees with international status as opponents of American war policies. Yet Sweden had a much more foreign culture than Canada, and it was an ocean away from friends and families. Exiles could satisfy their day-to-day needs by speaking English, but a command of the Swedish language was required for all but the most menial jobs. The local life-style lacked the comforting reminders of home that exiles could find in Canada with its American-dominated culture. Even Sweden's bigger cities were not melting pots, and young Americans generally suffered the same second-class treatment given Yugoslavs, Greeks, and other foreigners. The Swedish government, for all its generosity, often exhibited much the same heavy-handedness that had soured the exiles on the United States.

The exodus to Sweden began in early 1967, when the government quietly granted asylum to a black deserter from Germany. A handful of others slipped into the country illegally over the next few months, but the exile movement really began later that year with the widely publicized voyage of four sailors from the aircraft carrier *Intrepid*. In October 1967, they met in a Tokyo coffeehouse and agreed not to return to ship because of their opposition to the Vietnam war. With the help of "Beherein," the Japanese underground, they were smuggled away on fishing boats and delivered to the Russian coastal patrol. For two months, the Soviet Union treated them as celebrities. They were given the Lenin Peace Prize, 1,000 gold rubles, vacation trips, press conferences, and other amenities—all to the benefit of host and guest alike. But the four sailors, whom another deserter described as "whacked-out freaks," then began to embarrass the Russians with criticism of the opulent life-style of Communist Party members and comments like "Lenin, oh yeah, you mean John." The Russian Vietnam Committee negotiated with other countries to find a place to send them, and eventually the Swedish Vietnam Committee convinced its government to grant asylum.

The "Intrepid Four" were instant celebrities and drew considerable attention from the international press, which pleased the Swedes. But they also drew the attention of other deserters, which the Swedish government had not anticipated. As a later-arriving exile recalled, "the publicity those cats received helped guys who were fed up and refused to do any more killing for Sam. Now they knew there was at least one country in the world which would let them live like human beings." All of a sudden, Sweden became the deserters' mecca.

About a dozen soldiers and sailors from Southeast Asia followed the path cut through Japan and the Soviet Union by the Intrepid Four. They were shuffled in and out of taxis and buses by Beherein ("the slickest operators since Al Capone and his boys") and treated like heroes by the Soviet Union ("we were probably better excuses for partying than for making propaganda"). Others came from Southeast Asia via India and Afghanistan. As exiles in Sweden began to get attention in the American press, home-based deserters starting heading for Scandinavia. A few stowed away on ships, and one jumped off a Norwegian freighter and swam to safety. Some simply flew to Stockholm; one deserter showed up at an SAS reservation counter in his military uniform, bought a one-way ticket to Sweden, and took off that same day.

By far the largest migration came through West Germany and Denmark. With clothes and documents from the German underground, deserters could reach the Danish border without difficulty. Denmark

did not let them stay, but guaranteed safe passage to Sweden. Sometimes, deserters found help in unusual places. Butch Dodson planned
to flee to Sweden with his British fiancée, but she was killed in an
automobile accident. Distraught, Dodson told his commanding officer
of their plans to elope. The colonel gave him $100 and drove him on
the first leg of his journey.

Sweden accepted the flurry of deserters with ambivalence. Olaf
Palme's government extended a warm welcome to the Intrepid Four,
but others were treated coolly. Deserters were usually put in jail upon
arrival, sometimes in the drunk tank, while Swedish police made sure
they were not wanted for more serious crimes. Until 1969, Sweden
accepted deserters only from Vietnam or with orders for the war zone,
and it rejected draft resisters altogether. Some observers attributed this
restrictive policy to Sweden's own policy of universal conscription for
able-bodied men. In 1901, the year compulsory service was introduced
in Sweden, one of every seven draft-eligible men fled to other countries,
many to the United States—leaving the Swedish government with a
dim view of American draft resisters. But more important, Sweden was
a neutral nation with close economic ties to the West. American steve-
dores refused to unload Volvos because of Sweden's acceptance of
deserters, and other economic consequences began to be felt. At first,
Palme's government chose to move carefully. Its ambassador to the
United States commented that "nobody likes deserters," while the
interior minister said that offering asylum to deserters was "necessary
for humanitarian reasons," but "not an unfriendly gesture toward the
United States."

Deserters who came to Sweden in 1968 paid the price of this ambivalence. They were given little help in finding jobs, housing, or language
training, and were excluded from some social services available to other
immigrant groups. Welfare benefits amounted to only $15 per week,
and many turned to begging or stealing. The exiles became so discouraged that a delegation of twelve visited Copenhagen to inquire
about moving the entire community to Denmark. But public demonstrations and political pressure from Sweden's left wing induced
Palme's government to adopt a more positive attitude. After February
1969, all draft resisters and deserters were accepted at the border upon

a simple declaration of opposition to the Vietnam war, and Sweden instituted generous social services to help them adjust. Welfare benefits were doubled to about $30 per week, prompting accusations from the United States Congress that Sweden was "subsidizing" desertion. At about the same time, Palme firmly declared his government's opposition to American involvement in Vietnam, regardless of any threats of economic retaliation. Until the United States withdrew from Vietnam, official Swedish policy remained on the side of the exiles.

No one can say how many draft resisters and deserters chose exile during the war years. Popular estimates of the number of Vietnam-era exiles reflected the political hyperbole of those years. Richard Nixon referred to exiles as "those few hundreds," and antiwar spokesmen often used a figure of 100,000. Each side tried to tailor the exile phenomenon to suit its own political purposes. Both the Defense Department and the Swedish government had unreliable counts, and Canada's more precise immigration tally made no distinction between fugitives from justice and other draft-age male immigrants from the United States. It is difficult even to estimate how many illegal immigrants and international drifters never settled permanently in any country. The available evidence suggests that the grand total was about forty thousand—twenty thousand landed immigrants and ten thousand illegal aliens in Canada, one thousand each in Mexico and Sweden, and the rest scattered around the world. A few thousand were not American citizens, but resident aliens who typically fled to their countries of origin rather than serve in the American armed forces.

In one sense, the 100,000 figure of the antiwar movement was close to the truth. Draft resisters and deserters were the core of a much larger American exile community that included tens of thousands of other young people who had grown disenchanted with life back home. Many went to Canada or Sweden as an act of solidarity with the fugitives. Gregg Williams had planned to refuse induction, but his Kansas City draft board gave him an unexpected physical exemption. He went to Canada anyway, living as a subsistence farmer in Ontario. Friends, brothers, wives, and girl friends often accompanied fugitives across the border and never came back. Broken engagements and divorces were epidemic in the exile community, but American women often stayed in Canada or Sweden and married other exiles.

Nor were these young Americans the only draft-age refugees. Greece, West Germany, and Portugal produced thousands of their own draft resisters, some of whom settled in the United States until they discovered they were subject to the American draft. One man refused induction in Poland, West Germany, and the United States before volunteering for the Israeli army. European countries had experienced this phenomenon for centuries, and they cared little about it. Holland even paid its draft exiles $200 to help them settle elsewhere, promising to welcome them back at age twenty-six if they changed their minds. Australia and South Vietnam produced hundreds of their own anti-Vietnam-war exiles, many of whom emigrated to Canada. To the extent that this international exile population could be called a "community," the American fugitives were its leaders, partly because of their greater number, but also because they attracted by far the most attention.

Taken as a whole, these exiled Americans were much more of a cross-section of their nation's youth than any other category of Vietnam-era offenders. Draft counselor Arlo Tatum noted that their politics varied "from very conservative to revolutionary leftist to hippie, with heaviest representation between these extremes." They were "ambitious and lazy, unkempt and neat, strange and ordinary, married and single, nervous and self-confident."

Yet some aspects of their background set them apart from their peers back home—and from each other. Draft and military exiles had very little in common, a fact that they and their host countries soon discovered. Draft resisters usually emigrated between 1965 and 1970. They were predominantly white, middle-class, and fairly well educated. Their political views were diverse, typically left-of-center but well within the American mainstream. The radical *Amex-Canada* magazine labeled them "Bobby Kennedy or McCarthy types." By contrast, deserters took exile at the height of the war, between 1968 and 1972; they were younger, had far less education, and came from more disadvantaged backgrounds. Instead of being "clean for Gene," they tended to be either apolitical or intensely radical. A Canadian social psychologist classified deserters into four groups: "nonactivists," who deserted primarily for personal rather than political reasons (over 50 percent); "refugees," who were young, unskilled, frightened, and living underground as illegal aliens (30 percent); "organizers," who were college-educated radicals (less than 15 percent); and a "salvage group" of emotionally disturbed young men who often committed serious crimes in addition to desertion (less than 5 percent). Deserters were usually more hostile than draft resisters toward the United States, but much less capable of coping with life in a foreign country. Over time, their organizations became significantly more vocal and radical.

Some draft resisters went to Canada as the last recourse after an unsuccessful campaign to avoid induction. One North Carolina youth tried three times to get a physical exemption—by falling off a bridge on his motorcycle, grazing himself with a shotgun blast, and rupturing his Achilles' tendon with a pistol. Nonetheless, he passed his preinduction physical and went to Canada. Some, like the exile who trained Saudi Arabians to use Nike-Hercules missiles, were anything but conscientiously opposed to war.

Others were violent radicals, like the Puerto Rican accused of murdering a San Juan police officer in an antiwar riot, and the two brothers charged with the bombing of a University of Wisconsin building which killed a research assistant. To quote another, "I had already been convicted and sentenced to three years for assaulting two FBI agents. I was indicted for inciting to riot, for riot, and for burglary. With new charges against me arising out of an anti-imperialist strike at the University of Buffalo, I decided that to spend the next thirty years in jail would be a waste of time." These, however, were the unusual cases, hunted as much by the Canadian Mounties as by the FBI.

For every exile who was an unprincipled draft evader or an international outlaw, there were several who refused to submit to the draft or to participate in the war on moral grounds. About one-third of all exiled draft resisters refused to accept deferments and exemptions for which they apparently qualified. Joe Britt was an A student at a top-ranking university, but his student deferment gave him ethical problems. He quit school, sent his draft card back to his local board with a "letter of resignation," and took a last tour of America on a Greyhound pass before heading for Canada. John McDermott completely ignored his draft board, refusing to play the "game" of finding an acceptable way out of the draft: "I refuse to grovel! I could try numerous dodges, but I will not lower myself to that. Groveling puts the registrant's life in the hands that have no moral right to control it and presumes that the draft board's power is legitimate."

These exiles were similar to the draft violators who stood trial for refusing induction on moral principle. What distinguished them, however, was their rejection of the Gandhian principle that one must be prepared to accept the legal consequences of one's actions. Larry Allison, now a professor of philosophy at a major Canadian university, said that he

> never intended to weasel out of the draft. Going to Canada was the only moral option available to me. I was not willing to go to jail, because the country was wrong; I wasn't. I thought civil disobedience would be futile and harmful to my life. I saw bumper stickers saying "America, love it or leave it," and well, I just chose the second option.

Many deserters were equally motivated by principle. The organizers of numerous antiwar coffeehouses and newspapers *(Head-On, The Last Harass, Gig Line, Shakedown,* and *Fatigue Press)* ended up in Canada, as did the young Marine who feared for his safety after *Life* magazine printed his name and picture in an exposé about brig conditions in Camp Pendleton. A number of deserters took exile after completing full tours of Vietnam, usually because of their growing doubts about the war. John Sheehan deserted for Canada with just four months left in his tour because he refused to "wear the label" of an "honorably discharged veteran of the Vietnam war" for the rest of his life. Gene Brooks considered finishing the remainder of his tour, but he "just felt that maybe there was a more desirable place to live without going back to a situation where there's all this social unrest, and everything from pollution to discrimination to riots to political situations. The American way of life just lost appeal to me."

Most draft exiles could have escaped conviction and avoided the draft without leaving the country, but they were ignorant of their legal alternatives. Colonel Nathan Corman, Virginia state director for Selective Service, "felt sorry" for sons of the Old Dominion who took exile: "If they had looked into all their possibilities, things might have been different." But looking into all possibilities required counseling, and many mistakenly thought that meant high-priced, untrustworthy lawyers. Stu Beecham of Miami went to Canada without looking for help, because "when you're not used to dealing with lawyers, how do you know how to find the right one?" Draft counselor Michael Brophy insisted that "upwards of ninety percent of all the men who are in Canada are there because they were unable to obtain accurate information and competent, responsible counseling." Many draft-age men who might otherwise have gone to Canada had last-minute meetings with draft counselors that kept them out of the draft. Two Los Angeles youths packed their car, closed out their bank accounts, and visited draft counselor Steve Houston to ask what to do when they got to Canada. Houston convinced them that they had other options, so they went home and eventually avoided the draft without having to leave the country.

Lack of counseling also affected exiled deserters. Half of all deserters never made any effort to solve their problems through military channels, and many of the rest never had the patience to follow through. Paul Davidov applied for in-service conscientious objector status, but he fled to Canada without waiting to see what happened to his application. He later learned that he had been granted CO status, but by then he was a deserter.

The tendency to flee before seeking help stemmed from a distrust of draft boards and commanding officers. Orin Lathrop left Minneapolis for Winnipeg because he felt "attacked all the time" by his draft board. "I was too paranoid to try to find out about anything." Don Masters was so "disillusioned and bitter about the whole process" that he never bothered to inquire about exemptions and deferments. Today, he regrets his haste, "but I felt very strongly and didn't want to spend the energy to get things resolved." Carl Scheuer tried to deal fairly with his draft board. He thought he qualified for a physical exemption, but he fled in despair when "they didn't play fair in return."

Lathrop, Masters, and Scheuer were career-oriented college graduates from middle-class families, no different from the millions who safely avoided the draft through legal devices. But their bad relationships with draft boards, coupled with their staunch opposition to the war, left them in a state of confusion and fear. They fled in haste, and they now live with the knowledge that their many years of exile were probably unnecessary. As Lathrop noted, "a lot of doors were open to me at the time, but I didn't know about them—so I guess they really didn't exist."

American-Canadians and American-Swedes

When exiles crossed the border, most were determined never to go back: "I'm a twentieth-century runaway slave, not a draft dodger. There ain't no way I'd ever go back to the United States, except to destroy it." They had to forget the past and create new identities for themselves in Canada: "Once I moved to Canada, I no longer regarded myself as evading the draft. I was immigrating. I had broken my ties with the United States." It was impossible for these men to equip themselves psychologically for the possibility of coming home, lest that interfere with their adjustment to Canadian or Swedish life. A 1970 survey of exiles in Toronto discovered that 78 percent intended to remain in Canada permanently, regardless of the outcome of the war or any subsequent amnesty. They did not consider themselves exiles; they were expatriates, American-Canadians or American-Swedes, no more interested in returning to their homeland than are foreigners who immigrate to the United States. The Toronto bus station was their Statue of Liberty, the exile organization their Ellis Island.

Today, no more than one-fourth of the original forty thousand exiles remain in their adopted countries, and they tend to be the ones who have made the most successful adjustments. They are doctors, lawyers, university professors, reporters, musicians, movie stars, skilled mechanics, teachers, farmers, craftsmen, storekeepers, accountants—every imaginable trade. One patented an invention and is now a self-made millionaire. Many have Canadian or Swedish wives and children, and one married into the Swedish nobility. They have homes, mortgages, insurance policies, and other attributes of the middle-class life they would have led in the United States.

These successful exiles responded to the challenge of immigration with an élan and self-reliance that reflects well on the adaptability of

American youth. Americans are used to moving from one place to another, shaping a new environment and making new friends. Going to Toronto or Stockholm as a refugee was more difficult than moving to another American city, but the challenge sometimes added to the determination to succeed. "It's remarkable how unremarkable it was," commented Larry Allison, now a professor at a Canadian university. "The only difficult part was the decision itself. Being an immigrant wasn't hard at all."

Even many who still scratch for a living have found personal fulfillment with life as immigrants. Pat Simpson, barely supporting himself with a part-time job loading crates onto boxcars, insists that "Canada is a good place to be a working man. I suppose I'm doing what I would have done if I'd stayed in the States, but I get more respect here." Hundreds of exiles are frontiersmen or bush farmers, working in the summertime and living for the rest of the year off Canada's generous unemployment insurance. Some exiles to Sweden have settled in the Arctic tundra, helping the Lapps with their reindeer herds. Bush land still sells for just a few dollars an acre in remote sections of Canada and Sweden, and a number of exiles have become landowners. A counter-culture shoemaker joined a hundred-acre Ontario commune and built his own house for around $6,000: "I can fulfill the American dream better in Canada than in the States. I can buy some land, build a house, and settle down. How many Americans my age can do that?"

Success rarely came easily, however. Exiles had to be resourceful to survive. Carl and Anna Scheuer were college graduates from suburban Minneapolis whose combined income exceeded $15,000 per year in 1969. In 1970, after Carl's draft board denied him a physical exemption, the Scheuers left for Toronto. "Right at the start, they told me that coming to Canada meant a five-year setback in my career plans. That's exactly what happened." Neither of them could find a job in Toronto, so they moved to Calgary. Despite their willingness to work at almost anything, it took Carl three months to find a job, and Anna a full year. Their savings vanished, and they lived in an underheated lower-class housing complex. Two years after arriving in Canada, their combined income was half what it had been in Minneapolis, and they had a newborn baby to care for. Over the next three years, Carl graduated from accounting school, changed jobs twice, and finally established himself in a promising career. The Scheuer family income is now close to $20,000 per year, and recently they bought a comfortable house in a Calgary suburb. Carl and Anna Scheuer spent six years accomplishing what they could have done in one year back in Minnesota.

The trip across the border was a pivotal point in the life of almost every exile. For Larry Allison, the decision "made me more prone to stay in control of my own life. As a philosopher, I might call myself more 'morally autonomous.' I think I'll be better off in the long run as a result." Orin Lathrop insisted that coming to Canada was the "shock therapy" he needed to get away from thinking in conventional, programmed terms. "It brought out my strengths and weaknesses, teaching me how to organize my own life." Immigration may be an acquired skill, and many exiles speak of moving from Canada or Sweden to another country if they ever hit the doldrums. They share a strong sense of individuality and self-confidence born of crisis, perseverance, and eventual success against heavy odds.

However, for every one who made the adjustment, three others did not. They came back to the United States, some to prison. Many went home after a few days or weeks. They were unable to muster the skill, hard work, or good fortune necessary to establish a home in a foreign country. Part of the problem was economic. In Canada, jobs were scarce and low-paying, especially during the recession of the early 1970s. American-owned businesses often refused to hire exiles, and some Canadian employers were not inclined to hire Americans when able-bodied Canadian workers could be found. Work could be found more easily in Sweden, but most of the available jobs were those the Swedes themselves did not want.

Deserters had the most difficult time. Young and unskilled, they had to compete with West Indians, Yugoslavs, and other immigrant groups for menial jobs—washing dishes, sweeping floors, or driving taxis if they were lucky. The job market was hopeless for the thousands who were illegal immigrants; they had to resort to exploitation labor or petty crime to survive. Illegal immigrants risked deportation if they were caught, so they had no recourse if they were paid less than the minimum wage—or not paid at all, as sometimes happened.

In Toronto, Stockholm, and elsewhere, young Americans begged in the streets, slept in the parks, and gathered empty bottles to collect the deposits. Some began to "rip off" everything and everyone they could. Leaders of the Swedish exile community granted a contrived interview to a right-wing Texas broadcaster in exchange for $2,000. Hospitable Canadians and Swedes began to notice the disappearance of valuable possessions. A few exiles resorted to bootlegging liquor or peddling drugs, creating a public nuisance that affected the reputation of the entire exile community.

Almost every exile was mentally prepared to suffer misfortune for a while, but many began to wonder whether resistance was worth indefinite sacrifice. Friends at home were leading normal lives, starting families, and prospering in careers, while exiles were still hanging in limbo. Even those who were gradually building new lives were bitter about the years they were sacrificing in the process. A former Army doctor found that his deserter status prevented him from holding all but the lowest-paying medical jobs: "Look at me. I live in a crummy house. Here I am the doctor of the family, and all my brothers have better houses than I can afford."

Separation from families back home was another source of hardship. During an exile's first few months in Canada or Sweden, the event of the day was the arrival of mail from home. Many parents supported their sons' decisions, but that often increased the agony of separation. Some parents paid a price for that support. Terry Morton's father lost his American Legion membership, and his business orders fell so dramatically that he almost went bankrupt. Paul and Roger Hodgkins were taken to Canada by their father. He took ill and died shortly after the FBI threatened to prosecute him for helping his sons flee the country. (The Justice Department later dropped all charges against his sons.)

The strain of having a son in exile was aggravated by constant reminders that events had conspired to set otherwise law-abiding families on the wrong side of the law. FBI agents often interviewed neighbors and friends, and they had a habit of visiting at Christmastime to see if the son had come home. Many exiles had to remain in Canada or Sweden when family members died, because family funerals were a favorite hunting ground for the FBI.

Yet support from one's family often meant the difference between success and failure as an immigrant. Toronto psychiatrist Saul Levine discovered that almost every exile who came to him in deep depression had parents who disagreed with the decision and had given no moral or financial support. Parents sometimes actively helped the FBI find their sons, or else sent vitriolic letters disowning them: "You have disgraced your family and your country. . . . We never want to hear from you again except to have the money back we lent you to fly back to your base. . . . We burned your birth certificate and your insurance policy. You are no longer a son of ours."

Some exiles wondered whether they were indeed as bad as their parents and others said they were. "We were taught as children that deserting the Army was the most cowardly thing anyone could ever do. We usually thought that what we did was right, but sometimes you can't help believing a little bit of what people say about you." According to Levine, guilt was pervasive in the exile community—guilt over abandoning parents and friends, guilt over leaving the country they had been brought up to love, or guilt over not having taken a firmer stand by going to prison or fighting the war effort through the underground.

What kept their spirits up amidst the economic, family, and psychological pressures was the firm belief that resisting the war was the right thing to do. However, even that conviction eventually brought disappointment. Many exiles had hoped that their sacrifices could somehow help to end the Vietnam war. As the war raged on and on, most exiles sensed that their personal sacrifices had made little difference. They remained confident that history would record their stance as morally correct, but that was little solace: "The war ripped hell out of my life for ten years, and Nixon still got his 'peace with honor.' "

The grimmest time came between 1970 and 1973. Jobs were harder than ever to find, especially for deserters, and the American pullout from Vietnam was frustratingly slow. Canadians and Swedes began to sour upon the young Americans they once glorified as moral and political heroes. The local press featured stories about deserters convicted of robbery and drug dealing, and there was a growing fear that exiles were carriers of American disease: crime, drugs, and hippie culture. Just a few dozen were imprisoned or deported, but the entire community felt the sting.

Canadians began to change their attitude as they came to perceive the young Americans more as exiles than as immigrants. Anti-American feelings were muted so long as exiles did not act like Americans. But when they began to voice counterculture philosophies, they were looked upon as cultural imperialists. Much of the criticism came from left-wing Canadian nationalists, who accused Americans "of taking Canadian jobs, money, and places in schools, of denying a Canadian identity, of spreading the American way of life, and of not learning about Canada."

Exile organizations and publications often exacerbated anti-American sentiments. *Amex-Canada* magazine, for example, commented that "we are a brand new kind of immigrant, and Canadians will have to get used to us. Maybe with a little bit of luck, they'll listen seriously to a bit of what we're trying to tell them." *Amex* was replying to a Toronto *Daily Star* editorial which warned that "unless the young Americans for whom *Amex* speaks revise their priorities, . . . they risk arousing a growing hostility and suspicion among ordinary Canadians." The radical image of *Amex* and other groups was hard for politically moderate exiles to shake. "They give an unfair and unrealistic view of expatriates," Carl Scheuer complained. "They make all our legitimate arguments sound bad."

Much of the exile community's image problem came from the Canadian media. A CBC-TV episode of *McQueen,* entitled "Home Is Where the Draft Ain't," showed an immigration official turning back a would-be exile with the comment, "He's a weirdo, a draft dodger. . . . We don't need his kind." The Canadian film *Explosion* told a story with homosexual overtones of two American youths, one a draft-deferred psychotic and the other an exile, who went on a car-stealing, cop-killing spree. Conservative Canadians began to blame the exiles for the defiant behavior of their own children: "Canadian policemen are not pigs. You will say, 'But it is Canadians who use the word.' I will ask, 'Where did they learn it?' " The heaviest criticism was directed at deserters, whom Toronto *Telegraph* editorials portrayed as full-fledged criminals who deserved no shelter in Canadian society.

The Swedes, for their part, did not want the exiles to be unobtrusive; they considered the young Americans to be heroes and international celebrities. Almost all Swedes were opposed to America's Vietnam policies, and the exiles offered a showcase for that attitude. Leaders of the exile community were the toasts of parties. But through it all, the exiles felt that they were being used, and that the Swedes showed little regard for them as individuals: "We had to be chameleons. If we were talking to a revolutionary, we had to be a revolutionary. We couldn't be ourselves." Exiles complained that the Swedes "seemed to be playing games" with their fate: "Sweden wanted all the political credit for accepting the American war resisters, but little of the responsibility for job training, housing, and schooling."

Ironically, the Swedes' favorable attitudes began to change as their government became more generous. Largely by coincidence, the counterculture came to Sweden at about the same time as the Americans: 1968 was the year of the "Stockholm summer," when hippies from Europe and the United States descended on the country. A Swedish newspaper ran a front-page article about Americans and drugs, with a color picture of an arm hemorrhaged from mainlining. Fourteen Americans were deported for drug violations, and dozens were arrested for other serious crimes. The Swedish image of American deserters shifted from antiwar hero to heroin-shooting hippie.

During the next few years, there were enough page-one stories about Americans convicted of robbery or drug peddling, or engaging in radical political activity, to feed Swedish suspicions of the exiles. Headlines like "Deserters Selling Drugs to Swedish Youth" and "Americans Lead Narcotics Subculture" regularly appeared in newspapers. A magazine asked, "If we accepted them so they would not have to kill in Vietnam, why are we allowing them to kill our children?" In Norrkoping, exiles demonstrated against the building of a Dow chemical factory by burning Swedish and American flags sewn together. Swedes began to ask why American deserters were welcome when their own sons had to perform obligatory military service.

The Americans, for their part, resented being made scapegoats for Sweden's drug culture, and became increasingly hostile toward their hosts. They complained about the "standardized and repressed" Swedish society, the Garboesque reserve of the Swedish people, and the values of a society that let speeding drivers go free while fining someone

$60 if his dog ran loose: "I've just learned to sit back, stay cool, and laugh at whatever the hell these Swedes do when they're drunk. Because when they're sober, there's not much to laugh about."

The growing alienation from Canadian and Swedish society contributed to a distinct split within the exile community. In Canada, the division was largely between deserters and draft resisters. Deserters who were having little success as immigrants became more radical and political. Organizations like the Canadian-based American Deserters' Committee and *Amex-Canada* began to abandon efforts to help exiles with their adjustment problems, turning more toward ideological attacks against their hosts and their homeland. By contrast, draft resister organizations adopted a more pragmatic "priority counseling" strategy to help exiles succeed as immigrants; they discouraged other Americans from coming to Canada and adding to the exile community's problems. The two parts of the exile community became increasingly estranged and class-oriented. Each side accused the other of vandalizing its files or carrying on "vicious whispered lobbying" behind its back. *Amex-Canada* magazine condemned "draft dodger chauvinism," commenting that "many dodgers . . . have carved their little niche in the Canadian middle class. They wish to stay invisible and resent the visibility of field jacket and combat boot clad deserters trying to survive on the street and at the same time giving the exile a bad name." The Swedish exile community had a comparable split between those who were adjusting well and those who were having problems, but the distinction between draft resisters and deserters was not as sharp.

As the years passed, the less successful exiles either clung together in ghetto neighborhoods or drifted away to live in a personal no-man's land. One deserter bicycled through Canada for years, begging for handouts as he moved from town to town. Hundreds roamed the world with their duffel bags, out of touch with family and friends, living from day to day. If they looked at all to the future, it was to the end of the interminable war. Five committed suicide. But by far the most common solution for despair was to come home to the United States.

Coming Home

As refugees, the exiles' rejection of their homeland had always been a central part of their lives. Many of them were intensely anti-American when they left: "We said no to everything American when we crossed the border of no return. The illusion of the American Dream had been crushed." They were critical of the America First attitude that many believed had gotten the nation into the Vietnam war: "Americans are floundering in ignorance that their country is the best in everything. It's a good country, but not the best in all ways. By living in another country, you can see this more clearly." "Coming to Canada taught me to look at the world as just people, not the United States versus everyone else."

Yet despite their frustration over America's persistent involvement in Vietnam, and despite their belief that the country had not faced up to the lessons of the war, most exiles remained strikingly positive in their feelings about America. Withdrawal from Vietnam and the disgrace of Richard Nixon vindicated their decisions to leave, but it also made it harder to stay antagonistic toward their homeland. Larry Allison saw these events as evidence of the strength of the American political system: "It was easy to chuckle about the problems of Vietnam and Watergate, but that's all over now. Canada doesn't have problems on the same scale, but it's often bogged down in petty squabbling. There's a joke that Watergate could never happen in Canada, because they'd never be caught. Unfortunately, that's true."

Many exiles, including some of the most radical, had a love-hate attitude toward the United States. They continued to criticize the nation's social and political problems in the apparent hope that they could make some difference, yet their separation gave them a new respect for America's social and cultural qualities: "You have to separate people from policy. Taking exile was not an anti-American move; it was an antigovernment move." They criticized Canada for its "lack of creative spirit" and Sweden for its "gray mediocrity." Others acknowledged that their own characteristically American qualities of independence and resourcefulness had helped them as immigrants. Their circles of friends often included many Americans, a fact that gave Carl Scheuer an uneasy feeling: "I find that I am both attracted and repelled by other Americans. Basically, I like them—they're doers, and they remind me about my nostalgia for the States. But at the same time, they remind me of part of my life—and myself—that I'd rather forget."

These exiles accepted the fact that their homeland would always be part of them. When McDonald's opened a branch in Stockholm, it quickly became a popular hangout for exiles. Red, White, and Blues, an all-deserter rock group, played American music to rave reviews throughout Sweden. Jack Leeds, practicing law in Toronto, described himself as "partly American, but I don't know what part."

Their vision of the United States remained much as it was when they crossed the border. Images of revolutionary politics, racial riots, and college unrest formed permanent snapshots in their minds. They kept track of major events like the Watergate scandal, but avoided the American media: "I couldn't bear to watch the Bicentennial celebration on television. I was afraid of what my feelings might be, and I didn't want to let myself get too homesick."

Some exiles maintained a deep, festering hatred for their homeland, whose war policies they considered symptomatic of fundamental social flaws. Occasionally, this attitude was given violent expression. A clandestine exile group wrote a manual for antiwar activists, explaining how to attack draft boards with time bombs and Molotov cocktails. Exiles periodically vandalized American embassies and consulates, and Richard Nixon reportedly canceled a visit to Toronto and Montreal because of advance word that American war resisters posed serious security risks. The most dramatic act occurred on June 30, 1970, when the "Northern Lunatic Fringe" led one thousand exiles across the border to lay siege to Blaine, Washington. This was the first invasion of the continental United States since 1916, when New Mexico defended itself against Pancho Villa with a National Guard troop that included the young Lewis B. Hershey. But General Hershey was not there to defend Blaine, and the incursion caused an estimated $1,000,000 in property damage before the "NLF" was chased back to British Columbia. No one was arrested.

Blaine was near the site of the "Ho Chi Minh Trail," a 250-yard swamp that was a favorite route for border jumpers until electric devices were installed. There were easy crossings elsewhere, especially in the prairie provinces, but few were willing to risk freedom for a trip home. Dave Bosman slipped across to see his family in Tennessee, and he "really freaked them out. Everybody was awfully nervous, and they talked me into going back right away." Family get-togethers usually occurred in Canada or Sweden, or not at all. The long trips were financial hardships for families with modest incomes, and impossible for the poor.

Most exiles at first expected to remain permanently in their adopted countries. Coming home was seen as an inherent admission of failure. Yet over time, some came to the conclusion that what they had done was wrong: "I've learned a lot of things about myself during the months I've been up here. I thought it was because I disapproved of the war in Vietnam that I decided to come, but looking back on it, I can see it was more just a rebellion against authority than anything else." Others grew homesick, like Roy Brasile, who quit his $15,000 job as editor of a Montreal magazine to go back to Massachusetts: "I want to go home. Even if it costs me some time in jail, it's worth the price." But most returning exiles simply concluded they could not survive as refugees. They saw a better future at home, regardless of the legal consequences.

The American government took an active interest in the exiles. After the Intrepid Four incident, American diplomatic, military, and law enforcement officials made concerted efforts to monitor the exile community. Many law-abiding exiles were visited or followed by the Canadian Mounted Police, who sometimes advised the FBI of their whereabouts. The Swedish police did not cooperate with the United States government, but leaders of the exile community insisted that American officials engaged in covert activities to undermine their reputation. Periodically, exiles in Sweden were visited by self-proclaimed "Trotskyite revolutionaries" or "Weathermen on the run," who claimed to be from the European underground. With money and contacts, they gained the exiles' trust by helping those in need. But they later were accused of taking advantage of that trust to sabotage the community.

The individual most commonly suspected of having been an American agent was a central figure in the Stockholm-based American Deserters' Committee. He radicalized the exile community and helped alienate it from the Swedish left wing, whose leaders he accused of having pro-Nazi backgrounds. Just before leaving Stockholm, he was accused of undercutting efforts to coordinate an International Exile Day by telegraphing the wrong date to Canadian organizations. Other alleged American agents were accused of giving free drugs to Swedish exiles to set them up for arrest. One exile was given 750 liquid grams of mescaline for safekeeping, but he feared a trap and flushed it down a toilet. The next day, his apartment was ransacked. Leaders of the exile community blamed infiltrators for a major part of their drug problem and the ensuing loss of reputation among the Swedish people. They accused the American government of a deliberate effort to undermine the political impact and overall well-being of the exile community.

American intelligence agencies never confirmed or denied charges of American undercover work made by the Danish and Swedish press. One observer of the Swedish exile community commented that "if these people were government agents, they were not very good ones." But covert activities of this kind were consistent with the CIA's Operation CHAOS. CIA foreign stations were asked to accumulate information on "illegal and subversive" connections between domestic antiwar activists and "foreign elements." In 1968, CHAOS was made a "high-priority program" and specifically expanded to include surveillance of draft resisters and deserters. By the end of Operation CHAOS in 1972, agents had accumulated more than 7,200 files on overseas Americans, including information that the 1976 Select Senate Committee Intelligence Report called "wholly irrelevant to the legitimate interests of the CIA or any other government agency."

The most visible American government activity was the effort to induce exiles to come home. The American embassy in Stockholm acknowledged reporting "names and other information" about exiles to military intelligence officials, who sometimes made surprise visits to Sweden. Capitalizing on momentary despair, the officials tried to persuade exiles to return right away. They occasionally succeeded. "It was funny," one exile recalled. "There were people, and then there weren't people. All they took with them were the clothes on their backs." A deserter who was heading to Sweden through the Soviet Union met an American girl in Moscow, went out for a date with her that same night, and disappeared. No one knows what happened to him.

Deserters generally expected that they would spend years in prison if they returned. In 1966, a deserter who fled to China for ten days had been sentenced on his return to five years in military prison. But in 1968, the Roy Brown case signaled an apparent change in policy. Brown had been the first deserter to go to Sweden, and his charge of racial discrimination in the American Army was extensively covered by the Swedish press. In early 1968, the European editor of the *Army Times* made several trips to convince him to surrender. Brown was guaranteed no more than a six-month sentence and told that he would never be able to come home if he refused. After repeated threats and intimidation, Brown accepted the offer. His court-martial gave him a four-month sentence, encouraging other exiles to consider making their own deals.

Prompted by the Brown case and offers of leniency from military agents, twenty deserters abandoned exile by the spring of 1968. Only one was sent to prison for more than six months, and six avoided prison altogether. One was given a $15 fine and returned to his unit. This, however, led Senator Daniel Inouye of Hawaii, who lost an arm fighting in World War II, to conduct hearings before the Armed Services Committee to inquire about the "very light sentences" imposed on deserters. Alfred Fitt, the Defense Department's assistant secretary for manpower, acknowledged that "this is awfully lenient for these people who have gone off and made a disloyal spectacle of themselves, . . . but there is another side to it." Fitt indicated that the armed forces wanted these men back, and it did not wish to "reward" any deserter "by giving him punishment which in effect will remove him from the hazards of combat." Yet of the twenty returning deserters, only two were sent to Vietnam.

Inouye's committee report sharply criticized the military's bargain with Brown, commenting that "the attitude of some Defense officials in handling this case does justice to no one. . . . It should not be in the character of those entrusted with the administration of military justice to negotiate with deserters." For a short time thereafter, surrendering exiles were dealt a harsh surprise. James "Daddy" Lovett, a thirty-five-year-old Army cook, was greeted with a four-year prison sentence when he returned from Sweden. His case rekindled the exile community's fear of stiff punishment.

After a few months, however, the military returned to its original lenient policies toward exiled deserters who surrendered quietly. But those who came home amidst press conferences and antiwar statements still risked tough sentences. In 1972, the Defense Department reported that 640 deserters had surrendered from exile, and fewer than 150 had been sent to prison. The rest were returned to their units or, more and more often, given administrative undesirable discharges "for the good of the service." The Army also gave discharges *in absentia* to deserters who were aliens and had returned to their countries of origin.

Even the appearance of severity often included a private measure of leniency. In an open display of strict punishment, Tim Poirrot, the Marine deserter who surrendered on the floor of the 1972 Republican National Convention, was tried by general court-martial and sentenced to a year in prison. However, Poirrot had negotiated a maximum five-month sentence through a pretrial agreement. Out of the spotlight, the Marines reduced his sentence accordingly.

In the years after 1972, few deserters who returned from exile went to jail. Most received Undesirable Discharges, and some were even given General or Honorable Discharges. A few came home to learn that the military did not classify them as deserters. One exile's wife received a military dependent's allowance the whole time her husband was in Canada. Civilian counselors tried to convince exiles to end their fugitive status by accepting Undesirable Discharges, but many remained fearful that they would be victimized by a sudden change of policy. Others never came home because "it just wasn't worth the hassle."

Similarly, exiled draft resisters benefited from the lack of interest of most U.S. Attorneys in prosecuting Selective Service cases. But the government kept the truth about its prosecution practices so well hidden behind a mask of enforcement that many exiles never realized they were no longer fugitives from the law. Arlo Tatum's well-respected *Guide to the Draft* warned draft fugitives that "you are almost certain to be reported for prosecution to the U.S. Attorney. A warrant for your arrest will be in time issued, and it will be waiting for you if you ever return to American territory. There is no time limit; it will be outstanding indefinitely." Tatum's warning was correct in theory, but not in practice. After the courts made induction orders virtually unenforceable in 1970, federal prosecutors dropped tens of thousands of their pending cases, including many exile cases.

Unfortunately for the draft resisters, there was no requirement that they be informed when their cases were dropped. Prosecutors thought draft boards had to tell them, and draft boards thought prosecutors had to tell them. On one occasion, a state Selective Service director canceled an induction order and asked the local board to advise the exile of its action. The board never did so, and it took the individual three years to discover that he could come home. A U.S. Attorney who dropped thousands of draft cases acknowledged that his staff never considered contacting the exiles: "If you're going to take off and go to Canada, you should keep your intelligence network to find out what is happening in your case." Few exiles had lawyers, and they rarely had reason to doubt Arlo Tatum's warning that they would be prosecuted no matter how long they stayed away. After all, Ramsey Clark, who had been U.S. Attorney General when many exiles refused induction, stated in 1974 that "more than fifty thousand young men stand charged or convicted of violating the law."

Many had had enough exposure to the criminal justice system to think it unimaginable that no charges were outstanding against them. A draft resister from Marion, Indiana, signed papers at an induction station stating that he refused to enter the military. He was interviewed by a U.S. commissioner, sent to a federal medical center for two months for psychiatric observation, and put in jail to await trial. After obtaining bond, he fled to Canada. A few years later, suddenly and quietly, his case was dropped, but no one ever told him.

Occasionally, a draft exile discovered that he was a free man. One found out from a family friend who happened to be an FBI agent. Another called up the U.S. Attorney in his district "on a hunch" and learned that his case had been dropped a year earlier. Still another learned that his Michigan draft board had been bombed; when he contacted his prosecutor, he learned that his records had indeed been destroyed and his case dropped ("Whoever did it, hey, thanks a lot!"). His draft board may actually have been responsible, because Selective Service accidentally disposed of many records that prosecutors needed to obtain convictions. Wally Krentz discovered in 1973 that his name "wasn't in the book of bad people" at the border. After two years of repeated inquiries, he was told that his file had been mistakenly destroyed and the charges dropped.

Thousands of men spent unnecessary years on the run in the mistaken belief that they were fugitives from justice. Victor Cole of Wyoming lived in Canada for nine years before learning that no charges nad ever been filed against him. Andy McCoy challenged his induction, complaining to his Michigan draft board that they had unlawfully denied his CO application. But the board wrote that it refused to reopen his case because it was "in the hands of the U.S. Attorney." McCoy then panicked, spending the next several years living in the underground in six different states, fearful of visiting his family because of several trips the FBI had made to his house. Events were later to prove that McCoy had been right: it was the draft board, not McCoy, that had broken the law.

By 1972, word began to spread about the weakness of the cases against most draft fugitives. Draft attorneys Daniel Kallen and Curry First wrote *Amex-Canada,* alerting the exile community that "anywhere from a sizable minority to a slight majority [of draft fugitives] can safely return to this country." William Smith, a Los Angeles lawyer, traveled across Canada at his own expense to encourage exiles to inquire into their cases. Those who came in contact with Kallen, First, or Smith almost always received good news. Inquiring on behalf of eighteen clients in Canada, First discovered that fifteen no longer faced charges.

However, not many exiles asked for help. A good many were scattered across Canada, did not subscribe to *Amex,* and were not part of a formal or informal grapevine. Ignorance and suspicion were widespread, and rumors persisted that secret indictments had been issued to trap the unwary. Not many exiles knew how to get legal advice at a reasonable price. Dave Bosman called an attorney "friend" in Texas, who told him it would cost from $500 to $2,000 to look into his case. It was not until 1975, in the midst of President Ford's clemency program, that the exiles finally got reliable information about their cases. Of approximately 17,500 draft fugitives who still thought they were in legal trouble, 13,000 learned that they were no longer fugitives.

The reaction to this news was a mixture of disbelief and deep emotion. Some broke into tears of joy, realizing that they could finally come home after six or eight years of exile. But according to counselor Steve Pither, others broke into "tears of rage that they had wasted the last two, or four, or seven or more years underground or in exile because of Selective Service processing errors and . . . failure to let them know of their innocence once it was concluded that they committed no crime." To one embittered exile, the deceptive enforcement policy was "another indication of the moral corruption of the United States." Others were just angry with themselves for never having bothered to keep informed.

Some exiles had trouble adjusting to their changed legal status. Believing that he could be arrested by the FBI even though he was in Canada, Bob Grevey had covered his tracks for years by developing a completely new identity. He had a credit rating and an employment history, and was well established in his community. After he learned that charges against him had been dropped, he found it impossible to return to his old identity.

Most decided to stay in Canada or Sweden. Chris Parker had married a Canadian woman and started a family in Toronto: "When I left, I had to set my mind to the fact that this was a permanent change in my life. I can't turn back the clock now." Terry Morton went home in 1976 to campaign in the Wisconsin Democratic primary, but was so discouraged by his experience that he returned to Manitoba to live in a frontier town. Roy Brown returned to Sweden after serving his sentence and finding America not to his liking. Many exiles saw no reason to pick up roots and start over for the second time in their lives, especially since they feared the reception they would get when they returned: "If, after many trials, you have won a foothold, why would you want to go back? Why would you want to be an exile in your own country?"

Because the Justice Department was derelict in not informing them that their cases had been dropped, many draft exiles accepted foreign citizenship under the mistaken impression that they were subject to prosecution. They later felt that they had been tricked into paying a penalty for an alleged "crime" of which they were legally innocent. Before Carter pardoned them in 1977, the five thousand expatriates who had adopted Canadian or Swedish citizenship were unable to return to the United States, even if no charges were pending against them. They were subject to exclusion or deportation as "aliens" who avoided military service during a period of declared national emergency. This law was originally aimed at foreign nationals who tried to avoid the World War II draft, but the Justice Department enforced it against native-born Americans whom it could not prosecute for draft evasion.

Stu Beecham, a Ph.D. candidate, lived in Toronto with his American-born wife, Joanne, and their two children. Charges against him were dropped shortly after he came to Canada because his draft board had unlawfully denied his CO application. But no one told them this, and the Beechams became Canadian citizens. For years, Joanne took their children to visit grandparents in Florida, but Stu was barred from joining them. Joanne wondered, "Why couldn't they let us love both countries at the same time?" Their entire exile was unnecessary.

Whether they stayed away or came home, most fugitives paid a heavy price for their draft or desertion offenses: "Man, it'll weight you down." Five or ten years on the run or in exile did more than leave them in new places; it wholly recast their lives. They made irreversible decisions and endured irremediable sacrifices. The Vietnam war left its mark on all of them.

VI | AMNESTY

Morality and Mythology

In 1964, the year Congress passed the Tonkin Gulf Resolution, Australia enacted a conscription law to raise troops for Vietnam. Its draft was simple and precise; about 100,000 youths turned twenty each year, one-tenth of whom were chosen by lot to serve in the army. At the height of the war, eight thousand Australians were in Vietnam. As a proportion of national population, this was the equivalent of 130,000 American troops.

The draft and the war were heated issues in Australia. There were peace vigils, public demonstrations, draft card burnings (which were not against the law), and open defiance of the draft. Roughly fifteen thousand youths never registered, and seventy-five publicly refused induction. Yet only six people were ever convicted for violating the National Service Act, all of whom were sentenced to eighteen-month prison terms.

By 1972, more than 250 draft violations were pending in the courts. When Gough Whitlam of the Australian Labour Party campaigned for prime minister, he promised to end the draft, withdraw from Vietnam, and declare an amnesty for all draft resisters and deserters. Aided by newly enfranchised young voters, Whitlam was elected, and within ten days he fulfilled his promises. He also allowed draftees to resign from military service, and three-quarters of them did so. The Vietnam war and the amnesty debate quickly faded from the public's mind.

The United States found its problems with the draft, the war, and amnesty more difficult to solve. President Nixon ended the draft and withdrew American troops in early 1973, but the amnesty issue lingered for years. By 1977, when President Carter extended the largest and perhaps last measure of relief, it was too late for hundreds of thousands of people. Their lives had been permanently altered, and the American public had fixed ideas about who they were and what they represented. To some, they were conscientious antiwarriors; to others, the worst of traitors. Those in between regarded them with the same wary compassion commonly offered parolees from prison. Draft resisters and deserters had become permanent victims, not just of the Vietnam war, but of myths that personified the unresolved public debate about the war.

The stereotypes originated in the mid-1960s, when the draft-card burners of the early Resistance movement were much in the news. White, educated, well-to-do, and intensely antiwar, they were like tens of thousands of other activists who were challenging the war on the campuses and streets of the nation. By 1967, a number of draft resisters began to leave for Canada. They were a diverse group, but the ones who generated publicity were radical activists, much like the earlier draft card burners. Most exiles wanted privacy and a chance to blend into Canadian life, but the activists considered themselves symbols of the moral issues raised by the war. They were more accessible to the media, and made better press. When David Susskind's representative came to Toronto to select the right person for his show, one exile he interviewed was disgusted when "out of all the people in the room, he had to pick the most spooked-out radical, the weirdest character in the group."

When Eugene McCarthy first raised amnesty as a campaign issue in 1968, the image of the draft resister as a white, well-educated radical was firmly fixed. McCarthy described them as the best of their generation, promising to declare a "kind of amnesty" if elected President. The other presidential candidates avoided the issue. Amnesty in the midst of war had some precedent in American history. Abraham Lincoln issued two general amnesties for deserters during the Civil War, on the condition that they return to the front lines. But in 1968, the war itself overshadowed the fate of a handful of middle-class radicals in exile.

As President Nixon began his gradual deescalation of the war, interest in amnesty began to spread. Church groups passed amnesty resolutions, and "universal, unconditional amnesty" joined the list of demands of striking students. Tom Wicker, Julian Bond, and Richard Cardinal Cushing were among the first to call for the President to act. But the exiles themselves wanted no part of an amnesty. At a Montreal conference of exiles in early 1970, a visiting Tom Hayden drew sharp criticism when he brought up the subject. "Amnesty," wrote *Amex-Canada* magazine, was

> a dirty word inasmuch as it can be interpreted to mean that exiles . . . would be magnanimously forgiven for a crime we never committed. . . . Who wants amnesty? Liberals. . . . Like other liberal issues, it asks for sympathy and trustworthiness from the world's most viciously heavy-handed and conniving regime. Worse yet, it gives the impression to the enemy that the movement is running on nothing more threatening than simpering warmheartedness, by people who are not capable of shaping their lives themselves.

Many exiles agreed with *Amex*'s position. In 1969 and 1970, the Canadian economy was healthy, and American refugees were still the toast of Sweden. Many wanted to go home, but a mid-war amnesty would have put them on the spot. At the time, amnesty seemed an empty gesture which would have made them look like selfish draft dodgers, vindicating their detractors and depriving their resistance of all meaning. As a deserter in Sweden explained, the exiles saw amnesty as "just the start of our problems and not, as some believe, the end."

Thereafter, the antiwar orthodoxy saw amnesty as a "salve for the conscience of liberals who were silent as the war was being expanded and exiles were making their decisions not to go." Attitudes began to change in 1972, however, as the end of the war came in sight and life in exile began to sour. Noting that "the situation has changed fundamentally," *Amex-Canada* reversed its earlier position:

> For some time now, many exiles in Canada have known that many have been unable to adjust to exile life. More important, many have been unable to get landed immigrant status and have lived underground; this certainly has not been healthy, physically or psychologically. Now the

question of amnesty has been raised by others, and we have recognized that there is a very serious need for it.

That endorsement made amnesty more acceptable for the antiwar community back home. New lobbying groups were soon founded by clergymen, draft counselors, antiwar veterans, and the exiles themselves.

Originally, as *Amex* indicated, amnesty was a pragmatic cause, a way of relieving suffering and reuniting families. As the war wound down, however, most of those who could not cope with life in exile quietly drifted back to the United States, paying less of a penalty than they expected. But the antiwar community found itself increasingly frustrated by Nixon's elusive "peace with honor." The government was pulling out of Vietnam slowly and reluctantly, without acknowledging that the war was wrong. The antiwar community wanted the American people to make a clear judgment about the immorality of the war.

Amnesty offered one last chance to force the issue. Where exiles once had interpreted amnesty as an admission of their own wrongdoing, they now saw it making "the moral point that our government was wrong and these young men were right." It was, as one advocate observed, "a powerful tool to make the American people aware of the character of the war that was waged in their name." The pragmatism and compassion that had launched the amnesty movement became unacceptable; the proper basis for amnesty now was as a moral condemnation of the war. "In order to lead a principled fight," *Amex-Canada* remarked, "it is necessary to make judgments about the types of arguments we put forward. . . . We have a historic duty to perform—not only winning total amnesty but also explaining the unjust nature of the Indochina War. It is that duty, not shortsighted pragmatism, which must guide our work."

The integration of amnesty into the moral and political debate over the war had four important consequences. First, it left the movement vulnerable to excess. The more radical groups embraced amnesty with zeal, tying it to the rest of their platform and giving a politically extreme cast to the whole discussion. As one activist commented:

Most of us think that not only the war and the draft, but the whole American military empire which spawns these evils is an affront and a danger to humankind. This empire must and eventually will be dismantled. I believe —though at times I will not say this too loud—that an amnesty would be a small step in this dismantling.

Second, it kept the public's attention riveted on the most politically active exiles. Few people knew or cared much about the day-to-day problems of the great bulk of the half million or more who might have benefited from an amnesty—especially nonregistrants and veterans with bad discharges, many of whom were black, low-income, and poorly educated. By making amnesty an ideological issue, the movement eliminated the possibility of obtaining substantial active support from civil rights groups, liberal unions, and other potential allies. Even those who were sympathetic to the amnesty cause were unwilling to accept the antiwar orthodoxy that the movement demanded. As one movement participant observed, amnesty forces

> failed to develop a centrist core, though it is an issue that could sustain support by a broad coalition. Ideological orthodoxy is exacted at the expense of communicating with the people who will have to vote to return to office those Congressmen who dare to vote for amnesty.

Third, tying amnesty to the debate about the war encouraged strong emotional responses from the other side. As Washington *Star* columnist Mary McGrory noted, this meant "asking . . . middle-aged men with glorious memories of military service in a popular war to admit they were wrong about Vietnam." The Nixon administration capitalized on that point to turn public opinion against amnesty. "Now that the antiwar movement has collapsed, all those idle protestors have to have something to shout about," Spiro Agnew told a VFW convention. Amnesty was out of the question for "draft dodgers who bear a deep-seated and unabating grudge against their country, who revile its principles and its traditions, and who see nothing wrong in ducking out on their obligations." As for deserters, said Agnew, "it almost makes one ill to hear about how . . . they fled from an immoral war."

Fourth, the ideological orthodoxy of radical advocates created intense internal conflicts within the movement, frustrating efforts to develop sound and politically acceptable amnesty proposals. Individuals who raised more moderate, pragmatic arguments were often subjected to public calumny from those who should have been their allies. The amnesty movement finally paid the price for years of intransigence when President Carter's military program came under attack in Congress. Legislation repudiating that program was passed, with only eleven dissenting votes. Outside of Carter's inner circle, just two voices urged a veto of this new legislation.*

The ideological grounds upon which amnesty was proposed invited counterarguments that could not be overcome. The movement's quarrel was with the government, not with Vietnam veterans, but anti-amnesty forces used the veterans as the basis for their moral case against amnesty. Victim was set against victim. Rather than seeing all of these men as casualties of Vietnam, the American people were asked to make a choice. Nixon told the country where its values should lie. Amnesty, he said, was "the most immoral thing I can think of. . . ."

> I can think of no greater insult to the memories of those who have fought and died, to . . . those who have served, and also to our POWs, to say to them that we are now going to provide amnesty for those who deserted the country.

Administration spokesmen openly ridiculed amnesty advocates like Congresswoman Bella Abzug, who contended that draft resisters and deserters were "the finest, most conscientious, most creative young people." Drawing as sharp a contrast as possible, Nixon aides labeled them as the very worst of their generation. Speechwriter Patrick Buchanan called them "malingerers, opportunists, criminals, and cowards," and Charles Colson echoed that they were "victims of their own character deficiencies." Spiro Agnew lumped them in with "malcon-

---

*The Washington *Post*, which had earlier approved of the legislation, belatedly editorialized against it. Father Theodore Hesburgh, President of Notre Dame, sent Carter a personal telegram recommending a veto.

tents, radicals, incendiaries, civil and uncivil disobedients, . . . yippies, hippies, yahoos, Black panthers, lions, and tigers—I would swap the whole damn zoo for a single platoon of the kind of young Americans I saw in Vietnam."

An American Legion spokesman confidently predicted that the nation would never decide that "those who violated the law have the superior moral position to the President, the Congress, and the men who served." He was right. Washington *Star* columnist Smith Hempstone pleaded that "it simply isn't so . . . that men who spent the war comfortably living off remittances from Mom and Pop in Toronto coffee houses are the cream of their generation. . . . They want America to accept their image of themselves and their version of history, and this no self-respecting nation can grant."

As the antiwar movement reconstituted itself into the amnesty lobby, supporters of the war formed their own antiamnesty organizations. The Young Americans for Freedom sponsored a nationwide "No Amnesty Campaign," but most of the effort came from the older generation— the Veterans of Foreign Wars, the American Legion, the POW-MIA lobby. The leader of the opposition was President Nixon, who viewed the issue as an opportunity to take the offensive against his liberal enemies. "Never, never will we grant amnesty," he said during his reelection campaign. "Until this war is over, until we get the POWs back, those who chose to desert their country . . . can live with their choice."

Chiding Democrats for their contrary views, Vice President Agnew invited them to "seek [their] future leaders in the deserters' dens of Canada and Sweden." "Amnesty, Acid, and Abortion" was a slogan used against George McGovern in 1972, just as "Rum, Romanism, and Rebellion" had helped Republicans beat Democrats in earlier times. Under pressure, McGovern retreated from his original call for a general amnesty to a much more limited position, requiring alternative service and excluding deserters altogether.

McGovern's defensiveness and the political vulnerability of the amnesty lobby's moral arguments were no match for Nixon's political acumen. In June 1972, a Harris poll found that the public opposed amnesty by a 3–2 margin. By the following March, that margin had grown to 3–1. As the Watergate scandal undermined his moral and political authority, neither Nixon nor his spokesmen said much more about amnesty. But even in the midst of Watergate, the amnesty community could not gain the upper hand.

Out of the unsuccessful effort of the 1972 campaign, however, ground was laid for a compromise approach later embodied in President Ford's clemency program. In 1971, a conservative Ohio doctor wrote Senator Robert Taft, Jr., suggesting that draft resisters be amnestied if they worked for four years on public service jobs. Taft believed the idea had political promise because it sidestepped the ideological arguments for and against amnesty, and he sponsored a bill patterned on the idea. At the time, there was a widespread recognition that any form of amnesty was premature until all American troops and prisoners-of-war had returned from Vietnam, and Taft's bill attracted little open support. President Nixon derided the idea of making a "junket in the Peace Corps" a substitute for punishment.

After America's disengagement in 1973, "clemency" became increasingly popular among moderates of both political parties. Several bills and resolutions were introduced in both houses of Congress proposing some form of clemency. Two former Nixon administration officials, Melvin Laird and Robert Froehlke, who had been respectively Secretary of Defense and Secretary of the Army, publicly called on the President to institute a compromise program.

The debate, however, remained divided between advocates of universal, unconditional amnesty, and those who insisted that nothing be done. With amnesty still entwined with arguments over the merits of the Vietnam war, most political leaders were reluctant to take a position on the issue.

Clemency, Not Amnesty

A few days after Gerald Ford became President in August 1974, his son Jack suggested that he begin his administration by declaring some sort of amnesty. Given the circumstances of his accession to the presidency, Ford was eager to reestablish public confidence in the fairness of government, and he liked his son's idea. He asked the White House staff to assemble all relevant policy papers prepared by the Nixon administration. Except for speeches, there was nothing but a Defense Department study of AWOL, useless as a policy guide. The new President thus had to rely on his instincts. A close friend of Melvin Laird, with whom he had served in Congress, Ford was attracted to the compromise "clemency" idea that Laird had been urging on his predecessor.

Rather than wait for official studies, the President announced his intentions immediately and left the details to be worked out later. To a surprised and antagonistic VFW convention, the same forum that had earlier cheered Spiro Agnew's tough antiamnesty statements, Ford called for "the restoration of the essential unity of Americans, within which honest differences of opinion do not descend to angry discord, and mutual problems are not polarized by excessive passion." Ford's appeal to moderation as a means of "binding the nation's wounds" drew a strong positive response from the public. For many, this was the finest hour of his presidency.

The President's speech and the new era it promised engendered a mixture of anticipation and skepticism among amnesty forces. They viewed the Ford initiative as one of great promise, but even greater risk. Their principal fear, born of years of distrust of the government, was that a clemency compromise would prove empty of meaning, leaving draft resisters and deserters to pursue existing remedies through normal government channels.

The spirit of reconciliation fostered by Ford's speech was swept away in the outrage over his surprise pardon of Richard Nixon in early September. When he announced the details of his clemency program a few days later, he drew an angry reaction from all sides. To conservatives, many of whom were disturbed by the Nixon pardon, Ford's clemency action added one mistake to another. To liberals, the clemency program was a political gesture, intended mainly to ease the public reaction to what looked like an unsavory deal between Nixon and his successor. To amnesty forces, the limited terms of Ford's clemency offer, contrasted with the leniency granted Nixon, seemed an outrageous double standard of justice: "For his very real and very serious crimes, Richard Nixon has received an unconditional amnesty—plus a posh pension. For their justified resistance to an illegal and immoral war, war resisters must still pay a penalty."

To the general public, however, the clemency program seemed a reasonable and attractive solution to the amnesty problem. As the newly created Presidential Clemency Board concluded in its final report a year later, "clemency, not amnesty" was the "course of moderation. . . . No program at all would have left old wounds festering. Unconditional amnesty would have created more ill-feeling than it would have eased." Ford's "limited, conditional, case-by-case clemency" offered "a reasoned middle ground."

The Washington *Post,* which later became critical of the Ford program, initially praised it as "a reasonable balance between the view that calls for complete amnesty and the view that calls for no amnesty or clemency at all." The Philadelphia *Bulletin* noted that "the fact that the hard-liners on each side of the amnesty issue dislike President Ford's proposal could be proof that it is a moderate and workable approach."

Unfortunately, this view of the Ford program as a fair compromise between continued punishment and unwarranted generosity was heavily influenced by the public's widespread ignorance about the way the government was currently enforcing the law against draft resisters and deserters. By the time Gerald Ford became President, lenient treatment for offenders was the rule, not the exception. In fact, the Ford program offered little or no improvement over remedies that were already available. As the mother of an exiled draft resister observed, "Since 1970, whenever the FBI came around, they said Kenny had three choices: the service, jail, or alternate service. Now they're offering the same thing, and they call it amnesty. So what is different?"

Under Ford's program, fugitive draft resisters could sign up with their local U.S. Attorneys, perform a maximum of twenty-four months of alternative service, and then have their charges dismissed. Draft counselors knew, however, that those who refused clemency and pursued their cases in court had about a 90 percent chance of getting charges dismissed without having to do alternative service, and about a 99 percent chance of avoiding prison.

The President invited military fugitives to appear at a special clemency processing center at the Fort Harrison Army base near Indianapolis. Once there, they received immediate Undesirable Discharges, thereby ending their fugitive status and any threat of court-martial and military prison. They could also earn Clemency Discharges by performing up to twenty-four months of alternative service. This brand-new discharge was given under "other-than-honorable" conditions, just like an Undesirable Discharge and, like the latter, it bestowed no veterans' benefits. By 1974, however, the military had virtually stopped court-martialing deserters. Deserters who turned down the clemency program were all but guaranteed quick Undesirable Discharges if they surrendered at lenient Army bases like Fort Dix and Fort Sill. In fact, deserters discharged outside the Ford program had a ten times greater chance of receiving a General or Honorable Discharge, entitling them to veterans' benefits; they also incurred no obligation to do alternative service. All they lost was the dubious opportunity to earn a Clemency Discharge.

Convicted draft resisters and discharged deserters could receive presidential pardons from the Clemency Board, conditioned on the performance of periods of alternative service that rarely exceeded six months. Most draft resisters were already eligible to apply to the U.S. pardon attorney for the same pardon without alternative service, and none of the handful who had earlier done so had been refused. Deserters were also offered Clemency Discharges via the Clemency Board. Outside the Ford program, almost all deserters were eligible to apply through normal military review procedures, where they stood about a one-in-three chance of getting upgraded to General or Honorable Discharges entitling them to veterans' benefits. The Clemency Board could not grant these remedies.

Outraged by the inadequacies of the Ford program, amnesty groups labeled it a "dangerous trap," a "cynical smokescreen," and "shamnesty." Many did what they called "repatriation counseling," helping thousands to take advantage of remedies inside or outside the clemency program. However, the rest of the amnesty community declared a formal boycott, publicly discouraging people from applying. They feared that high application figures would persuade the public that the program was a success, dooming future prospects for a more comprehensive amnesty.

Their fears had some basis in recent history. After World War II, Americans favored a general amnesty for draft resisters by a three-to-one margin, and Congress began considering legislation to grant them relief as a class. In response, President Truman appointed an amnesty board and asked it to review all cases individually. After a year's work, the board granted relief only to those whose offenses resulted from religious beliefs, accusing the rest of having "no respect for the law or the civil rights to which they might have been restored." But it also refused to pardon Jehovah's Witnesses, because "to do so would be to sanction an assertion by a citizen that he is above the law, that he makes his own law, and that he refuses to yield his opinion to that of organized society. . . ." The Truman board recommended less than 10 percent of its 15,805 cases for presidential pardons. When its work was done, the public and the Congress believed that every case had been fairly decided, and the issue was forgotten.

For his part, President Ford appeared quite willing to let his program run its course and be forgotten. Although he privately indicated his desire for a successful and generous program, he delegated near-total responsibility to Justice and Defense department officials and paid little attention to the program they devised. Neither they nor the White House staff ever personally supported the President's idea. They wished only to have a quick and quiet program that interfered as little as possible with their own interests.

After the program had been formulated, former Senator Charles Goodell, a personal and political friend of Ford's from their days together in the House of Representatives, was chosen to head the Clemency Board. Goodell had been a staunch critic of the Nixon administration's war policies, and the administration had publicly opposed his reelection because of his stand. His appointment appeared to signal a real desire on Ford's part to make the program work. Goodell believed he would be the spokesman for the entire program, exercising authority over all its phases on behalf of the President. When, however, he tried to assert this authority, even over matters pertaining only to the Clemency Board, the President did not support him, and the White House staff worked against him. Evidence that the program was headed for failure made little impression. "The program was a success the day it was announced," observed the junior White House aide charged with overseeing its operation, who saw no political advantage in trying to make it better. As one spokesman commented, the clemency program was "about as important as the spat over the President's swimming pool."

Ultimately, only 6 percent of the roughly 350,000 eligible persons ever applied to the program. This was more the result of widespread ignorance, distrust, and lack of interest than a consequence of the amnesty community's boycott. Surveys found that most of the ninety thousand eligible deserters with bad discharges never knew they could apply, thinking instead that the Ford program was just for fugitives in Canada. Others were disdainful of the meager benefits of the program, or resented the necessity of what Attorney General William Saxbe called "acts of contrition"—signing an oath of allegiance, cooperating with Selective Service, and doing alternative service work. As one draft resister commented, "They want me to shuffle and scrape and mumble, 'I'm sorry, folks, I shouldn't of done it—please forgive me,' all so Ford can feel good about letting Nixon off the hook. They can cram it."

Of the 21,500 who applied, just 8,000 eventually received the formal clemency offered by the program (see Figures 8 and 9). President Ford later said it was "tragic" that so few participated, and Board chairman Goodell called the program "a partial success, at best."

The major effect of the Ford initiative was the reinforcement of several of the myths that had long plagued the amnesty issue. The program was tailored to suit the public image of draft resisters and deserters as conscientious war objectors, who were supposedly being given a second chance to satisfy the requirements of CO status by doing alternative service. Above all, the Ford program reinforced the mistaken view that Selective Service, the Justice Department, and the Defense Department had enforced the law strictly and fairly throughout the Vietnam era. This was the natural consequence of their dominant roles in the planning and implementation of the program, roles given them despite their long-standing antagonistic relationships with draft resisters and deserters.

Selective Service was chosen to supervise alternative service, just as it had supervised similar work by conscientious objectors during the war. Many of its top officials despised the people they were supposed to help. But without the Ford program, according to one official of the Office of Management and Budget, "Selective Service might have been zero-budgeted right out of existence." As it was, supervising alternative service became the main task of an agency that was fast being phased out.

It was a singularly poor choice. Not only unwilling, Selective Service proved incapable of performing its task of finding and overseeing thirteen thousand alternative service jobs. Part of the problem was that many draft resisters could not forget the unfair treatment they had previously received from these very same officials. One exile signed up for the program and went home to San Diego, only to get immersed in a series of quarrels with Selective Service: "I came back to the U.S. because I thought the purpose of the President's program was reconciliation. I found, instead, that Selective Service officials used the program to retaliate against me. If I'd known what to expect, I would have stayed in Canada."

Officials in the Defense and Justice departments had a more tolerant disposition toward the program, if only because of their interest in trimming backlogs of fugitive cases. As one Pentagon planner recalled, "We all wanted to wash our hands of these people as quickly as possible."

The Defense Department accomplished this largely through what became known as the clemency loophole. Contrary to what the public believed, deserters were rarely court-martialed after 1970. Instead, they were quickly given administrative Undesirable Discharges and sent home (see Part IV). The clemency program continued this practice, with one new twist. Applicants had to sign promises to do alternative service, thereby risking possible prosecution if they dropped out.

Most deserters had no desire to perform this service. A few publicly declared their intention, prompting antiamnesty critics to insist that all dropouts be prosecuted. Defense officials were well aware that they lost jurisdiction to court-martial these men once they received Undesirable Discharges, and that the Justice Department had little hope and no intention of prosecuting them as civilians. Fearful of admitting openly that the clemency program was unenforceable, Defense Department

FIGURE 8: AMNESTY—CIVILIANS

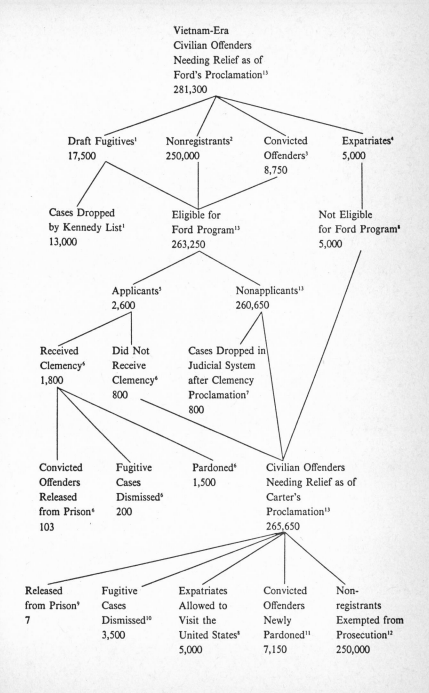

Vietnam-Era
Civilian Offenders
Needing Relief as of
Ford's Proclamation[13]
281,300

Draft Fugitives[1]
17,500

Nonregistrants[2]
250,000

Convicted
Offenders[3]
8,750

Expatriates[4]
5,000

Cases Dropped
by Kennedy List[1]
13,000

Eligible for
Ford Program[13]
263,250

Not Eligible
for Ford Program[8]
5,000

Applicants[5]
2,600

Nonapplicants[13]
260,650

Received
Clemency[6]
1,800

Did Not
Receive
Clemency[6]
800

Cases Dropped in
Judicial System
after Clemency
Proclamation[7]
800

Convicted
Offenders
Released
from Prison[6]
103

Fugitive
Cases
Dismissed[6]
200

Pardoned[6]
1,500

Civilian Offenders
Needing Relief as of
Carter's
Proclamation[13]
265,650

Released
from Prison[9]
7

Fugitive
Cases
Dismissed[10]
3,500

Expatriates
Allowed to
Visit the
United States[8]
5,000

Convicted
Offenders
Newly
Pardoned[11]
7,150

Non-
registrants
Exempted from
Prosecution[12]
250,000

FIGURE 9: AMNESTY—MILITARY

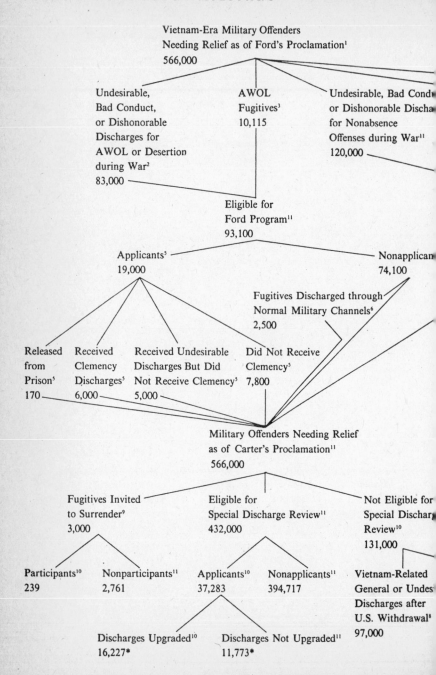

Vietnam-Era Military Offenders
Needing Relief as of Ford's Proclamation[1]
566,000

Undesirable,
Bad Conduct,
or Dishonorable
Discharges for
AWOL or Desertion
during War[2]
83,000

AWOL
Fugitives[3]
10,115

Undesirable, Bad Cond
or Dishonorable Discha
for Nonabsence
Offenses during War[11]
120,000

Eligible for
Ford Program[11]
93,100

Applicants[5]
19,000

Nonapplican
74,100

Fugitives Discharged through
Normal Military Channels[6]
2,500

Released
from
Prison[5]
170

Received
Clemency
Discharges[5]
6,000

Received Undesirable
Discharges But Did
Not Receive Clemency[5]
5,000

Did Not Receive
Clemency[5]
7,800

Military Offenders Needing Relief
as of Carter's Proclamation[11]
566,000

Fugitives Invited
to Surrender[9]
3,000

Eligible for
Special Discharge Review[11]
432,000

Not Eligible for
Special Dischar
Review[10]
131,000

Participants[10]
239

Nonparticipants[11]
2,761

Applicants[10]
37,283

Nonapplicants[11]
394,717

Vietnam-Related
General or Undes
Discharges after
U.S. Withdrawal[8]
97,000

Discharges Upgraded[10]
16,227*

Discharges Not Upgraded[11]
11,773*

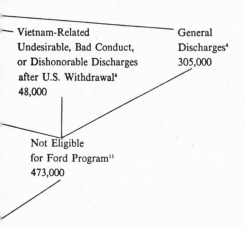

— Vietnam-Related
Undesirable, Bad Conduct,
or Dishonorable Discharges
after U.S. Withdrawal[4]
48,000

General
Discharges[4]
305,000

Not Eligible
for Ford Program[11]
473,000

— Court-Martial
Discharges[7]
34,000

*As of October 1977, approximately 9,000 cases remained to be processed.

General Counsel Martin Hoffman publicly warned applicants to perform alternative service or face prosecution for fraud. Military lawyers began giving applicants equivocal advice, like "Maybe there's a loophole, but the Department's policy is to prosecute people," or "It's a dangerous area; you be the jury and think about it."

Almost 90 percent of the fugitive deserters who applied for clemency never completed alternative service, and no one was ever prosecuted. However, some were intimidated by Hoffman's warning. John Walters, a deserter from Kansas, found an alternative service job working for his hometown government. After local veterans' groups intervened to get him fired, Walters was unable to find another job that met the standards of the program. Eventually, Selective Service officials convinced him to sign a statement declaring himself a clemency program dropout, and they told him that the statement would be forwarded to prosecutors. For months, Walters lived with the same day-to-day fear of arrest he had known for so many years as a deserter.

Don Kuzier leased his Winnipeg house and abandoned his one-man trucking business to find an alternative service job in Kalamazoo, Michigan, his old hometown. But because he was a deserter, no one offered him a job. Kuzier had to sell his truck to support his family, and his wife suffered a collapsed lung. Discouraged, the Kuziers moved back to Canada, but not into their own house. They had given a binding two-year lease to someone else.

Through the clemency program, the Defense Department cut its fugitive list by almost two-thirds. The Justice Department accomplished the same thing, also in a manner that avoided any serious inquiry into its record of enforcement. At the start of the clemency program, approximately 17,500 draft resisters still believed they faced prosecution. But when the first clemency applicant surrendered amidst press fanfare in San Francisco, the U.S. Attorney told him that his case had already been dropped. The Justice Department then released a list of only 6,200 men still wanted for draft offenses. Several weeks later, however, a number of persons not on this list were indicted by a Boston grand jury, and concern spread that the list was a trap.

Prompted by complaints from amnesty groups, Senator Edward Kennedy demanded a final, closed list of all persons still wanted for draft offenses. In January 1975, the Department produced what many called the "Kennedy list," with 4,522 names. Except for unidentified nonregistrants, everyone else was free of prosecution, including the overwhelming majority of Canadian exiles. Although expatriates who had accepted foreign citizenship were still excluded from returning to the United States, some thirteen thousand people received what amounted to unconditional amnesty.

Despite an official commitment from Washington that those not on the Kennedy list were now relieved of prosecution, some U.S. Attorneys began to file additional cases. They complained that they had not realized the lists were final and binding. In Oregon, the U.S. Attorney had distributed most of his files to defense attorneys to update their materials, and these cases were inadvertently left off the list he sent to Washington. One draft resister wrote a letter to his Virginia prosecutor, saying "fuck the clemency program." The prosecutor left his name off, believing he had no intention of applying for clemency. In Wisconsin, two unrelated draft resisters had identical first and last names. The state Selective Service director got their files mixed up, so the U.S. Attorney notified the wrong one that his name had been left off the Kennedy list. U.S. Attorneys across the country eventually produced more than eight hundred cases they claimed had been omitted by mistake. But Edward Levi, the new Attorney General, refused to add their names. The eight hundred received an inadvertent amnesty, but amnesty nonetheless.

Ironically, the alternative service loophole and the Kennedy list meant that those who benefited the most from President Ford's clemency program were not the ones who conscientiously earned clemency. The pardons and Clemency Discharges were, at best, symbolic measures of forgiveness, of little practical value to most recipients. General Donald Connally, commander of the clemency processing center at Fort Harrison, said that earning clemency was "like making up a grade from D to an A," but few agreed with him. Charles Goodell told a press conference at the end of the program that he would never advise anyone to work for two years to earn a Clemency Discharge.

Those who did try to earn clemency encountered constant difficulties. Qualifying jobs were hard to find, and those who found them were often subjected to intense local opposition. The Veterans Administration, despite the President's personal plea for cooperation, publicly refused to help clemency applicants find alternative service jobs. The Arizona state legislature passed a special resolution denying state employment to all persons granted clemency under the Ford program. In Palm Beach, Florida, a draft resister lost his job after complaints like the following from the mother of a soldier killed in Vietnam: "I lost a son and all I got was a flag. This man hid, and now he has a good-paying job."

Many of the problems in the design of the Ford program became apparent to officials responsible for implementing it, but they were powerless to make changes. Vernon Jordan, head of the National Urban League and a member of the Clemency Board, recalled how surprised he was when "the conventional image of the spoiled rich kid who ran away to Canada to beat the draft just didn't hold true." After reading case after case of poorly educated, low-income people, many of them Vietnam veterans, the Clemency Board recommended to the White House that the program be liberalized, making it of real value to those who merited relief. The Board wanted Clemency Discharges to be "neutral," not given under "other-than-honorable" conditions, and it wanted pardons to be accorded full respect by all federal agencies. The Clemency Board also wanted to give discharges under honorable conditions to veterans with good combat records, making them eligible for veterans' benefits.

These recommendations were either rejected or ignored by President Ford. Yet, even had they been implemented, they would have brought only marginal improvements in the program. More sweeping changes were never suggested, largely because of the Board's desire to preserve its fragile consensus. Many members feared that substantial modifications in the "earned clemency" concept would produce open dissension and embarrass the President.

Despite the Board's growing sense that the program was fundamentally flawed, only Vernon Jordan resigned in protest. Marine General Lewis Walt and three others, complaining that the Board had a pro-amnesty bias, wrote an angrily worded minority report. The majority stayed on, some for no purpose other than preventing the program from deteriorating further. At the end, many of them were discouraged. Like

Board member Joan Vinson, they found in retrospect that they had worked on "a totally hollow program." Through an elaborate case-by-case process, costing $10,000,000 and requiring a full-time staff of six hundred, the Clemency Board drew careful but essentially irrelevant distinctions among its fifteen thousand cases. It offered meaningless relief to people who needed far more.

The military lawyers at Fort Harrison also tried to liberalize the program after encountering deserters with "the goshawfulest stories we ever heard." Elvin McCoy had been in the service more than five years when his two brothers were killed, one in a car accident and the other in Vietnam. McCoy was wrongly denied discharge as a sole surviving son, and he went AWOL to return to his family. He qualified for better than an Undesirable Discharge under standard military policy. After seeing a number of cases like McCoy's, military lawyers eventually prevailed on the Fort Harrison commanding general to deal with meritorious applicants outside the framework of the formal clemency program and discharge them under his normal authority as commander. They could thereby receive General and Honorable Discharges, with full entitlement to veterans' benefits.

This alternative was much more time-consuming than the one-day clemency program, and few returning deserters were willing to stay the weeks or months it usually required. Paul Elias was addicted to heroin when he enlisted in the Army. He was qualified for a medical discharge and veterans' benefits, but only if he were willing to spend several weeks at Fort Harrison. Elias was undergoing methadone treatment in New York City, and no one could find a methadone source in Indianapolis. Rather than undergo withdrawal, he accepted an Undesirable Discharge and went home.

Just 1 percent of the 5,555 returning servicemen who passed through Fort Harrison endured the long waiting period and received better than an Undesirable Discharge. Military lawyers estimated that ten or twenty times as many could have been helped if every file had been carefully reviewed without delay. One official called the Fort Harrison clemency process an "in-by-nine, out-by-five dry cleaning operation," more efficient at discharging people than at giving them the relief they deserved.

Both the Fort Harrison staff and the Clemency Board issued comprehensive reports that described the applicants sympathetically. The Defense Department never publicly released the Fort Harrison report, which was critical of the leadership problems that contributed to many AWOLs. At the insistence of one Board member who was a former Selective Service official, the Clemency Board deleted from its report language sharply critical of the draft system. The White House later issued the Board's report in a way that minimized its public impact. When the Government Accounting Office conducted an inquiry into the clemency program, the White House claimed executive privilege and barred it from speaking with Clemency Board officials. As a result, the public gained no better understanding of the individuals who had committed draft or military offenses.

Despite its shortcomings and the constant criticisms from all sides, the Ford initiative did achieve its narrow political purpose of deflating the amnesty issue. A Gallup poll in August 1975, near the end of the program, showed that a majority of Americans supported conditional clemency and did not want it broadened. Most believed a fair offer had been extended, making it no fault of the President's if the resisters turned him down. Ford himself helped cultivate this view. When asked about his program, he said, "I think we gave them a good opportunity. I don't think we should go any further." This reinforced the widely held belief that non-participating draft resisters and deserters were selfish and uncompromising.

A new measure of scorn was now afforded the 97 percent of the draft resisters and deserters who never applied for clemency or who failed to complete alternative service. To a senior attorney in the Fort Harrison clemency program, they were "double deserters," who had twice demonstrated poor citizenship. One veteran with an Undesirable Discharge was about to be granted limited benefits by the Veterans Administration, but when the VA learned that he had been discharged by the Fort Harrison clemency program and had not done his assigned alternative service, it turned him down.

The end of the Ford program saw the collapse of much of the vitality of the amnesty movement. Many of the more visible exiles had solved their immediate legal problems through the Kennedy list, the Fort Harrison loophole, or the government's lenient discharge and prosecution policies. The long effort to achieve amnesty left others exhausted and dispirited. The American Civil Liberties Union ended its amnesty project for want of funds, depriving the movement of a major source of legal support and an important bridge to liberal opinion. Legislative efforts by Congressmen Robert Kastenmeier and Edward Koch succeeded in moving an amnesty bill past its first stages, but their efforts faltered more from lack of interest than from outspoken opposition.

The old arguments pro and con no longer excited the public. The radical members of the community combined amnesty with new lists of demands. The American Deserters Committee pressed for amnesty, "vigilance against U.S. aggression in the Middle East, and an end to the dictatorial government of the U.S. puppet regime in South Korea." The National Council on Universal, Unconditional Amnesty demanded amnesty, "a single type discharge for all veterans, jobs or income for all, and no more imperialist wars." On the other side, James Wagonseller of the American Legion repeated the argument that any further forgiveness was "a direct insult to the millions of Americans who served honorably during the Vietnam war and an even greater insult to those who died, were incapacitated, or are still missing in action."

A month before he left office, President Ford called Jane Hart after the death of her husband, Senator Philip Hart of Michigan, a close friend of Ford's and a leading proponent of amnesty. When Ford asked her if there was anything he could do, she told him there was—he could declare the amnesty that her husband had not lived to see. Hopes then grew that Ford might end his Presidency by declaring a general amnesty. Ford had considered this step before, after South Vietnam collapsed in the spring of 1975. But at the urging of his White House advisers, he rejected the idea. His election defeat removed the political constraints that had weighed heavily on his mind. The President had before him the example of Harry Truman, whom he liked to consider his spiritual mentor, and who had issued a Christmas pardon to peacetime deserters in his last month of office. Ford would thus relieve his successor of a major source of controversy, lift the amnesty issue from partisan politics, and accomplish his original goal of "binding the nation's wounds."

The President had also been urged by Charles Goodell to take several steps short of amnesty that would have benefited large numbers of people. Ford rejected all but one of Goodell's suggestions. Just before disbanding in September 1975, the Clemency Board had recommended that the President upgrade the discharges of five hundred Vietnam combat veterans, or at least make them eligible for medical benefits to care for their service-incurred injuries. President Ford had originally turned down this suggestion, and the Defense Department agreed only to give these cases priority treatment if the individuals applied to the discharge review boards. Fifteen months later, only eight applications had been reviewed, five of which were granted upgrades. In his last week as President, Ford ordered yet another case-by-case review of these combat veterans.

Blanket Pardons

In 1973, a year before President Ford launched his clemency program, the annual convention of the Association of the U.S. Army went on record opposing "blanket amnesty," but left the clear impression that pardons for draft resisters and deserters might be acceptable.

Despite the legal distinctions between "pardon" and "amnesty," there is little practical difference between the two. In an amnesty, it is the pardoning power of the Constitution that gives the President his authority to act. Certificates of pardon signed by the President are formal evidence of the relief directed to amnestied persons. Nonetheless, the terms assumed an important political and emotional significance in the Vietnam context. Amnesty came to connote relief for groups of persons whose violations were grounded in political or moral opposition to the government. An amnesty was said to reflect official recognition that the acts in question were not fundamentally criminal, and might be excused or even justified in the interests of political reconciliation. A pardon, by contrast, is directed to individuals. It does not distinguish between ordinary felons and those who acted out of political or moral conviction. Furthermore, the law traditionally requires that a pardon be accepted, and this acceptance is technically regarded as a personal acknowledgment of guilt. For these reasons, the amnesty movement never considered pardons to be acceptable for war resisters.

Mindful of the political importance of these emotion-laden terms, Jimmy Carter capitalized on the distinction drawn by the AUSA. Campaigning in Iowa two years later, he gave it a new twist. "Amnesty says what you did was right," he explained. "Pardon says whether what you did was right or wrong, you are forgiven for it." Legal scholars questioned his semantics, and the Republican vice-presidential candidate, Robert Dole, later looked vainly through his Webster's for the Carter definitions. An "amnesty," said his dictionary, is "a general pardon." Dole was right, but that did not detract from the political significance of Carter's formulation.

Carter had once opposed amnesty in any form, but he changed his mind apparently at the urging of his draft-age sons, one of whom had a General Discharge from the Navy for smoking marijuana. In what he later described as the "single hardest decision" of his campaign, Carter came to the conclusion that resisters, right or wrong, had suffered enough. He promised to grant them "blanket pardons" during his first week in office.

More than any other major political figure, Carter addressed amnesty not as a question of ideology, but as a matter of national reconciliation:

> I think it is time to get the Vietnamese war over with. I don't have any desire to punish anyone. I'd just like to tell the young folks who did defect to come back home with no requirement that you be punished or that you serve in some humanitarian capacity or anything. Just come back home, the whole thing's over.

But Carter's desire to "get the war over with" excluded a significant portion of those who needed help. More important than his distinction between "blanket amnesty" and "blanket pardons" was the line he drew between draft resisters and deserters. The latter, in his view, were less deserving.

Many of the early amnesty proposals, including Senator Taft's 1971 bill, had also excluded deserters. Senator Philip Hart once characterized deserters as "guys who take off with the company cash," and most people perceived of them as common criminals. A Howard Johnson place mat, for example, warned diners that picking up hitchhikers was dangerous because many were AWOL soldiers.

It was not until Senator Edward Kennedy's amnesty hearings in 1972 that deserters began to be considered in the same terms as draft resisters. A number of witnesses argued strongly that deserters were the military equivalent of antiwar draft resisters, and stressed the fact that deserters more often came from disadvantaged backgrounds. The hearings had the important result of blending the two groups together in the public mind. During the next four years, few suggested that the two should be treated differently, and in this spirit President Ford's clemency program tried to deal with them comparably. Throughout the 1976 presidential campaign, Carter was the only candidate of either party who distinguished between them.

Carter's justification for a "blanket pardon," moreover, seemed to argue for more sympathy toward deserters, not less. In a conversation with the editors of the Washington *Post* in March 1976, he acknowledged the special seriousness with which he viewed desertion, but he also recognized the large measure of class injustice in the way America had fought the war

> In the area of the country where I live, defecting from military service is almost unheard of. Most of the young people in my section of Georgia are quite poor. They didn't know where Sweden was, they didn't know how to get to Canada, they didn't have enough money to hide in college. They thought the war was wrong. They preferred to stay at home, but still they went to Vietnam. A substantial disproportion of them were black. They had never been recognized for their service to the country. They had often been despised, characterized as criminals, they were never heroes, and I feel a very great appreciation to them. They were extraordinarily heroic, serving their country in great danger even if they didn't have the appreciation of their fellow citizens and even if they felt the war was wrong. It's very difficult for me to equate what they did with what the young people did who left the country.

Yet Carter never acknowledged that many deserters were like the Georgians he described. As candidate and later as President, he persisted in drawing a sharp distinction between draft resisters and deserters.

During the Democratic Convention, amnesty forces, led by former peace activist Sam Brown, lobbied the platform committee for a plank that treated both groups equally. When the Carter forces held firm, they had to settle for a compromise that offered a "case-by-case review" for deserters. The language was vague enough to mean anything from including deserters in a nearly universal amnesty to excluding them from any special program. It committed Carter to nothing. "Candidly," admitted former Ohio Governor John Gilligan, chairman of the committee's foreign policy task force, "the question of covering desertion was so controversial that we walked away from it."

In one of the more emotional events of the convention, Ron Kovic, a severely crippled Vietnam veteran, gave a moving and powerful speech about amnesty in nominating Fritz Efaw, a fugitive draft resister, for Vice President. After attending the convention as an alternate delegate for overseas Americans, Efaw surrendered a few days later in Oklahoma. His case was dropped at the prosecutor's request because of draft board irregularities.

A few weeks later, Carter reaffirmed his plans to pardon draft resisters in a speech before the American Legion convention. Not surprisingly, the Legionnaires' reaction was strongly negative. Except for a passing exchange during his first televised debate with President Ford, Carter said little more during the campaign, and did not clarify his position on deserters. Ford never pressed him on the issue; the failures of his own clemency program left him vulnerable to counterattack, and his private polls showed that the American people had scant interest in the subject.

Two weeks after the election, President-elect Carter met with Father Theodore Hesburgh, president of the University of Notre Dame, and McGeorge Bundy, president of the Ford Foundation. They presented him with what they called a program of "reconciliation" and strongly urged that he change his mind about deserters. He promised to study the proposal, but warned them, "You know, I may not agree with you."

The amnesty movement knew this was probably its last opportunity. Its lobbyists showed a new sense of pragmatism, arguing less for public vindication than for meaningful relief for a half million or more individuals. Some even supported the idea of excluding deserters who fled from combat, the principal heroes of the early days of the movement. Much of this new-found pragmatism evaporated, however, when Charles Kirbo, Mr. Carter's closest confidant, invited leading advocates to a discussion of the issue. The group that went to see him included what one participant later called "a very unfortunate choice of people" —the mother of a well-known deserter who had fled to Sweden through the Soviet Union, a radical deserter-at-large who told Kirbo that any amnesty program should include billions of dollars in reparations to Vietnam, and other voices reminiscent of the radicalism of the 1960s. Their approach clashed with the old-fashioned patriotism of Kirbo and Carter.

The debate within Carter's inner circle split almost precisely on generational lines. The younger members of his staff suggested broad relief for deserters and other military offenders, while Carter's contemporaries—Kirbo, Defense Secretary-designate Harold Brown, and Attorney General-designate Griffin Bell—urged a more cautious approach.

As Carter's inauguration approached, news leaks suggested that the President-elect was changing his mind about deserters. In mid-December, Carter's transition staff released a statement that "substantial agreement" had been reached on a plan offering broad-based relief for 250,000 deserters and other military offenders, and Charles Kirbo commented that as many as 800,000 Vietnam-era veterans might get upgrades to Honorable Discharges. But this was not to happen.

On January 21, 1977, his first full day in office, the new President issued a "blanket pardon," offering total relief—in effect, unconditional amnesty—for draft resisters. Except for a handful who used "force or violence," 7,150 convicted draft offenders were pardoned,* and all of the 3,000 remaining fugitives had their cases dropped. The immigration

---

*The 1,600 convicted draft offenders previously pardoned by President Ford received nothing new from President Carter.

rules were eased to allow some five thousand expatriates to visit the United States. A quarter of a million nonregistrants were assured that they no longer faced prosecution upon discovery. In all, roughly 265,000 people were affected (see Figures 8 and 9). For deserters, Carter announced only that he had asked the Defense Department to study their situation.

Carter's program drew very little praise. *Pravda* hailed it as an official admission of American wrongdoing in Vietnam. Conservatives were furious, as Carter himself had predicted. Senator Barry Goldwater said it was "the most disgraceful thing a President has ever done." The chairman of the Republican National Committee called it "a slap in the face of all Americans and families who did their duty." "It's the saddest day in American history," complained the director of the VFW, "even sadder than Watergate and Vietnam itself." Veterans' groups in some parts of the country threatened to circulate blacklists of pardoned offenders among local employers.

The amnesty community had a mixed reaction to Carter's policy. Some spokesmen called it "hopeful" or a "first step." But others accused the President of a class bias, forgiving draft resisters but not the disproportionately black, low-income, and poorly educated military offenders. Many Vietnam veterans, some of whom opposed pardons for draft resisters, were particularly angered by the exclusion of servicemen, which they regarded as yet another example of the nation's insensitivity to the men who had served in uniform during the war. Yet most of the protests were feeble. As one pardoned draft resister said, "I'm sorry, but I'm happy." The heart had gone out of the movement. In Toronto, only two hundred of an expected four hundred attended what many regarded as the last amnesty conference. *Newsweek* called it "the last major battle by opponents of the Vietnam war." They feared their cause and their sacrifices would be forgotten.

For most draft resisters, Carter's pardons made very little difference, even though he offered them all the legal relief within his power. By 1977, few convicted draft resisters were any longer in prison or on probation. Nonregistrants were extremely unlikely to be found and punished. Exiles had established permanent homes outside the United States; they expected to visit their families now and then, but few had any intention of coming back permanently. In the first six months after Carter's announcement, just ninety-nine individuals asked the Justice Department for pardon certificates, and only 85 exiles returned permanently to the United States.

Meanwhile, the Defense Department conducted the deserter study requested by the President. The Carter administration was relying for advice here on some of the same Pentagon officials who had helped shape President Ford's clemency program. The first proposal submitted by the Defense Department was rejected by the White House as too stringent, and the plan finally adopted was a compromise between competing views within the administration.

In late March, the Defense Department announced a "Special Discharge Review Program" through which 432,000 veterans with Undesirable or Clemency Discharges were invited to apply for upgrades via existing discharge review boards. Those with Undesirable Discharges who had completed tours in Vietnam, had two years of good service, or had received Clemency Discharges under the Ford program were virtually guaranteed automatic relief. The boards were directed to "reexamine" other cases in a "spirit of compassion." Yet large categories of veterans were excluded. Those who had deserted from Southeast Asia were automatically barred, even though many of their offenses involved conscientious war resistance, combat fatigue, or other extenuating circumstances. The program also failed to cover the 22,000 individuals who were discharged by court-martial for offenses against military discipline, even though Defense Department officials acknowledge privately that their misconduct was generally no worse than that of the 130,000 who accepted Undesirable Discharges as plea bargains. In fact, many of the most conscientiously motivated individuals had refused to plea-bargain, maintained their innocence, and insisted on standing trial.

A fundamental weakness in the Carter program for military offenders was its requirement that eligible veterans apply within a six-month period. During the six and a half months of President Ford's program, only 15 percent of its ninety thousand eligible veterans with bad discharges had applied. The Ford program offered fewer benefits than Carter's, but its top officials believed that the low application level resulted mainly from ignorance, apathy, confusion, and distrust of the government—problems no less serious in 1977 than in 1974. Father Hesburgh and McGeorge Bundy had warned the President that any program requiring applications or imposing deadlines would help relatively few people. They further suggested that the President order a comprehensive file review at the military records center to assure that his program reach as many people as possible. However, Carter chose to follow the advice of Pentagon officials who rejected the Hesburgh-Bundy approach as an "administrative nightmare." Those same Defense Department officials forecast that only about 120,000 of the 432,000 eligible veterans would apply, and that roughly 70,000 would get upgrades. For them, and apparently for the President, those numbers were sufficient.

The Carter program required that fugitive deserters also apply in person—Defense Department officials rejected the idea of granting them Undesirable Discharges "in absentia." As before, fugitives could surrender at any military base and be virtually assured of an immediate administrative discharge, but many still feared they would be court-martialed and sent to prison. In contrast to the 1974 program, they stayed away in droves.

The Defense Department estimates proved wildly optimistic. The Carter program attracted a scant 9 percent of the 432,000 eligible veterans, far below the 19 percent proportion who had applied to the less generous Ford program. As of October 4, 1977, the date the program ended, the Defense Department had received only 37,283 applications. Of 28,000 cases processed, 16,000, or 60 percent, received upgrades.

The Defense Department had originally planned to spend $200,000 on a public information program to stimulate applications, but Congress prohibited any expenditures for advertising. Congressional opposition to Carter's program also persuaded many eligible veterans to follow the advice of pro-amnesty veteran's counselors, who warned that applying to the program might only compound their problems. Carter seemed content simply to announce his program and then let his policy fare as best it could without any further effort to enlist public support. Candidate Carter had spoken eloquently about the social inequities of the war, but President Carter said nothing. As it was, the public perceived Carter's military program more as an unfair windfall for deserters than as an effort to correct the injustices of the Vietnam era.

Working through Congress, conservative veterans' groups mounted an attack against the program. In the weeks before the President's inauguration they fostered a Senate resolution condemning any kind of amnesty policy. This was stymied only because the new President announced the pardons for draft resisters his first day in office. Then, in rapid succession, Congress enacted legislation which attempted to prohibit the use of funds for processing returning exiles, for issuing pardon certificates, and for the dropping of draft prosecutions. And to prove that politics does indeed make for strange bedfellows, Alan Cranston, a liberal Senator who had been sympathetic to the amnesty cause, joined with Strom Thurmond, a longtime opponent, in a particularly vindictive bill which denied veteran's benefits to those who had received upgrades under the special rules of the Carter program.

Arguing that the Vietnam war was no different from other wars, and that its veterans deserved no special treatment, the bill's supporters challenged the basic premise of the Carter program. Taking advantage of the administration's inept, halfhearted defense, legislators on the House and Senate Veterans Committees succeeded in moving the bill through both houses of Congress. The President pondered whether to sign the legislation for the full ten days constitutionally allotted him, and Secretary of Defense Harold Brown, Attorney General Griffin Bell, and top White House aides all urged him to veto it. Other Carter aides, however, had inadvertently committed the President to acceptance of the bill, in the mistaken belief that the somewhat less stringent Senate version had been adopted. Reluctant to renege on his commitment to House Speaker Tip O'Neill and concerned that a veto might not be sustained, President Carter ultimately decided to sign it. The distinction between draft-evaders and deserters he had drawn during the campaign was thus reaffirmed.

Carter offered more significant relief to more people at less taxpayers' expense than Ford. Unlike his predecessor, President Carter had full access to the facts about draft resisters and deserters when he constructed his program, he was personally and politically committed, and he enjoyed a far stronger mandate to effect a fair solution. Yet, his must stand as the greater disappointment. Ford's concept of "earned re-entry" may not have been a satisfactory approach, but it did reflect an understandable personal philosophy and an internally consistent response. Carter, by contrast, offered total amnesty for draft resisters but, by signing the Cranston-Thurmond bill, provided very little for their military counterparts, who deserved no less and needed far more than the civilians.

Both Presidents, however, must share equal responsibility for the government's failure to secure what draft resisters and deserters needed most—a change in the public's longstanding misconceptions about who they were and what they had done. Both Gerald Ford and Jimmy Carter failed to use the prestige of their office to change public attitudes and bring about a true national reconciliation.

The Next War

Throughout the amnesty debate, fear was often expressed that any measure of official forgiveness, no matter how limited, would undermine America's ability to fight future wars. When talk of amnesty spread through Congress in 1972, Congressman William Jennings Bryan Dorn of South Carolina warned his colleagues that "amnesty would be a severe blow to the defenses of our nation. It would be a step toward anarchy, chaos, and a breakdown of all discipline so necessary for the survival of our democratic institutions." Later, Congressman Sonny Montgomery of Mississippi led the opposition to President Carter's blanket pardons by warning that a future generation of draft-age men might refuse induction or desert from the military on the assumption, born of the Vietnam era, that they would be amnestied a few years later. Carter's own distinction between draft resisters and deserters reflected his concern about the military's ability to maintain discipline in future wartime situations. When Charles Kirbo met with amnesty advocates before Carter's decision, he asked them, "Well, what do we do when the next war comes?"

Throughout its two-hundred-year history, America has fought almost a dozen wars. Many of the conflicts were divisive, engendering considerable war resistance. Most were followed by some form of amnesty. The experience of each war left its imprint on the public. But the amnesties were quickly forgotten and had little, if any, bearing upon the nation's subsequent ability to mobilize troops. During the Vietnam war, draft resisters and deserters seldom broke the law with a view to history, confident that they, like Whiskey Rebellionists or Confederates, would eventually be amnestied. Years from now, when historians look back to the post-Vietnam amnesties, they will probably find them to have had little influence on resistance or evasion in subsequent military crises. It is hard to imagine future war resisters taking much solace in the official measure of relief that followed the years of anxiety, exile, and social disgrace of Vietnam-era offenders.

If the legacy of Vietnam should affect a future wartime mobilization, the reason will not be President Ford's clemency or President Carter's blanket pardons. If draft-age men are unwilling to serve, it will be less in hope of another amnesty than because of a fundamental skepticism about the government in time of military crisis. The Vietnam generation's experiences with the war—the antipathy to military service, the inequities of the draft, and the widespread belief that war resisters were right when the government was wrong—have shaken the nation's confidence that it can order young people to fight in anything short of an unquestioned national emergency.

Some view this as a blessing. One of the original goals of Vietnam resistance and the amnesty movement was to force legal and political acceptance of the individual's moral right to decide for himself whether to fight in any given war. According to a spokesman for the pacifist Mennonite Church,

The United States government may wish to wage a major unpopular war requiring more personnel than the active armed services and the reserves can supply, a war which does not have the support of the American people and for which volunteers would not be forthcoming. . . . In a democratic system, however, the justification for fighting such a war seems dubious at best.

Thus would a form of pure democracy determine the nation's defense policy and prevent future Vietnams. This has some appeal in theory, especially for those who loathe the memory of Vietnam. But could America fight such a "democratic" war when its long-term security but not its immediate survival is at stake?

Despite court challenges to the Vietnam-era draft, it remains the law that one may not legally refuse to fight in a particular war, no matter how morally based the decision. The Supreme Court, in the 1971 *Gillette* decision, held that there is no constitutionally recognized principle of "selective conscientious objection." In the Court's view, such a principle is incompatible with the need of the country to defend itself.

The *Gillette* case may have denied the legal principle of selective objection, but Vietnam-era policies condoned the practice. A draft-age man could be selective, not as a matter of conscience, but as a matter of conscientious avoidance. Millions selected themselves out of the war by lawful avoidance, safe military service, or unlawful but unpunished evasion. Their conduct reflected the public's general distaste for coercion in a free society, a distaste that eventually led to the end of the draft.

In 1971, the same year as the *Gillette* decision, the Gates Commission reported to President Nixon that an all-volunteer force was desirable and feasible for the postwar period. The Gates report drew strong attack from an uncommon alliance of liberals and conservatives. The former, led by Senator Edward M. Kennedy, feared that the armed forces would become disproportionately poor and black and that a professional military would lose the leavening influence of civilian soldiers. Conservatives, led by Senator John Stennis, complained that an all-volunteer force would give the nation inadequate flexibility to meet an emergency. Notwithstanding these warnings, President Nixon and Defense Secretary Melvin Laird endorsed and later implemented the Gates Commission recommendations. When the all-volunteer force came into being in 1973, the principle of selective objection became national policy. In effect, each individual could selectively object simply by not volunteering for military service. Temporarily, at least, this resolved the tension between personal freedom and the needs of the government.

The all-volunteer force has also led to significant reforms that might not have happened in a conscripted army. The military has had to compete in the marketplace like any other employer, and it has quickly learned that increased pay and a reduced risk of combat are not enough. The memories of the earlier army—of makework tasks, poor leadership, and excessive discipline—are still fresh in the minds of nineteen-year-olds. "Today's youth," warned Peter Hauser in *America's Army,* "just will not join that sort of organization—at least not in the quality and quantity necessary to accomplish the Army's mission." So, to enlist men and retain them once they are trained, the military has tried to improve its image and, in particular, its treatment of recruits.

During the Vietnam era, volunteers were often promised the opportunity to learn new skills. But for too many, the only skill learned was combat. In the all-volunteer force, enlistment contracts have been made binding. Recruits now know what they are getting into and what is expected of them. If the government fails to deliver, or if recruits prove unqualified for the specialties they want, they can leave the service with Honorable Discharges.

The life of a soldier is far better than it was just a few years ago. Barracks have given way to dormitories. Longer haircuts, mustaches, and other expressions of individuality are permitted more widely than before. What soldiers used to call the "Mickey Mouse" aspect of military life has largely disappeared. Civilians have been hired for KP and the other kinds of menial labor that soldiers have always resented. There is increasing talk of a serviceman's union. Day-to-day relationships between officers and enlisted men have improved; drill sergeants, in particular, have become less abusive. New human relations programs have been devised to help soldiers with personal problems. "We're trying to approach men with a concept of mutual trust," commented General George Forsythe, coordinator of the Army's shift to a volunteer force. "A man old enough to fight and die is old enough to be trusted."

Some of the more far-reaching reforms have come in the area of discipline. The draft provided a cheap and apparently inexhaustible supply of manpower resources. If an individual did not perform well, he was punished, sent to the stockade, or put to demeaning and unproductive chores. It cost little to keep him around, and his punishment was thought to discourage others from misbehaving. Poor performers were kept in the service until their petty offenses led to major offenses, resulting in court-martial convictions and bad discharges. By contrast, every soldier in the all-volunteer force has become an expensive and scarce resource, and the military can ill afford to keep those who are unproductive. Since 1970, the annual cost per soldier has tripled. The cost of tolerating and punishing poor performers has been estimated to be about $1 billion a year. "Suddenly," said Roger Kelley, former assistant secretary of defense for manpower, "the armed forces have had to become efficient managers of people."

The military has begun to deal with poorly performing recruits the same way private sector employers do with poorly performing employees—by firing them, or by trying not to hire them in the first place. All branches of service have tried to be more selective in the hiring of marginally qualified young men with AFQT scores in Category IV. Compared to the Vietnam era, a much greater effort is made to screen out potential disciplinary problems, but a number of poorly educated, low-IQ recruits are still accepted. Otherwise, despite the presently high unemployment rate among nineteen-year-olds, enlistment quotas could not be filled.

An important change in the approach to discipline has come with the introduction of what some soldiers call the "I quit" or "you're fired" discharge. The initial training months are now regarded as a trial period. If the recruit or his commanding officer decides that the new soldier is not suited for military life, either can take the initiative to sever the military contract in a matter of days. The "trainee discharge" that follows is usually an Honorable and never worse than a General Discharge. This enables the services to dispose of potential disciplinary problems quickly. In some branches of the service, as many as 20 percent of new recruits are separated before the end of the initial training period. First-term servicemen who complete their training period but then begin to present disciplinary problems can be eliminated almost as easily under the "expeditious discharge" program. These discharges are similarly either Honorable or General, and they qualify an individual for veterans' benefits after six months of service.

In fiscal 1977, almost 30 percent of all new recruits failed to finish two years of service.

The AWOL soldier can still receive an Undesirable Discharge, but even this reflects the military's decriminalization of unauthorized absences. This lenient treatment began in the latter years of the war, gaining impetus when the loophole of the Ford clemency program guaranteed returning deserters automatic administrative discharges. Since the end of the Ford program, court-martial trials for absence offenders have become rare. In 1975 and early 1976, only one hundred deserters were sentenced to prison terms, almost all at Fort Gordon, Georgia. However, the sentences were commuted by the Pentagon shortly after the men arrived at Fort Leavenworth prison. Fort Gordon eventually complied with the prevailing policy of giving AWOL soldiers nothing worse than immediate Undesirable Discharges. Today, the military looks at AWOL as a problem more of management than of discipline, and even the official terminology has changed. Soldiers who go AWOL are no longer "deserters"; they are "absentees."

The changing military attitudes have also had a retroactive impact on veterans of earlier times. Post-discharge review procedures have been liberalized in recent years, making it easier for veterans with bad discharges to have them upgraded to General or Honorable. President Carter's special discharge review program for Vietnam-era veterans was in some respects a codification of existing policies, but it also reflected a continuing liberalizing attitude toward veterans with bad discharges from all eras. The military has established a number of regional discharge review boards, enabling applicants to pursue their cases without making long and expensive trips to Washington. Under pressure of a lawsuit, the boards have agreed to issue detailed reasons for each decision. This should improve the consistency of decisions and may reduce the wide disparity among branches of service and individual commanders who make original discharge decisions.

The changes in discharge review are partly the result of a proliferation of veteran counseling organizations. Staffed by Vietnam veterans and the remnants of the draft-counseling community, some two hundred organizations have been established since the war. The result has been a dramatic increase in the number of veterans applying to discharge review boards. At the Army board alone, the number of monthly cases has increased tenfold in the last several years. Even before the announcement of the Carter program, discharge review boards were expecting as many as fifteen thousand applicants annually. By 1977, their backlogs had grown to seven thousand cases, straining the review process to the breaking point. But success rates have been higher than ever before, ranging from 29 percent at the Army board to 49 percent at the Air Force board. Applicants who appear in person and have experienced counselors do even better, with an upgrade rate approaching 50 percent. During Carter's discharge review program for deserters, 80 percent of the eligible applicants were upgraded.

Continued public criticism of the military's discharge system, reinforced by the rapid increase in the numbers of veterans seeking upgrades, has increased the pressure on the services to reform the current five-tiered system. Throughout the armed forces, there is a growing awareness of the long-term social and economic costs of less-than-Honorable discharges, especially those imposed administratively without the due process safeguards of court-martial trials. Yet the military has continued to resist this most basic of reforms.

The progress made by the post-Vietnam military is partly the product of the war and partly the product of the all-volunteer force that followed it. But the future of the nonconscript army is hardly secure. Enlistment quotas have not been reached without accepting more high school drop-outs. But retention of these drop-outs has become a serious problem, with more than 50 percent of them failing to complete their initial three-year enlistment. An anticipated drop in the number of eligible eighteen- and nineteen-year-olds will aggravate the problem in the 1980s. Manpower officials are pleased with the positive attitude of recent recruits, but they complain of a growing difficulty in attracting men with special talents and high aptitudes—the same men who once could be lured into noncombat assignments by the threat of induction. The all-volunteer force has not been as predominantly black and low-income as many had feared, but it still does not represent a true cross-section of American youth.

The commitment to the all-volunteer force has never been universal. Many defense leaders question whether it will ultimately prove feasible even in peacetime. The economic arguments in favor of a draft are regaining popularity. Questions are also asked whether an all-volunteer system can provide the necessary troops to meet a military emergency of more than a few months. Under the current "total force" concept, the reserves are seen as the necessary backup to the active duty force in the event of a crisis. But with the end of the draft, there has been difficulty in attracting reservists, and the deterioration of reserve strength is expected to grow more severe in the coming years. William Brehm, formerly assistant secretary of defense for manpower and reserve affairs, testified to Congress that today's active forces could supply less than half of the combat troops that a major ground war in Europe would require. Even if the President activated all combat-trained reserves, Brehm believed that there still would be a shortage of 250,000 combat troops. The 1976 Defense Manpower Commission likewise warned that "in the event of sudden major hostilities, our volunteer forces would be weakened by casualties without adequate loss replacements. In time they would be unable to conduct sustained operations, and would be annihilated."

Theoretically, at least, the anticipated shortage could be solved through the marketplace by increasing combat enlistment bonuses beyond their $1,000–$2,500 peacetime levels. However, bonuses might have to reach extraordinary levels in time of war. The underlying dilemma about defense manpower policy has not been solved; it has only been postponed.

Whatever the fate of the all-volunteer force during peacetime or limited conflict, there is widespread acknowledgment that a prolonged conflict would require a return to a draft. It remains to be seen how many of the recent military reforms would survive conscription. Binding discharge contracts, trainee and expeditious discharges, and leniency toward absentees might all become casualties of a reversion to a conscript army, especially during hostilities.

The public attitude is certain to dictate the success or failure of any future draft system. The social and political environment of a future crisis cannot be predicted. It is possible that the next draft-age generation will exhibit the same eagerness to serve and willingness to sacrifice that characterized World War II. Avoiders, evaders, and professional draft counselors may be held in disrepute by their peers. Draft boards, prosecutors, and judges may enforce the law strictly and effectively.

But the next set of parents and national leaders will come from the Vietnam generation, almost half of whom thought they were treated unjustly by Selective Service or the armed forces. According to the Notre Dame survey, four of five lost respect for the government as a result of what happened to them or their friends. No one can say what effect this will have on the nation's long-term defense posture, but there will be an impact. World War II conditioned the responses of the older generation toward Vietnam; Vietnam will likewise affect the younger generation's response to future wars. Part of this conditioning will be political, affecting the kinds of declared or undeclared wars the nation is willing to fight. Another part will be personal, affecting the individual's willingness to serve—or have his children serve—in time of need.

Over the next twenty years, the 53 million men and women of the Vietnam generation will have their own children come of age. Family discussions in the 1990s will seldom recall national sacrifice, a dedicated response to the call to arms, or the generosity of a grateful nation toward those who served in its name. Millions of draft-age youths will know that their fathers were avoiders, war resisters, or disillusioned veterans. This is not the stuff upon which to build an ethic of unquestioning patriotism.

The offspring of the Vietnam generation may inherit or even magnify the skeptical values of their parents. As one advocate of amnesty warned, a generation of disillusioned parents will produce sons and daughters who "will question the actions of the military before they get involved," and they may do so earlier and to a greater extent than their fathers did during Vietnam.

When the nation's youth are next called upon to fight, the ultimate legacy of Vietnam may be a widespread attitude that the draft and the armed forces are not to be trusted. Isolationist and pacifist sentiments may be strong, prompting a revival of the resistance and draft-counseling network. A renewed guerrilla war against the draft might have greater success in paralyzing draft boards, jamming the courts, and destroying discipline in the armed forces. The whole system of conscription might break down, and the United States might not be able to raise an army.

At present, little thought has been given to the obstacles confronting a return to the draft. Since 1975, draft-age men have not been required to register with Selective Service and draft boards have been disbanded. All that is left of the Selective Service system is a small caretaker staff, much of whose time is spent disposing of old records. Nonetheless, present contingency plans assume that an immediate registration would enable the drafting of 100,000 men within four months and a half million by the eighth month, through a system nearly identical to the one abandoned in 1972. These plans are predicated on the successful mass registrations of World Wars I and II. World War I registration began seventeen days after the enactment of a conscription law, and 475,000 men were drafted within six months. The World War II draft registered 16,500,000 men within thirty days, and mass inductions began just one month later. But history offers little assurance, given the fresh memory of Vietnam and the residue of the antidraft movement.

In the Vietnam era, just 1 percent of all draft-age men failed to register, and another 1 percent refused induction. Still, the draft barely survived the challenge. In the next war, if 10 percent or even 5 percent of all draft-age persons do not register, there might indeed be a "snowballing" effect like the one the Resistance movement tried, unsuccessfully, to catalyze in the late sixties. That prospect is a very real threat. In early 1976, Selective Service announced plans for a one-day mass registration of eighteen-year-olds, and draft resistance groups quickly organized a boycott. The plan was canceled, ostensibly for budget reasons; had it been carried out, the combined effect of the boycott and public apathy might well have produced an alarmingly low turnout.

The effective functioning of a post-Vietnam draft hinges on a number of other optimistic assumptions: the overnight mobilization of a draft structure that is presently nonexistent, the fair application of laws and regulations by draft boards whose Vietnam-era performance did not withstand judicial scrutiny, swift and certain criminal enforcement by a judicial system that dismissed more than 90 percent of all Vietnam-related cases, and the absence of a concerted resistance effort by pacifist groups who oppose conscription as a matter of principle. Most important, it requires a reversal of the present antipathy toward the idea of a draft. "Going back to the draft would upset the whole country," conceded Byron Pepitone, Director of Selective Service during the Ford administration. "The mothers of America have learned to like the past four years."

Unless the nation wants to gamble its security on these optimistic assumptions, it has to develop reasonable, publicly acceptable plans for coping with a military crisis. At the same time, it must design manpower and enforcement policies which avoid the social inequities, disrupted lives, and permanent stigmas of the Vietnam era.

The all-volunteer force may be the nation's choice. If so, the high cost of emergency mobilization has to be acknowledged in advance, along with the risk that low-income youths may do a disproportionate share of the fighting. Alternatively, all draft-age youths could be ordered to perform two years of civilian or military service, the minimum time the armed forces consider necessary for a useful military tour. Jobs would have to be created for eight million young men and women, the great bulk of them in the civilian economy. The cost would be staggering. Americans would also have to accept what many consider the dangerously totalitarian notion that the government has the right to demand involuntary civilian service of its citizens. The problem of conscientious objection would still exist, and rules would have to be developed for determining who fights and who stays at the homefront.

Selective conscription, modeled after the Vietnam-era lottery, is the third alternative. However, the experience of Vietnam suggests that any system with status-based deferments and exemptions would again encourage manipulative behavior, legal challenges, and social inequities unless all subjective decision-making were eliminated. As long as anyone can contrive to flunk a physical exam or persuade a draft board that he—or she—is a conscientious objector, the draft system would be vulnerable to abuse and legal challenge. Yet if incapacitated persons and conscientious objectors are pressed into military service, thousands of draft offenses would occur.

In any system of limited conscription, the issue of selective objection has to be faced and resolved. As one possibility, anyone unwilling or unable to perform military service might be permitted to excuse himself at his own initiative, without having to demonstrate his sincerity. This would be similar to the CO provision in the West German draft law. New York Congressman Jonathan Bingham has proposed a scheme whereby selective CO's would have to declare themselves before becoming subject to a draft lottery. In doing so, they would commit themselves to alternative service regardless of their lottery numbers. In effect, this would build on the Vietnam-era precedent of offering noncombat assignments to draft-age men who enlisted for three or four years in the Navy, Air Force, or Coast Guard. But unlike the Vietnam era, anyone could become a selective objector, regardless of his background, education, or social status.

Reconciling personal freedom with national security will never be easy in America's democratic society. It is part of the legacy of Vietnam that the nation may find itself unprepared in a future military crisis.

VII | LEGACIES

Half a decade has passed since the last American troops left Vietnam. The debate about the war has moved from the newspapers to the history books. Former Johnson administration officials who helped shape the nation's Vietnam policy are now sharing power in the Carter administration with a number of activists who opposed that policy. With a collective sigh of relief, the nation has closed a tragic chapter of its history.

The 26,800,000 men of the Vietnam generation are preoccupied with building careers, raising families, and making their way in American life. But their experience with the war can never be erased. Few can forget the decisions, compromises, and sacrifices they had to make. Nor can they forget what happened to their friends and peers who fared perhaps better, perhaps worse than they. The war may fade in everyone else's mind, but not in theirs. In *We Are All POW's,* Vietnam veteran Gary Wood was asked by his co-author, convicted draft resister Chuck Noell, whether America would ever "work through" Vietnam. His answer: "No. The rest of society will pretend it never happened. Or they'll pretend that it isn't important. And our generation will go on reliving Vietnam until it dies off."

Combat veterans, especially, cannot forget. While others stayed home, they were uprooted from their loved ones, subjected to the rigors of military training, and sent to fight for a cause that had little meaning for many of them. Most were lucky and returned without wounds or bad discharges. But there were few parades, ceremonies, or even notes in their local newspapers. They came home, that was all.

They are the orphans of the war. To some, they represent a defeated army, losers of a war that could have been won. One veteran recalled getting in a fistfight with a Legionnaire who blamed him and his buddies for the loss of Vietnam: "I fought just as well as he did, maybe better. Guys like him always talked a lot about how great the war was, and how everybody should support it, but deep down they had no respect for grunts like me who had to fight it."

To others, they are the criminals of My Lai, killers of women and children, the spreaders of defoliants, napalm, and cluster bombs. A Chicano from Los Angeles found that "everyone I talked to was negative. 'What is it like to kill? How does it feel?' Questions like that. A lot of it was just well-founded curiosity, I think, but a lot of it was twisting it in you. It was like—hey—you're really a loser." An Ohio veteran, militantly antiwar himself, was shamed and ridiculed whenever he wore his army uniform around town: "People just look down on you. They treat you altogether different when you're in uniform. I went up to the campus to see my girl, and I got called pig and murderer and all kinds of things just because I was in uniform."

Vietnam veterans have learned through bitter experience that military service did not gain them personal honor or a headstart in life. Their time in the military taught them few useful skills. All too many had serious problems finding jobs when they returned and, even now, unemployment remains disproportionately high among disabled, minority, and younger veterans. As Michael Marks explained:

> Stuck with the stigma of being a Vietnam vet, I couldn't get a job for a long time. TV commercials were begging business people to hire Vietnam vets, but where in the hell was a job for *me?* Sure, I made it back, unscathed by combat wounds, alcoholism, or drug addiction. But my personal pride was at an all-time low.

Their peers are years ahead of them in building careers and families. Understandably, many veterans resent those who saw the war only from living rooms. One recalled getting a letter from a college-educated friend:

"Harry," he wrote, "maybe we're doing a terrible thing, trying to destroy a whole way of life, trying to impose Catholicism and Americanism on Asia. Think about it, Harry." Think about it? I never answered him, the son of a bitch. Here he was, deferred as a schoolteacher, and me getting shot at. What did Asian culture mean to me? What about my men, some of whom were still in Vietnam and might never come home alive? Here I was, sitting among draft dodgers and flag-waving sons of bitches, none of whom took the trouble to go and fight for the country they say they love so much, and all a bit drunk and holding their girls' tits, and my men, my buddies, far away, abandoned, left to decay in a place that didn't exist for me anymore.

Another recalled his anger at coming home to an antiwar demonstration:

I ran into a "Resist the Draft" rally on the street. At first I smiled; kids at it again, just a fad. Then I started gettin' sore. About how I had to go and they could stay out. My Negro buddy didn't like the war, but he went in too. I just stood there and got sore at those spoiled rich kids tellin' people to "resist the draft." What about us poor people? For every guy who resists the draft, one of us gotta go, and he gets sent out into the boonies to get his backside shot at. One of their signs read, "We've Already Given Enough." And I thought, "What *have* they given?"

Paul Starr interviewed hundreds of veterans for *The Discarded Army,* his book about post-Vietnam adjustment problems. Starrr found "they feel overwhelmingly that people who were not in Vietnam have no right to judge them, that such judgments are a luxury of those who stayed at home and had nothing to do with the situations they confronted."

As Starr noted, combat veterans rarely feel guilty for doing what they did—"they believe they were much more sinned against than sinning." But they also feel little pride in having done the fighting for others. When they are called heroes, it is usually for a cause other than their own—as an argument for opposing amnesty, for example. What the

Vietnam veteran wants, and what he has not gotten, is understanding. As psychologist Dr. Peter Bourne commented, "It is not so important that he be treated as a hero, but that some recognition be given to the experiences and suffering he has endured."

Just as the American people have forgotten the Vietnam veteran, so too have they forgotten that every member of the generation is, in a very real sense, a veteran of Vietnam. Ron Bitzer, a former combat infantryman who is now a veterans' counselor, laments that "the American people seldom realize that Vietnam veterans and deserters are very similar; sometimes, in fact, they are one and the same. If people really cared about any of us, they would care about all of us." Bitzer's "all of us" includes the entire generation, not just the relative few who saw combat or paid a price for breaking the law.

Except for the few who considered military service an honor and privilege, and except for the lucky ones who saw fate pass them by, every draft-age man had to choose from among a number of unpleasant choices. The alternatives—combat, avoidance in or out of service, evasion, desertion, or exile—each involved the possibility of sacrifice, punishment, or moral guilt. This was a difficult decision for a young man to make.

In the late 1960s, Eddie Correia, Jim Fallows, and John Foote each had the opportunity to escape the draft by means of a physical exemption. Correia knew from childhood that he would be disqualified, no matter what he did. Fallows was in excellent health, but won an exemption by exploiting the system. Foote turned down a near-certain disqualification to become an infantry officer in Vietnam. Here are their accounts:

Eddie Correia

The war. My generation called it then (and now) simply The War. To our parents it was the "war in Vietnam"—the latest in a series of wars they and the nation had to endure. While the honor of serving in this war might not be so honorable, and the heroes of this war not so acclaimed, it was to them a war much like other wars. But to my generation, it was more a political and personal phenomenon than an effort to defend our country.

Vietnam, at least for three or four years, hovered over my life and the lives of those around me. It was the source of scores of discussions about the folly of our involvement and the focus of shared views about how drastically wrong political leaders could be. It was, I believe, the strongest force driving young people to distrust their leaders and to destroy what they felt was worst about American life.

The war was the center of heated arguments between us and our parents and their contemporaries. I remember speaking to a men's civic club about American involvement. Those men, who, on other days, were proud and supportive of us, seemed to despise me that day. Their frustration and anger poured over me. These arguments across the age and experience barrier were to be repeated many times, and I believe some scars remain. In our desperate efforts to convince each other, we almost always failed and almost always felt some bitterness.

I, as most others, I think, passed through a period of reflection and confusion—first about the rightness of the war, then about the meaning of fighting in it. I, as many others, came to doubt the war more and more strongly until the conviction became an emotional one.

But in the most crucial way of all, the war passed me by. I always knew I would not have to serve in Vietnam. I have a handicap, a mark of childhood polio. It left one leg smaller and weaker—not enough to make me inactive, but more than enough to make a physical exemption certain. I know now this handicap was, in one important sense, a luxury. My lottery number, 83, was low enough so I would have been drafted had I not been exempted. As the lottery was based on chance, so was my physical disability. In my case, chance spared me the dilemma faced by millions of others. That dilemma—the critical choice whether to serve if drafted—was confronted by many of my friends. Some of them were terrified.

One of my closest and most sensitive friends chronically wrestled with the prospects of prison or flight to Canada. His fears were very real. He believed he would be in Canada all his life, or, if he went to prison, his life would be destroyed. He once told me he feared he would be homosexually raped in prison, and he felt he should prepare himself psychologically. Although he was the most conscientious of objectors, his religious beliefs did not fit the Selective Service's standards. I believe he would not have fought in the war, and I believe some of his fears would have come true. As with many of us in the white middle class, however, he won his reprieve. After long and, it seemed, desperate efforts, he got a physical exemption. When he received this news, it was a time of rejoicing for him, for me, and for everyone who knew him.

Would I have gone to Vietnam if I had been forced to make the choice? Going would have meant fighting in a war I hated and, perhaps, killing others under circumstances I believed were inhuman. Going would have meant betraying myself by failing the first important moral test I created for my iife. Going would have meant risking death for nothing.

Yet I do not know. Resisting would have led to prison or a life in another country. It would have meant imposing a grief on my family from which they never fully would have recovered. Resisting would have meant destroying a career I hoped (and expected) to be a successful and satisfying one. It would have meant creating a suspicion in myself that I was a coward.

Most choices in life, I believe, lend themselves to weighing one course against the other. The war seemed to present alternatives that were so bleak, so empty, and so destructive than any rational decision-making was pointless. I do not know what I would have done. That I was not forced to choose caused me some guilt and, I believe, caused my friends some unspoken resentment.

I am sure, however, I cannot judge what any of my friends did or what any of the millions of my contemporaries I will never know chose for themselves. I am simply thankful I did not have to decide. And I am thankful the war is over.

Jim Fallows

In the fall of 1969, I was beginning my final year in college. As the months went by, the rock on which I had unthinkingly anchored my hopes—the certainty that the war in Vietnam would be over before I could possibly fight—began to crumble. It shattered altogether on Thanksgiving weekend when, while riding back to Boston from a visit with my relatives, I heard that the draft lottery had been held, and my birth date had come up number 45. I recognized for the first time that, inflexibly, I must either be drafted or consciously find a way to prevent it.

In the atmosphere of that time, each possible choice came equipped with barbs. To answer the call was unthinkable, not only because, in my heart, I was desperately afraid of being killed, but also because, among my friends, it was axiomatic that one should not be "complicit" in the immoral war effort.

Draft resistance, the course chosen by a few noble heroes of the movement, meant going to prison or leaving the country. With much the same intensity with which I wanted to stay alive, I did not want those things either. What I wanted was to go to graduate school, to get married, and to enjoy those bright prospects I had been taught that life owed me.

I learned quickly enough that there was only one way to get what I wanted. A physical deferment would restore things to the happy state I had known during four undergraduate years. . . .

Although, on the doctor's advice, I made a halfhearted try at fainting spells, my only real possibility was beating the height and weight regulations. My normal weight was close to the cutoff point for an "under-weight" disqualification, and, with a diligence born of panic, I made sure I would have a margin. On the morning of the draft physical I weighed 120 pounds. . . .

I stepped on the scales at the very beginning of the examination. Desperate at seeing the orderly write down 122 pounds, I hopped back on and made sure that he lowered it to 120. I walked in a trance through the rest of the examination until the final meeting with the fatherly physician who rules on marginal cases such as mine. I stood there in socks and underwear, arms wrapped around me in the chilly building. I knew as I looked at the doctor's face that he understood exactly what I was doing.

"Have you ever contemplated suicide?" he asked after he finished looking over my chart. My eyes darted up to his. "Oh, suicide—yes, I've been feeling very unstable and unreliable recently." He looked at me, staring until I returned my eyes to the ground. He wrote "unqualified" on my folder, turned on his heel, and left. I was overcome by a wave of relief, which for the first time revealed to me how great my terror had been, and by the beginning of the sense of shame that remains with me to this day.

It was, initially, a generalized shame at having gotten away with my deception, but it came into sharper focus later in the day. Even as the last of the Cambridge contingent was throwing its urine and deliberately failing its color blindness tests, buses from the next board began to arrive. These bore the boys from Chelsea, thick, dark-haired young men, the white proles of Boston.

Most of them were younger than us, since they had just left high school, and it had clearly never occurred to them that there might be a way around the draft. They walked through the examination lines like so many cattle off to slaughter. . . .

We returned to Cambridge that afternoon, not in government buses but as free individuals, liberated and victorious. The talk was high-spirited, but there was something close to the surface that none of us wanted to mention. We knew now who would be killed. . . .

On either side of the class divide, the war has left feelings that can easily shade over into mistrust and hostility. Among those who went to war, there is a residual resentment, the natural result of a cool look at who ended up paying what price. On the part of those who were spared, there is a residual guilt, often so deeply buried that it surfaces only in unnaturally vehement denials that there is anything to feel guilty about.

In a land of supposed opportunity, the comfortable hate to see the poor. Beneath all the explanations about self-help and just deserts, there remains the vein of empathy and guilt. Among the bright people of my generation, those who have made a cult of their high-mindedness, the sight of legless veterans and the memories of the Navy Yard must also touch that vein. They remind us that there was little character in the choices we made.

John Foote

I come from a conservative southern background, growing up extraordinarily conscious of the Civil War. When younger I could recite the order of march into the major battles of the war, and the names of the great generals were second nature to me. Viewed from the distance of a hundred years, it all seemed so incredibly romantic. Even the Second World War seemed somehow to have been reinforcement for the notions of duty, honor, and country. This romanticization of war, and the view of it as a time of anonymity and individual elevation through feats of arms, affected my whole perception of military service.

Both my parents, though not particularly warlike, were strong believers in the duty to serve and the honor that was associated with honorable service. They rarely spoke of Vietnam, or even of my impending service, in other than immediate terms (fear for my life), but my father once told me that if I chose not to serve, I should do so in the knowledge that his home would no longer be open to me. I never believed him, for such things would have been out of character, but the statement had an impact on me. He had served honorably in World War II, and is a reasonable man who believes himself a patriot.

My college life gave incredible reinforcement to my earlier training. Louisiana State University, an island of near-timeless beauty, was a remarkably womblike environment during the late 1960s. For most of my time there, Vietnam was nothing. It did not exist. Of course, my classmates and I were as aware as anyone who could watch the national news that things were getting progressively worse there, but none of us believed that this meant anything to us.

Like death, war was something that happened to someone else.

I cannot say with any certainty that I ever felt any serious "moral" reservations about the war, but I was troubled by it. I thought deeply about it, but I was totally unable to find any personally acceptable reason for refusal to serve. Although it galls me to acknowledge the shallowness of my sentiment, my opposition to military service was largely based on my personal distaste for leaving my girl friend of those days, and truncating my education, just as my antiwar feelings were principally a concern for the effectiveness of American policy: it was not "moral" revulsion.

I graduated from LSU in 1968, just as the draft calls were on the steady rise, and a friend of mine learned that he and I were at the top of the list. I would not be able to make it through my first year at law school. In July of that summer, I was summoned for my preinduction physical, and the war became a real part of my world. I was extremely bitter about the seeming helplessness with which I faced the draft.

It was around this time that I discovered that an allergy to bee stings was a surefire way to avoid induction, and I had a documentable case. It was clear now that I had an easy out, but despite the fact that I could now avoid service without danger, I began to wonder about the choice of doing *that*, just as much as I had wondered about the choice of refusing service.

Although still very much embittered that these forces beyond my control were moving at me, I began to see Vietnam as the preeminent historical experience of my lifetime, certainly of my youth. Wrongly or rightly, Vietnam had to be faced. And it seemed to me then that there were only three ways to face it honorably: go to war, go to jail, or go to Canada. I accepted that one's participation in the event could take the form of fighting the war or fighting against it. It was not necessary that one join up; it was fully enough to show the courage to fight against the war, and to take the consequence of one's actions. All other methods of legally avoiding service were somehow tainted, cowardly. They were to miss a participation, demanded of all, in this overwhelming historical event. War was, I knew it then and still believe it to be, a life-changing experience.

In the summer of 1968 my draft notice arrived. Although I went into the Army, I did not do it without remaining qualms. Ultimately, however, I was still unable to find any personally acceptable, principled reason to refuse service. Therefore, I believed that my only choice was to go to the guts of the matter and serve in the infantry: the quintessential military experience. But in the end, my time as an infantry officer in Vietnam was undistinguished. My services were marked by boredom more than bravery, and when it was over, I think I was half pleased, half not.

I suppose after all this reflection, and in the wake of personal criticism from those who refused to go, I do not believe my choice to serve was wrong. Indeed I believe that honorable service is an honorable thing and not to be derogated. But since I know the torment that went through my own mind in coming to my choice, I can appreciate and even admire the courage (if not the response) of those who made affirmative decisions different from my own.

(John Foote later became a top official in President Ford's clemency program, and a strong amnesty advocate. A close friend of Foote's at LSU, Blake Jones, was also allergic to bee stings. But unlike Foote, Jones saw a doctor, documented his case, and secured an exemption. After graduating from law school, he became one of the South's best draft counselors, never losing a case.)

The members of the Vietnam generation are now in their late twenties and thirties. Vietnam was and always will be their war, just as World War II belonged to their parents, and World War I to their grandparents. The war stories of older generations—stories about mustard gas, Guadalcanal, or the liberation of little French towns—have no meaning for those who came of age during Vietnam. Like Eddie Correia, Jim Fallows, and John Foote, these 27 million men have their own stories, but they are seldom told with pride. Their battles were with the police, their narrow escapes involved draft boards and courts, and the enemy was the government. Some feel guilty, others lucky. Many have a faint sense of disquiet from having been touched but not really touched, from having left the fighting and dying to others.

The war affected them in complex ways, but it engendered a strong sense of kinship. Vietnam was a crisis that they all faced—whether in the barracks, on the campus, or in the streets. Unlike other Americans, most members of the Vietnam generation are reluctant to judge a man by his personal response to the war. They know that the labels—loser, coward, evader, deserter—are part of the tragedy of Vietnam.

NOTES

In the following pages we set forth the citations of the material we have used from secondary sources. With a few exceptions, we have not cited anecdotes and quotes gathered in interviews. Textual and figure notes are presented separately.

I | THE VIETNAM GENERATION

The estimate of 500 Vietnam casualties for the "Kennedy generation" is derived from official Defense Department casualty statistics. The cost of the war is estimated from Department of Defense statistics cited in the *Congressional Quarterly* of January 27, 1973, p. 148. George Will's quote is from his column in the Washington *Post* of January 13, 1977. The Manchester quote is from *The Glory and the Dream*, p. 287. The breakdown of Vietnam casualties is from Emerson, *Winners and Losers*, p. 58, and Pilisuk, "The Legacy of the Vietnam Veteran," in the *Journal of Social Issues*, vol. 31, p. 9. The high-school survey is taken from Bachman and Jennings, "The Impact of Military Experience," in the *Journal of Social Issues*, vol. 31, p. 149. The Harris survey data is referred to in Helmer, *Bringing the War Home*, p. 92. The Glassman comment appears in the *Congressional Record* of March 23, 1976, p. 4023. James Fallows is the source of the *Harvard Crimson* story and the Rhodes scholar's comment, both of which appear in his article "What Did You Do in the Class War, Daddy," in the October 1975 issue of the *Washington Monthly*. The University of Michigan student is quoted in "The Draft: The Unjust vs. the Unwilling," *Newsweek*, April 11, 1966. The Delaware defense worker is quoted in Sanders, *The Draft and the Vietnam War*, p. 116. Kingman Brewster is quoted by Harry Marmion in *Selective Service: Conflict and Compromise*, p. 19. The doctor draft is described in Selective Service's *Semi-Annual Report* of January 1971, p. 6. The Fiedler comment appears in his article "Who Really Died in Vietnam," in the *Saturday Review* of November 18, 1972. The Marshall quote comes from Tax, *The Draft*, p. 64. Racial inequity data is from Little, *Selective Service and American Society*, p. 149, and Starr, *The Discarded Army*, p. 187.

The 1965–66 study of college draftees is from Davis and Dolbeare, *Little Groups of*

Neighbors, p. 12. The O'Konski survey is from Strickland, *Championship Debater's Complete Sourcebook,* p. 64. The Harvard experiences in World War II and Vietnam are from Fallows' *Washington Monthly* article. The comparative likelihood of Vietnam service by educational level is from Defense Department MARDAC data. The Long Island and other surveys on combat deaths are cited in Useem, *Conscription, Protest, and Social Conflict,* p. 108. The Badillo and Curry study, "Social Incidence of Vietnam Casualties," is published in volume 2 of *Armed Forces and Society,* May 1976, p. 397.

General Lewis Hershey contributed in a personal interview the fact that the Rockefeller brothers and other notables of class and wealth volunteered early in World War II. The quotes from Thurmond and Brophy come from their testimony in the 1972 Senate Selective Service and Amnesty Hearings, pp. 181, 241, and 319. The Nixon quote comes from Carl Rogers' written statement in the 1974 House Amnesty Hearings, p. 729. The Eddie Slovik quote is taken from William Huie, *The Execution of Private Slovik,* quoted in Hayes, *American Deserters in Sweden,* p. 50. The resister's quote about everyone being an evader is taken from William Wick's testimony before the 1974 House Amnesty Hearings, p. 648. Mrs. Diliberti is quoted in "Parents Personify the Amnesty Appeal," *Newsday,* March 31, 1974.

II | AVOIDERS

Channeling

The Milligan case comes from the March 1, 1976 issue of *The New Yorker.* Hershey's channeling quotes come from his 1965 memorandum "On Manpower Channeling," reprinted in the December 1966 issue of *Ramparts,* and from Davis and Dolbeare, *Little Groups of Neighbors,* pp. 21–22, 154. Hershey's "administrative or financial challenge" quote is from Chapman, *The Wrong Man in Uniform—Our Unfair and Obsolete Draft and How We Can Replace It,* p. 11, and his "selfish individual" quote from O'Sullivan and Meckler, *The Draft and Its Enemies,* p. 242. The military character of the Selective Service staff is described in Wamsley, *Selective Service and a Changing America,* pp. 73 and 99.

The Confederate and Union drafts are explained in Liston, *Greeting,* pp. 30–31; Miller, *Why the Draft: The Case for a Volunteer Army,* pp. 132–37; and William Wick's testimony in the 1974 House Amnesty Hearings, pp. 641–43. The World War I draft is described in Liston, pp. 36–40; Morris, *Why Draft Repeal?* p. 25; and the government report "War Department Policy with Reference to the Disposal of Draft Deserters," August 1920. The Wilson quote comes from O'Sullivan and Meckler, p. 128. The World War II situation is described in Ginzburg, *The Lost Divisions,* p. 36; and Marmion, *Selective Service: Conflict and Compromise,* p. 37. The worrisome postwar quotes are from Dr. M. H. Trytten, director of the Office of Scientific Personnel, National Academy of Science, and Betty Vetter, executive secretary of the Scientific Manpower Commission, quoted in Willenz, *Dialogue on the Draft,* pp. 46 and 54. The postwar draft and the accompanying quotes are described in O'Sullivan, p. 196; Gerhardt, *The Draft and Public Policy,* pp. 116, 154, 233, and 269–70; and Willenz, pp. 53–54 and 71.

The Vietnam-era draft exam is described in Sanders, *The Draft and the Vietnam War,* p. 38; and Little, *Selective Service and American Society,* pp. 46–47. Hershey's "mathematical" quote is from Chapman, p. 19; his "reclassification" quote from William Wick's testimony in the 1974 House Amnesty Hearings, p. 644; and his "bastard" quote from O'Sullivan, p. 213. The "accordion," "putting something over," "Boy Scouts," "trolley," and "slot" quotes are from Little, pp. 87, 92, and 98. His "all over my back" and "can't muddle around" quotes come from a personal interview. The Ann Arbor case is from Williams, *The New Exiles,* p. 17, and the Rudd case from Suttler, *IV-F: A Guide to Draft Exemption,* p. 101. The post-lottery jump in the physical rejection rate is described in Selective Service's *Semi-Annual Report* of January 1975, p. 80. The administrative details underlying the lottery loophole are discussed in Selective Service's *Semi-Annual Report* of July 1971, pp. 54–55. Curtis Tarr's testimony is in the 1972 Senate Selective Service and Amnesty Hearings, p. 370. The Truman's death escape is described in Selective Service's *Semi-Annual Report* of July 1972, p. 63.

Artful Dodgers

The 7% jump in college enrollments is calculated from a comparison of nationwide enrollment trends from 1965 to 1972 with straight-line increments from 1964 to 1973. The data come from the Commerce Department's *Statistical Abstract of the United States* (1973), Table 203, p. 130. The Emory prank is described in Sanders, p. 86; the business school survey in Tax, *The Draft,* p. 64; and the New York City teacher glut in Gaylin, *In the Service of Their Country,* p. 269. The Hershey "PhDs" quote comes from a personal interview. The Hamilton case comes from Chapman, p. 13, and Eisenhower's "babying out" quote from O'Sullivan, p. 215. The nationwide rise in marriage rates is described in Useem, *Conscription, Protest, and Social Conflict,* p. 101, and Canby, *Military Manpower Procurement,* p. 40. Colonel Smith's quote is from Strickland, *Championship Debater's Complete Sourcebook,* p. 67.

The *One Third of a Nation* report refers to the report of the 1963 President's Task Force on Manpower Conservation, p. 25. The .22 rifle case comes from William Wick's testimony in the 1974 House Amnesty Hearings. Draft Board #100 is described in Tatum and Tuchinsky, *Guide to the Draft,* p. 35; *Amex-Canada* magazine, vol. 2, no. 7, p. 10; and the May 16, 1966 issue of *Newsweek.*

Aid and Comfort

The O'Konski quote comes from the December 9, 1966, issue of *Life.* The Luci Johnson, proud mother, and "rotten, stinking war" quotes are all from Sanders, pp. 15, 61, and 76–77. The braking systems quote is from Little, p. 86; the presidential commission quote from Davis and Dolbeare, pp. 82–83; and the doctor quote from Suttler, p. 4. The Seeger case is cited as *U.S.* v. *Seeger*, 380 U.S. 163 (1965).

The Smith and Los Angeles prosecutor quotes are from Frank Slatinshek's testimony in the 1970 House Armed Services Hearings, p. 12839. Draft counseling sites are described in Schiller and LeBlanc, *Exiled*, pp. 78–109. The "sit down and think" quote is from "If War Is Hell," Central Committee for Conscientious Objectors (CCCO) Booklet No. 6, May 1972. Prepping at the Jane Addams Center is described in Miller, p. 32. The Denver draft board quote is from O'Sullivan, p. 224, and the *Newsweek* quote from the November 1, 1975 issue. Alternative service dropout statistics are from Selective Service's *Semi-Annual Report* of January 1975, p. 82.

The Peard, "investigating hippies," medical counselor, IV-F fraud, and "acting crazy" quotes are from Suttler, pp. 4, 12, 66–67, and 74. The "draft immunization" quote is from Lynd, *We Won't Go*, p. 96. The Caplan quote comes from *Newsweek*, November 9, 1970, and the NATO data from Strickland, p. 121. The "chronically injured athlete" quote is from Marmion, p. 6; the "dental cop-out" quote from John Wheeler's testimony in the 1970 House Armed Services Hearings, p. 12504; and the homosexual fakery quote from Sanders, p. 86. The homosexual bluff case comes from Chapman, p. 190, and the Chicago activist case from Ferber and Lynd, *The Resistance*, p. 63. The racial statistics for physical exam rejections come from Little, p. 144. The Bourne quote is from a personal interview, and the "pinch the wrong foot" quote from Thomas Elias' testimony in the 1970 House Armed Services Hearings, p. 12502.

Safety in Service

The New York Jets case comes from the December 3, 1965 *New York Times.* All other football cases (except the Detroit Lions case) are from the December 9, 1966 issue of *Life*, pp. 44–47. The National Guard racial statistics come from Walton, *The Tarnished Shield*, p. 157, and the college graduate statistics from the 1976 Defense Manpower Commission's *Report to the President*, p. 159. The Defense Department's comment about National Guard riot control and the 1968 callup are described in the June 5, 1971 *National Journal*, pp. 1212–13. The draft motivation for National Guard and reserves enlistment is discussed in Walton, pp. 180–81; Hauser, *America's Army in Crisis*, p. 155; and Cortright, *Soldiers in Revolt*, p. 8.

The noncombat specialty assignment rates for the Spanish-American War, World War II, and the Vietnam war come from Glick, *Soldiers, Scholars, and Society*, p. 42. The noncombat specialty survey is from the Opinion Research Corporation's "Reaction of 17–21 Year Olds to Military Service," p. xix. The "don't enlist to fight" quote, the risk of death for draftees versus enlistees, and the description of computerized assignments come from Glass, "Defense Report," in the August 15, 1970 *National Journal.* The draft-motivated college-graduate statistic is from Helmer, *Bringing the War Home*, p. 340 (citing a 1968 Defense Department survey). The death-risk statistics are taken from Canby, *Military Manpower Procurement*, pp. 64–65. The Air Force recruiter quote is from *Amex-Canada,* vol. 2, no. 5, p. 27; the "no Viet Cong submarines" quote from the April 11, 1966 issue of *Newsweek;* and the "Action Army" quote from Barnes, *Pawns,* p. 71.

The West Point combat volunteers are described in Sanders, p. 119. The counseling manual quote comes from Rivkin, *GI Rights and Army Justice,* p. 54. The data on CO approvals come from Cortright, pp. 15–17; General Leo Benade's testimony in the 1974 House Amnesty Hearings, p. 545; and CCCO "News Notes" for Autumn 1975, p. 6. The court-imposed CO standards are described in Polner, *No Victory Parades,* pp. 95–97. The Pacific Counseling Service activities are discussed in Cortright, p. 17. The "Getting Out" pamphlet was published by the CCCO.

The cases of the fourteen-year veteran, the deliberate wounds, and the sergeant who refused antimalaria pills are from Polner, *No Victory Parades,* pp. 69 and 115. The Oberstrom case is from *Amex,* vol. 2, no. 1, p. 21, and the Patterson case from "This Suit Doesn't Fit, Sarge," a CCCO pamphlet. The risks facing combat troops are extrapolated from the data in Figure 3. The "search-and-evade" quote is taken from Walton, p. 237, and the $350 bounty case is from Linden, "The Demoralization of an Army," in the January 8, 1972 *Saturday Review.* The "CYA" quote comes from Hauser, p. 102; the firebase reenlistment study from Williams, pp. 267–68; and the "million-dollar wound" quote from Woodstone, *Up Against the War,* p. 158.

The Resistance

The Mario Savio quote comes from Ferber and Lynd, *The Resistance,* p. 277. The quote from the St. Louis pact of joint resistance is from Lynd, *We Won't Go,* p. 146. Staughton Lynd's target of 100,000 acts of resistance was first printed in the April 1967 edition of *Liberation* magazine. The "Call to Resist Illegitimate Authority" is cited in Woodstone, *Up Against the War,* p. 58. William Sessions' quote came from his testimony in the 1970 House Armed Services Hearings, p. 12852. The O'Brien case is cited as *U.S.* v. *O'Brien,* 391 U.S. 367 (1968). The antiwar civil liberties cases decided contrary to O'Brien include *Tinker* v. *Des Moines School District,* 393 U.S. 503 (1969); *Schacht* v. *U.S.,* 398 U.S. 58 (1970); *Cohen* v. *California,* 403 U.S. 15 (1971); *Smith* v. *Goguen,* 415 U.S. 566 (1974), and *Spence* v. *Washington,* 418 U.S. 405 (1974). The Catonsville Nine account comes from Ferber and Lynd, p. 202. and Sessions' testimony in the 1970 House Armed Services Hearings, p. 12842. The other draft board raids are from O'Sullivan and Meckler, *The Draft and Its Enemies,* p. 227; *Amex-Canada,* vol. 4, no. 3, p. 9; and Ferber and Lynd, p. 33. The other references to the resistance and antidraft activities are taken from Useem, *Conscription, Protest, and Social Conflict,* pp. 7, 54–55, 60–62, and 165–67.

Surveys and anecdotes about individual threats of draft defiance come from O'Sullivan and Meckler, p. 225; Ferber and Lynd, pp. 93 and 286; and Williams, *The New Exiles,* pp. 33 and 37. The Seeger case is cited as *U.S.* v. *Seeger,* 380 U.S. 163 (1965). The lawyer's handbook with four hundred defenses was *The Selective Service and Military Guide for Attorneys,* published by Curry First. The "fine-tooth comb" quote was by Sessions in his testimony before the 1970 House Armed Services Hearings, p. 12873. The discussion about Selective Service's delinquency practice is partly taken from Williams, p. 31, and Ferber and Lynd, p. 280.

Breakdown

The comment about being "laughed out of court in New York" was from Michael Kennedy, quoted in the June 1, 1970 *National Observer.* The San Francisco dismissals for out-of-district draft board members emanated from *U.S.* v. *Machado,* 306 F.Supp. 995 (ND Cal. 1969). The antiwar activist sent to prison for challenging the "imperialist" system had his conviction sustained in *Harris* v. *U.S.,* 412 F.2d 384 (9th Cir. 1969). The case of the Washington, D.C. draft resister who forum-shopped in San Francisco is cited in Frank Slatinshek's testimony at the 1970 House Armed Services Hearings, p. 12839. The statistics about San Francisco declinations and dismissals come from a table submitted by the Justice Department to the 1970 House Armed Services Hearings, pp. 12858– 60. San Francisco U. S. Attorney James Browning is quoted in the June 1, 1970 *National Observer.* General Hershey's "call Ramsey" quote comes from a personal interview. Curtis Tarr's "splendid support" statement comes from the 1970 House Armed Services Hearings, p. 12480, and his "most difficult problems" statement comes from the Selective Service System's January 1972 *Semi-Annual Report,* p. 41. The William Sessions quote is taken from his testimony before the 1970 House Armed Services Hearings, pp. 12871– 72. Congress' expediting of Selective Service cases came through 50 U.S.C. App. 462.

The three landmark cases are *Gutknecht* v. *U.S.,* 396 U.S. 295 (1970); *Welsh* v. *U.S.,* 398 U.S. 333 (1970); and *Mulloy* v. *U.S.,* 398 U.S. 410 (1970). The Cassius Clay (Muhammad Ali) case is cited as *Clay* v. *U.S.,* 403 U.S. 698 (1971). The principal retroactivity cases are *U.S.* v. *Fargnoli,* 458 F.2d 1237 (1st Cir. 1972), and *Andre* v. *Resor,* 313 F.Supp. 957 (N.D. Cal. 1970). All sentencing statistics come from the various annual reports of the Administrative Office of the United States Courts. Five-dollar fines and one-day probations were ordered in a number of cases, but the one-hour probation came in *U.S.* v. *Feliciano Grafals,* 309 F.Supp. 1292 (DPR 1970). Chuck Noell's quote from *We Are All POW's* comes from p. 77. All statistics about 1967–70 declinations and dismissals are from the Justice Department's table in the 1970 House Armed Services Hearings, pp. 12858–60. The juror who could not ignore the war was quoted in *Brotsky,* "The Trial of a Conscientious Objector," a chapter in *The Relevant Lawyers,* edited by Ann Fagan Ginger and the Seattle juror was quoted in *Amex,* vol. 3, no. 7, p. 41.

The Ones Who Got Away

The Morton case is drawn from *Imus* v. *U.S.,* 447 F.2d 1008 (10th Cir. 1973). The "forget it" quote comes from Thomas Elias' testimony before the 1970 House Armed Services Hearings, p. 12499. The Jones story comes from Lynn, *How to Stay Out of the Army,* p. 102. Nonregistration conviction data is extrapolated from the Presidential Clemency Board's survey of civilian applicants, described in Chapter 3 and Appendix C of its final report. The Gutknecht quote comes from *Check Out the Odds,* a 1971 manual he coauthored through the Twin Cities Resistance. The Ford Foundation account of nonregistrants is taken from its 1974 report on amnesty, "Veterans, Deserters, and Draft-Evaders—The Vietnam Decade," p. 44. The Walker case is described in *Check Out the Odds.* The Minnesota survey of nonregistrants was conducted by the state selective service office, with findings published in the 1972 Senate Selective Service and Amnesty Hearings, p. 378.

The two-million nonregistrant estimate was made by former Attorney General Ramsey Clark, quoted in Richard Lyons, "Full Amnesty Apparently Has a Long Way to Go," in the January 25, 1976 *New York Times.* The "fools coming to our door" quote is from Woodstone, p. 73. The Census Bureau's undercounting of young men is explained in its publication "Evaluation and Research Program: Estimates of Coverage of Population by Sex, Race, and Age" (1975), pp. 29–30. The Hooton case comes from Gutknecht, *Check Out the Odds.* Data pertaining to the Justice Department's prosecution of nonregistrants come from Assistant Attorney General Henry Peterson's testimony before the 1974 House Amnesty Hearings, p. 37. The nonregistrant statute of limitations decisions are *Toussie* v. *U.S.,* 397 U.S. 112 (1970), and *U.S.* v. *Richardson,* 514 F.2d 105 (3d. Cir. 1975).

William Sessions' quote is from his testimony before the 1970 House Armed Services Hearings, pp. 12871–72. Statistics on declinations and dismissals in nondraft cases are taken from the Census Bureau's 1973 *Statistical Abstract of the United States,* p. 152. Curtis Tarr's contention was made on p. 44 of Selective Service's July 1972 *Semi-Annual Report.* Robert Mardian and Walter Morse made their contentions before hearings of the Senate Judiciary Committee, Subcommittee on Courts and Civil Liberties (1972), pp. 164 and 204. Stuart Loory's quote comes from his book *Defeated: Inside America's Military Machine,* p. 246. The *New York Times* survey was reported on April 16, 1971, and described in the 1972 Senate Selective Service and Amnesty Hearings, p. 464. The capitulating draft resister is quoted in Lynn, p. 111. The "our job is to prosecute draft dodgers" quote is from Judson Bowles, head of the Criminal Division's Selective Service unit, recounted in Woodstone, p. 65. The Justice Department's twelve-month sample of reasons for case closings is described in a letter from Kevin Maroney to Senator Edward Kennedy, reprinted in the Senate Subcommittee Report, p. 395. An additional analysis of dropped cases was made by John Schultz in his testimony before the 1975 House Presidential Clemency Program Hearings, pp. 96–97.

The Wheels of Justice

The Horn, orthodontist, Black, Ramirez, Johnson, Jackson, Blass, Allen, Wilson, Eckhart, Taliaferro, Greene, Craig, Daley, Hare Krishna, heroin addict, post office examinee, and disappointed law student cases all come from the Presidential Clemency Board's final report—cases 3–5, 3–13, 3–22, 3–7, 3–29, 3–33, 4–7, 3–37, 3–15, 4–6, 3–3, 3–4, 3–31, 3–36, 3–50, 3–52, 3–54, and 3–53, respectively. Data about the characteristics of convicted draft offenders are also taken from Chapter 3 and Appendix C of the Clemency Board's report. The Young Republican case comes from William Sessions' testimony in the 1970 House Armed Services Hearings, p. 12843. The FBI discovery of draft evasion organizations are described in "The Draft: The Unjust Versus the Unwilling," an article in the April 11, 1966 edition of *Newsweek*. The corrupt local board member story is from the "Draft Counselor's Handbook" of the Philadelphia-based Central Committee for Conscientious Objectors (CCCO). The Sisson case is cited as *U.S.* v. *Sisson,* 399 U.S. 267 (1970).

The Walker and Peters cases come from Polner, *When Can I Come Home?* pp. 165 and 116–17. The Lavelle case came from Lynd, pp. 100–103; the Wagler case from Gaylin, *In the Service of Their Country,* p. 274; the Jenkins and premature baby cases from Woodstone, pp. 39–40 and 58; the Tucker case from an oral presentation before the February 26, 1976 ad hoc Amnesty Day hearings in the United States Senate (unpublished); the James case in the April 17, 1974 New York *Post;* the Buford case in Willard Gaylin's testimony before the 1972 Senate Selective Service and Amnesty Hearings, p. 296; and the Halsted case in Sanders, *The Draft and the Vietnam War,* p. 81. The Justice Department's treatment of Muslims is described in a letter from J. Oscar Smith, quoted in Lynd, p. 233. The Clay (Muhammad Ali) quote also comes from Lynd, pp. 230–34. Sentencing statistics are taken from the annual reports of the Administrative Office of the U.S. Courts. The "threaten society," "opposed to conscription," "sacrifice to their principles," General Hershey, and Brooklyn judge quotes all come from "Sentencing Selective Service Violators: A Judicial Wheel of Fortune," *Columbia Journal of Law and Social Problems,* vol. 5, no. 2 (1969), pp. 190, 189, 175, and 174. The "Decline and Fall" quote is from O'Sullivan and Meckler. Kevin Maroney's quote comes from his testimony before the 1972 Senate Selective Service and Amnesty Hearings, p. 276.

The encouraging words about prison life come from Tatum and Tuchinsky, *Guide to the Draft,* p. 266, and from the Friends Peace Committee pamphlet quoted in the December 9, 1966 *Life* magazine. The "I am lonely," "who'd ever thought," "friends ask us," "massive mill wheels," and "duck the bullets" quotes all come from Lynd, pp. 107, 114, 52, 59, and 64, respectively. The Vincent McGee quote comes from his testimony before the 1972 Senate Selective Service and Amnesty Hearings, p. 342. The "jolly good felon" and "Antigone" quotes are from Chuck Noell in *We Are All POW's,* a book he coauthored with Gary Wood, pp. 266 and 32. The Morris and Jones cases and all other quotes from incarcerated draft resisters come from Gaylin, pp. 36, 59, 68, 84, 123, 129, 154, 157, 182, 212, 239, 274–75, 278, and 284.

IV | DESERTERS

Over the Hill

The description of desertion by the Senate Armed Services Committee is from the 1968 Senate report, *Treatment of Deserters from Military Service,* March 11, 1969, pp. 7–8. The reference to World War II deserters sentenced to death is from Barnes, *Pawns,* p. 280. The 100-troop disciplinary breakdown is from Cortright, *Soldiers in Revolt,* pp. 24–25. The Mason, Meaks, Morehead, and Nolan cases are taken from the final report of the Presidential Clemency Board, cases 3–81, 3–75, 3–74, and 4–31. The Gilman case is from Hayes, *American Deserters in Sweden,* p. 93. The Saunder case is from *Amex-Canada* magazine, vol. 2, no. 7, p. 9. The Gruening quote is from the 1974 House Amnesty Hearings, pp. 221–22. The references to Civil War deserters is from the Clemency Board's final report, p. 366. The data about World War II deserters are from Helmer, *Bringing the War Home,* p. 38, and originate in the clerk's office of the U.S. Army Judiciary. The figures for Vietnam-era courts-martial for desertion to avoid hazardous duty are from data supplied by the Court of Military Appeals, interviews with the U.S. Army Judiciary, and the Clemency Board's final report. The references to the difficulty of deserting in Vietnam are from Emerick, *War Resisters in Canada,* p. 161, and *Amex,* vol. 3, no. 4, p. 27. The estimate of deserters in "AWOL alley" is from *Amex,* vol. 4, No. 3, p. 39. The Hansen case is from Emerick, pp. 76–77.

The McAllen quote is from the 1972 Senate Selective Service and Amnesty Hearings, p. 338. The quote about the California missile base comes from Emerick, p. 86. The estimate of military families below the poverty level is derived from figures in the *Congressional Quarterly,* April 3, 1970, p. 931. The Steiger quote comes from Stuart Loory, *Defeated,* pp. 191–192. The number of congressional complaints is from hearings by the Special Subcommittee on Recruiting and Retention of the House Armed Services Committee, 92d Congress, p. 8117, quoted by Cortright, p. 23. The quote from the Ford clemency program comes from the Defense Department Joint Report to the Service Secretaries, p. IV-2, and the Clemency Board statistic appears on p. 127 of its report. The Smith and Watson cases are from Sherrill, *Military Justice Is to Justice as Military Music Is to Music,* pp. 30–31. The composite deserter is derived from data in the Clemency Board report and Bell and Houston, *The Vietnam Era Deserter,* a 1976 report for the Army Research Institute. The official AWOL film is described in Barnes, pp. 105–6. The official comparison of AWOL during the Korean and Vietnam wars is from the testimony of General Leo Benade, Deputy Assistant Secretary of Defense, in the 1974 House Amnesty Hearings, p. 540. The Vietnam deserter figures are from Cortright, p. 13. The frequency of absence offenses and their manpower equivalents are derived from data in the Senate Armed Services Committee report, pp. 24–25.

The Bottom Third

Much of the discussion in this chapter is based on Starr, *The Discarded Army,* pp. 185–97, and Barnes, pp. 66–68 and 258–59 (Matts case). The Peters case is from the Clemency Board report, case 3–62. The reference to Ginzburg's findings on high-school dropouts is from his *Patterns of Performance,* pp. 113–14. The discussion of pre-Vietnam military standards is from Gerhardt, *The Draft and Public Policy,* p. 220, and the Citizens Advisory Panel on Military Manpower Procurement, Report to the House Armed Services Committee, February 28, 1967, p. 9. The 1965 survey on black motivation for enlisting is from Little, *Selective Service and American Society,* p. 148. The Moynihan quotes are taken from Morris, *Why Draft Repeal?* p. 110, and Starr, p. 186. The General Nickerson and *Army Times* quotes are also from Starr, pp. 185 and 191–92. The Grant case is from Sherrill, p. 25. The Polner quote is from pp. 80–81 of his book *No Victory Parades.* The characteristics of Project 100,000 men are taken from Barnes, pp. 66–68; the Clemency Board report, Chapter 3; and Bell and Houston, *The Vietnam Era Deserter,* a 1976 Army Research Institute report. The 1964 study of Category IV military assignments is from Cortright, p. 195. Disciplinary problems of Category IV troops are from Sherrill, pp. 219–22; Clemency Board data; and 1972 House Defense Appropriations Hearings, p. 582. Data on post-Vietnam levels of Category IV are from Roger Kelley. The quote from Colonel Hays is from Tax, *The Draft,* p. 15.

Kooks, Heads, Brothers

Much of the material in this chapter comes from Haynes Johnson and George Wilson's *Army in Anguish.* The quotations that begin the chapter are from p. 116; the Froehlke quote is from p. 154; the references by the employee at the Vietnam rehabilitation center are from pp. 26–27; the quotes about black attitudes by the battalion commander and at the counseling session in Germany appear at pp. 37–38 and 48–49; and the quote about black views of military justice as white racism is from p. 47.

The general's description of Vietnam-era soldiers as "kooks" is from Finn, *Conscience and Command,* p. 15. The Cortright quote, the data on daily heroin usage in Vietnam in 1971, the discussion of drug treatment programs, and the references to the Black Caucus and NAACP racial survey are all from Cortright, pp. 31, 156, 174–75, and 207–13. The quote from Ward Just and the rest of that paragraph are taken from his book *Military Men,* p. 73. The data on marijuana usage are from a report of the Human Relations Research Organization, "Survey of Drug Abuse," pp. 72–78. The Harris survey is from Helmer, p. 190. The quote from the drug counselor comes from an article by Linden in the *Saturday Review* of January 8, 1972. The costs of marijuana and the statistics on drug enforcement in Vietnam are from the report of Army Judge Advocate General George Prugh, *Law at War,* pp. 106–7. The figures on pot smoking in 1967 and 1971 and the study of the demographics of addicts are from Helmer, pp. 75 and 87. The paragraph on alcoholism is from Loory, p. 204. The 1972 data on the usage and cost of heroin in Vietnam and the U.S. are from the *Congressional Quarterly* of January 22, 1972, pp. 145–46. The data on the Laird drug discharge upgrade program is from Glass, "Defense Report," in the *National Journal* of August 8, 1970, p. 1776. General Kerwin's quote comes from 1972 House Defense Appropriations Hearings, p. 571.

The pejorative description of black soldiers is from Glick, *Soldiers, Scholars and Society*, pp. 28–29. The 1971 Department of Defense racial survey is cited in the *Congressional Quarterly*, September 18, 1971 at p. 1943. The Urban League reference is from the testimony of Ronald Brown at the 1974 House Amnesty Hearings, pp. 411–12. The references to the Defense Department *Task Force Report on Military Justice* are from vol. I, p. 32, and vol. II, p. 14.

Vietnam and Back

The "tore the fabric" quote is from General Walter Kerwin in his testimony during the 1972 House Defense Appropriations Hearings, p. 554. The survey of attitudes toward the war is from Starr, *The Discarded Army*, p. 23, and the Polner quote appears on p. 36 of *No Victory Parades*. The Pacek story appears in *We Are All POW's* by Chuck Noell and Gary Wood, pp. 24–25. The material on prosecutions for antiwar activity is from Polner, pp. 98, 105–12. The Chadwick, Hodgkins, Dantlee, Cutter, Rainwater, McKuen, Jollie, Stokes, and Barajian cases are all taken from the Clemency Board final report, cases 3-78, 3-77, 3-92, 4-37, 3-83, 3-89, 3-93, 3-91, 4-70, and 7, respectively.

The statistics on fragging between 1969 and 1971 and the example of the general's parade are from Johnson and Wilson, pp. 92, 110–11. The raid on the officers' club and the quote that follows are taken from Linden's article in the *Saturday Review* of January 8, 1972. The story of the company that refused to retrieve the documents is from Hauser, *America's Army in Crisis*, p. 99. The Starr quote appears on p. 28 and the Emerick quote on pp. 161–62 of their respective books. The Cannille and Rathbone stories are from Barnes, p. 258, and Williams, *The New Exiles*, pp. 296–97 and 304. The Johnson story is from Killmer, *They Can't Go Home Again*, p. 81. The Lee story is from an article by Austin Scott, "Deserters Live Openly in the U.S.," in the Washington *Post* of October 12, 1974. The Johnson-Wilson quote appears on p. 73 of their book. The quote about military deserters processed under the Ford program is from the Defense Department *Report to the Service Secretaries*, p. IV-4. The Barnes quote appears on p. 124 of his book.

Canceling Them Out

The Shoup story is related in Sherrill, pp. 218–19. The 1971 study is *Leadership and Situational Factors Related to AWOL*, by McCubbin, U.S. Army CTF, Ft. Riley, Kansas, p. ii. The Westmoreland quote is cited in Johnson and Wilson, p. 81, and the Kerwin quote is from the 1972 House Defense Appropriations Hearings on Department of Defense Appropriations, p. 603. The references to young officers' attitudes toward the war is from Johnson and Wilson, pp. 119–20. General Berg's "cancel . . . out" quote is from the 1968 Senate Deserter Hearings, p. 66. The summary history of the military discharge system is from Admiral John Finneran's testimony of November 5, 1975, before the House Armed Services Committee (unpublished). The defense of the characterized discharge system was made by General Leo Benade, quoted in Frederick Smalkin's "Administrative Separations: The Old Order Changeth," Department of Army pamphlet 27–50–17. The reference to the deterrent effect of bad discharges is from the 1971 McCubbin study, p. 26. The quote from the *Report of the Task Force on Military Justice* appears at p. 33 of Vol. II. Leo Benade's explanation of the SPN system is from the 1974 House Amnesty Hearings, p. 542. The list of SPNs is reprinted in the *ACLU Practice Manual on Discharge Upgrading* by Addlestone and Hewman, p. 293. The quote by the Macy's representative is from Congressman John Downey's testimony at the 1975 House Armed Services Hearings. The veteran's story that follows is from testimony at the 1974 House Amnesty Hearings, p. 289. The figures on the disparity of discharges are from the *Task Force Report,* p. 355.

The Banks, Dodson, Sanders, Barnes, and Cook cases are taken from the Clemency Board report, cases 3–114, 3–121, 4–36, 3–116, and 3–117, respectively. The Duke case is from Loory, p. 200. Data pertaining to employer discrimination against veterans with bad discharges are from the Clemency Board report, p. 403. The NCO's gripe is from Johnson and Wilson, pp. 131–33. The observation on the difficulty of trials in Vietnam is from *Law at War,* p. 198. The statistics on Army Chapter 10 discharges are from the Department of Defense Office of Manpower and Reserve Affairs, reprinted in Baskir and Strauss, *Reconciliation After Vietnam,* p. 123. The Army warning against excessive use of Chapter 10's is from a *New York Times* story of September 10, 1972, quoted in *Amex,* vol. 3, No. 6, p. 40. The quote about undesirable discharges is from Fred Halstead, *GI's Speak Out,* a CCCO reprint, pp. 46–47. The story of the two GIs from Sweden comes from "Guide for the AWOL GI," a CCCO pamphlet. The comparison between undesirable discharges and punitive discharges is derived from unpublished Clemency Board statistics.

V | EXILES

On the Run

The flight of 80,000 Tories is described in Duscha, "Amnesty," in the December 24, 1972, *New York Times Magazine,* p. 15. Descriptions of the Udall and Agnew nephews are presented in *Amex-Canada* magazine, vol. 2, no. 6, p. 25, and vol. 2, no. 3, p. 20. Data about the proportion of draft and military offenders who took flight come from Chapter 3 of the Presidential Clemency Board's final report. The "self-retired veterans" quote comes from *Amex,* vol. 3, no. 4, p. 37. The listing of the positions of trust held by fugitive deserters comes from the Fort Harrison *Report to the Service Secretaries* (on the implementation of Presidential Proclamation 4313), p. VII-w.

The $25 bounty for captured deserters is described in Franks, *Waiting Out a War,* p. 214. The Berkeley City Council's asylum policy is mentioned in Loory, *The Defeated,* p. 250. The Seattle steelworker case comes from Fialka, Washington *Star,* Oct. 6, 1974; the oil wildcatter case from Scott, Washington *Post,* Oct. 12, 1974; and the termite case from Woodstone, *Up Against the War,* p. 80. The Santa Claus case, "little Canada," and the government's prosecution of those who "enticed" desertion are discussed in *Amex,* vol. 2, no. 2, p. 8; vol. 3, no. 7, p. 49; and vol. 2, no. 4, p. 25. The San Francisco "GI Help" program is described in Ferber and Lynd, *The Resistance,* pp. 231–32. The "deserter inducement programs" quote comes from Major Donald Kennedy's testimony at the 1968 Senate Military Deserters hearings.

Taking Exile

The capsule descriptions of Brazil, Haiti, and Venezuela come from Schiller and Leblanc, *Exiled,* pp. 11–15. The "brain drain" comment comes from a Canadian immigration official quoted in Woodstone, p. 92. The Mitchell Sharp quote is from *Amex,* vol. 1, no. 7, p. 8. The "frontier" and "big beautiful jail" quotes come from Lynd, *We Won't Go,* pp. 115–19. The Danielson, Csikor, Peters, and Swedish hijacking cases are all from *Amex,* vol. 5, no. 6; vol. 2, no. 2, p. 14; vol. 2, no. 2, p. 14; and vol. 2, no. 9, p. 14. Canadian immigration rules are described in Harrop Freeman's testimony before the 1972 Senate Selective Service and Amnesty Hearings, pp. 452–55, and Tatum and Tuchinsky, *Guide to the Draft,* p. 239. The "checking into a hotel" quote comes from "Amnesty for War Exiles," *Newsweek,* Jan. 17, 1972. The advertisement for Canadian women is described in *Amex,* vol. 2, no. 8, p. 29. The number of illegal immigrants amnestied in 1972 comes from an oral report from the Canadian Embassy in Washington, D.C.

The account of draft-avoiding Swedes, the story of the one-way SAS passenger, the Dodson case, the quotes from Swedish officials, and the description of welfare benefits for newly arriving exiles in Sweden are all from Hayes, *American Deserters in Sweden,* pp. 41–42, 100, and 141. The "live like human beings," "Al Capone," and "partying" quotes come from Whitmore, *Memphis-Nam-Sweden,* p. 169. The exile delegation to Denmark is described in Franks, p. 151. The accusation that Sweden was "subsidizing" desertion comes from the 1968 Senate *Treatment of Deserters* Report, p. 12.

Richard Nixon's "those few hundreds" quote is taken from the 1974 House Amnesty Hearings, p. 729, and the 100,000 estimate comes from materials submitted by the Amnesty Committee of the Center for Pursuit of Peace in the 1974 House Amnesty Hearings, p. 622. The triple-exile (Israeli volunteer) story comes from "Amnesty Plan —Story of Two Local Men," Ann Arbor *News,* August 17, 1975. Holland's subsidy for draft resisters, Australian and Vietnamese exiles in Canada, the "Bobby Kennedy" quote, the violent radical quote, the Puerto Rican accused murderer case, the antiwar editors in Canada, and the *Life* magazine case all come from *Amex:* vol. 2, no. 4, p. 13; vol. 2, no. 5, p. 23; vol. 2, no. 8, p. 5; vol. 2, no. 6, p. 17; vol. 3, no. 6, p. 53; and vol. 2, no. 3, p. 29. The four deserter categories are described in Loh, "An Analysis of Amnesty,"

Journal of Social Issues, vol. 31 (1975), p. 158. The Brooks case and the fact that one-third of all exiles qualified for deferments come from Emerick, *War Resisters in Canada,* pp. 72 and 81. The Britt and Sheehan cases are from Williams, *The New Exiles,* p. 337. The Brophy quote is taken from the 1972 Senate Selective Service and Amnesty Hearings, p. 319. The fact that half of all deserters never asked for help before leaving is from Bell and Houston, *The Vietnam Era Deserter,* a report of the Army Research Institute, July 1976.

American-Canadians and American-Swedes

The 'rɔrawa clave" quote, the vitriolic family letter, the "brand new kind of immigrant' quote, the Toronto *Daily Star* editorial, the *McQueen* and *Explosion* episodes, the "pigs" quote, the Toronto *Telegram* editorials, the Dow chemical demonstration, the "vicious whispered lobbying" quote, and the "draft dodger chauvinism" quote all come from *Amex:* vol. 2, no. 7, p. 13; vol. 2, no. 3, p. 27; vol. 2, no. 7, p. 7; vol. 2, no. 7, p. 6; vol. 2, no. 2, p. 23; vol. 2, no. 4, p. 25; vol. 2, no. 9, p. 5; vol. 2, no. 6, p. 14; vol. 2, no. 2, p. 5; and vol. 2, no. 9, p. 6. The Levine quote comes from Levine, "American Exiles in Canada: A Social and Psychological Follow Up," *Psychiatric Opinion,* November 1974, p. 24. The descriptions of vagabond life, Swedish antiwar sentiment, Swedish headlines, magazine quotes, and fast cars and unleashed dogs come from Franks, pp. 104 and 163–72. The facts about criminal activity and deportation come from Pat Buchanan, "The Facts on Exiles," *New York Times,* February 20, 1973 (quoting William Leth, Swedish Director of Immigration). The "stay cool" quote is from Whitmore, p. 185. The five suicides are described in Hayes, p. 190; Franks, p. 188; and *Amex,* vol. 2, no. 6, p. 24, and vol. 2, no. 9, p. 26.

Coming Home

The "American Dream" quote comes from Noell and Wood, *We Are All POW's,* p. 43. The Molotov-cocktails discussion and "rebellion against authority" quote are in Taylor, "Draft Dodgers in Canada," *The Reporter,* May 2, 1968. The cancellation of the Nixon trip, the story of the Blaine siege, the "Ho Chi Minh Trail," the Poirrot case, and the Kallen and First letters are from *Amex:* vol. 3, no. 4, p. 13; vol. 6, no. 6, p. 12; vol. 3, no. 6, p. 38; vol. 3, no. 5, p. 4; vol. 3, no. 7, p. 4. The Brasile case is from "Amnesty for War Exiles," *Newsweek,* Jan. 17, 1972. Operation CHAOS is described in the 1976 Senate report, *Intelligence Activities and the Rights of Americans,* pp. 99–102. The Brown case is described in Franks, pp. 57–58, and the Lovett case in Whitmore, p. 144. American embassy activities in Sweden, the China deserter case, the fate of the 20 exiled deserters, the $15 fine, the Inouye quote, the Fitt quote, and the fact that only 2 of the 20 returning exiles were sent to Vietnam are all from the 1968 Senate Military Deserters hearings, testimony from Alfred Fitt (Defense Department), Frederick Smith (State Department), and Commander Carlton Wilgus (Navy), pp. 5, 26, 41, and 65. The critical reaction to the Brown case comes from the 1968 Senate *Treatment of Deserters* Report, p. 19. The fact that fewer than 150 former exiles went to military prison comes from the 1971 House Administrative Discharges Hearings, p. 5872. The discharges *in absentia* are described in a written submission from General Leo Benade in the 1972 Senate Selective Service and Amnesty Hearings, p. 385. The Tatum quote comes from Tatum and Tuchinsky, p. 233. The calculation that 13,000 cases were dropped comes from a survey of about 3,000 telephone inquiries received by the clemency information center in the weeks following the list's release. The "tears of rage" quote is from John Schultz's testimony before the House Subcommittee on Courts and Civil Liberties, p. 205. The immigration statute barring reentry of aliens who avoided military service is U.S.C. App. 1182(a) (22). The "Man, it'll weight you down" quote is from Hayes, p. 43.

VI | AMNESTY

Morality and Mythology

The Australian amnesty experience is from "The Australian Clemency Program" by Wil Ebel in Appendix G of the Clemency Board's Final Report, pp. 379 ff. Tom Hayden's call for amnesty and the exiles' responses are from *Amex-Canada*, vol. 2, no. 4, p. 10, and vol. 2, no. 5, p. 3. The Swedish exile's observation is quoted in Hayes, *American Deserters in Sweden*, p. 46. The 1972 *Amex* proamnesty quote is from vol. 3, no. 4, pp. 44–45. The "moral point" quote is from former Oregon Congressman Charles Porter, who headed a group called "Amnesty Now," quoted in *Newsweek* of January 17, 1972. The "powerful tool" quote is from Shank, "Amnesty: Remembering the Past" in *Win* magazine, November 13, 1975. The "principled fight" *Amex* quote is from vol. 5, no. 3. The activist's quote on the larger significance of amnesty is from *Amex*, vol. 3, no. 6, p. 5. The "centrist core" quote is from William Yolton's testimony in the 1974 House Amnesty Hearings, p. 717. Mary McGrory's observation is from her column of March 12, 1974. The Agnew comments are from his remarks at a VFW congressional dinner of March 6, 1973; a VFW national convention on August 25, 1972; a Lincoln's Day dinner quoted in *Amex*, vol. 3, no. 7, p. 23; and a statement of February 10, 1970, cited in Lifton, *Home from the War*, pp. 369–71. Richard Nixon's "most immoral thing" quote and Agnew's "malcontents" quote are from Lifton, *Home from the War*, pp. 369–71. Bella Abzug's and Charles Colson's remarks are from the March 11, 1973 issue of the Baltimore *Sun*, and Pat Buchanan's comments from "The Facts on Exiles" in the February 20, 1973 *New York Times*. The Legion spokesman is John Geiger, former national commander, testifying at the 1972 Senate Selective Service and Amnesty Hearings, p. 242. Hempstone's column is from the Washington *Star* of March 20, 1974. The origins of Senator Taft's bill are described in the May 5, 1972 *Saturday Review*. Nixon's comment on the "Peace Corps junket" is quoted in the 1974 House Amnesty Hearings, p. 697. Froehlke's position is documented in his testimony before the 1974 House Amnesty Hearings, p. 371, and Laird's position in a letter to VFW Commander Ray Soden, reprinted in the 1974 House Amnesty Hearings, p. 339.

Clemency, Not Amnesty

Information regarding the formulation and operation of the final clemency program is largely based on the personal observations of the authors; the Clemency Board final report; the report to the service secretaries of the (Defense Department) Joint Alternative Service Board (April 11, 1975); the *After Action Report* by the Office of the Army Deputy Chief of Staff for Personnel (October, 1975); the hearings by the 1974 House Presidential Clemency Program Hearings and Report; and the General Accounting Office's 1977 report on the clemency program.

President Ford's speech to the VFW Chicago convention outlining his intentions on clemency was on August 19, 1974. On September 16, 1974, he sent a message to the VFW national commander further explaining his program. The "very serious crimes" quote is from the November 1974 issue of *Amex.* The excerpts from the Clemency Board report appear on page 1. The *Post* and *Bulletin* comments appear in their editorials of September 18, 1974. The comment by the draft resister's mother is from *Newsweek,* September 30, 1974. The material on the Truman board comes from its final report, reprinted in the 1974 Senate Clemency Program Practices and Procedures Hearings on p. 255, and from Harrop Freeman's "Amnesty Now," a CCCO pamphlet. The survey on knowledge of eligibility for the program is described in the Clemency Board's final report, pp. 20–23. Attorney General Saxbe's comment is cited in an article by Robert Seeley, "No Amnesty," a CCCO pamphlet. The draft resister's criticism of the program is from Noell and Woods, *We Are All POW's,* p. 10. President Ford's observation on the results of his program was made to a group of Durham, New Hampshire, students on February 8, 1975. Chairman Goodell's observations were made at his press conference of January 15, 1976. The San Diego exile's comments are from a letter to a 1975 issue of *Playboy* magazine. Hoffman's warning is from his news conference of October 3, 1974, reprinted in the *New York Times* of October 7, 1974. The Walters case was related in Senate Ad Hoc Amnesty Day Hearings, February 26, 1975. The surrendering draft exile's experiences appeared in *Newsweek,* September 30, 1974. The Arizona resolution is number 2004, filed April 10, 1975. The Palm Beach story is related in Noell and Woods, p. 79.

Vernon Jordan's comment was published in "Amnesty Still an Issue," an Urban League column reprinted by the National Council for Universal, Unconditional Amnesty. The estimate of the overall cost of the Clemency Board was disclosed in an interview with an official of the Office of Management and Budget. The White House claim of executive privilege on the GAO inquiry is alluded to in the GAO report, p. 2. The Gallup poll results are reprinted in the Clemency Board report, p. 389. President Ford's remark on his program came in an interview in *Newsweek,* October 4, 1976. The new demands of the amnesty groups are from *Amex,* vol. 5, no. 3, 1974. James Wagonseller's comment appears in the *Congressional Quarterly,* September 20, 1974. President

Ford's exchange with Jane Hart and his later clemency order are related in the Washington *Post* of December 29, 1976, and January 19, 1977.

Blanket Pardons

The resolution of the AUSA was reported in the *Army Times* article "Clemency Board Seen as King," September 25, 1974. The "amnesty" versus "pardon" debate is best explained in the Supreme Court case of *Burdick* v. *U.S.*, 236 U.S. 79 (1915), and the *New Republic* of June 26, 1976. Carter's Iowa remarks are reprinted in a March, 1976 compilation of campaign statements issued by his campaign office. His "get the Vietnamese war over with" and "defecting from military service" statements are reprinted in the Washington *Post* editorial of January 9, 1977. The Hart quote and Howard Johnson's place mat are described in "The Truth about Deserters," a CCCO pamphlet. The inclusion of deserters in the amnesty issue was discussed in the testimony of Amherst professor Henry Steele Commager at the 1972 Senate Selective Service and Amnesty Hearings, p. 182. Carter's discussion with the *Post* editors is included in that paper's editorial of January 9, 1977. The debate at the Democratic Platform Committee is summarized in the *New Republic*, June 26, 1976. Carter's promise of a blanket pardon came in his American Legion speech of August 24, 1976, and Dole's reply came at the same forum on the following day. Reactions to Carter's early intentions are described in the *New York Times* of August 26, 1976.

The preinauguration report that Carter would include military offenders appeared in ι   *k Times* of December 17, 1976. *Pravda*'s comment was reported on CBS radio on January 30, 1977. The reactions of Goldwater, the Republican National Committee, the VFW, and the amnesty community are quoted in the *New York Times* of January 22, 1977, the Washington *Post* of February 3, 1977, and the January 31, 1977 issue of *Newsweek.* The tally of pardon certificate requests comes from the U.S. pardon attorney's office, and the tally of returning exiles from the Immigration and Naturalization Service. All other tallies come from the Washington *Post* of October 5, 1977.

The Next War

Congressman Dorn's remark is quoted in the *Congressional Quarterly,* October 14, 1972, p. 2663, and Congressman Montgomery's in the *Congressional Record* of January 11, 1977, p. 11268. Kirbo's comment was related by a participant at the meeting. The Mennonite position is in a written statement submitted to the 1972 Senate Selective Service and Amnesty Hearings, p. 102. The Gillette case is cited as *Gillette* v. *U.S.*, 401 U.S. 437 (1971). The Gates report is formally known as the *Report of the President's Commission on an All-Volunteer Armed Force,* February 20, 1971. The Hauser quote is from his book *America's Army in Crisis,* pp. 158–59.

The costs of separating modern-day soldiers were estimated by Roger Kelley, former assistant secretary of defense for manpower. Category IV information is from the Commission's Defense Manpower report, p. 159, and Dr. William King's February 1977 report to the Senate Armed Services Committee, "Achieving America's Goals: Rational Service or the All-Volunteer Armed Force?" pp. 15 and 25. Information about the operation of the discharge review boards was obtained through interviews with Defense Department officials. Future manpower levels, current black representation in the volunteer army, and reserve problems are described in the Defense Manpower Commission's report, pp. 160 and 387, and "Achieving America's Goals," pp. 18 and 23. The Commission's "sudden major hostilities" quote comes from p. 427 of its report. Brehm's observation appears in the 1976 House Selective Service System Hearings, pp. 2 and 169. The Vietnam generation's attitudes about the draft and military are taken from the Notre Dame survey. The plans for the 1976 registration and Byron Pepitone's comment on the impact of a return to the draft are from personal interviews. Current contingency plans for emergency mobilization and the account of World War I and II registration campaigns are taken from the testimony of Byron Pepitone and Congressman Robert Drinan before the 1976 House Armed Services Hearings, pp. 28 and 104. The Bingham plan is described in his testimony in the 1970 House Armed Services Hearings, p. 12763. The figures for high school drop-outs come from a Department of Defense press release of November 15, 1977.

VII | LEGACIES

The Noell quote is from p. 82 of *We Are All POW's,* which he coauthored with Gary Wood. The Chicano's comment is from the Washington *Post* of January 23, 1977, and the Ohio veteran's is from Johnson and Wilson, *Army in Anguish,* p. 117. The "Harry" and "Resist the Draft" quotes are from Polner, *No Victory Parades,* pp. 77 and 29. The quotes from Starr and Bourne appear in Starr, *The Discarded Army,* pp. 33 and 35. Correia's and Foote's recollections are from personal communications with the authors; Fallows' story originally appeared at greater length in his article "What Did You Do in the Class War, Daddy," in the *Washington Monthly* of October 1975, and has been excerpted with his permission.

Figure 1: Vietnam Generation

[1]The Vietnam generation is defined to include anyone who was of draft-eligible age during the Vietnam war. Draft-eligible age is defined as 19, the age at which induction was possible, and up to (but not including) 26, the age at which induction was no longer a threat to anyone other than medical specialists. Specifically, those who were ages 23 through 38 on June 30, 1977, are considered part of the Vietnam generation. It should be noted that 18-year-olds did fight in Vietnam, but because of the phased pullout of American troops during 1972 and 1973, it is unlikely that more than a very few were to be part of the Vietnam generation as defined here. A much larger number of older

military personnel served in Vietnam, and they are excluded from the statistics wherever possible.

²These base statistics come from data in the *Statistical Abstract of the United States* (1973), Table 35, p. 31. To the base figures in the *Statistical Abstract* must be added 1.15%, to include those who died before the census was taken. According to the Census Bureau's "Estimates of Coverage of Population by Sex, Race, and Age: Demographic Analysis" (February 1974), the 1970 census undercounted the 16–31 male population by 860,000–960,000 and the 16–31 female population by about half that amount. To account for this underenumeration problem, the "men" and "women" tallies are augmented by 900,000 and 450,000, respectively.

³This is an error factor that cannot be accounted for elsewhere. Some of the statistics shown in these charts are quite precise, while others are extrapolations from a limited amount of clear evidence. The fact that the error factor shown here is small (0.5%) does not mean that all other statistics are nearly correct; it simply means that if one statistic is too high, another must be too low.

⁴Historical data are included from July 1, 1960, assuming that the average individual was drafted during his twenty-first year in the early 1960s. From July 1, 1964, through July 1, 1973, 1,773,000 were drafted. The others were drafted before then, some serving during the Vietnam war. *Selected Manpower Statistics,* DOD-OASD (Comptroller), May 1975, pp. 51–54.

⁵See Figure 3.

⁶See Figure 6.

⁷See *Selected Manpower Statistics,* p. 108, and *Statistical Abstract of the United States* (1973), Table 447, p. 275. National Guard and reserves computations assume 19-year-old enlistments, so historical data from July 1, 1959, are used.

⁸See Figure 2.

⁹See Figure 4.

¹⁰See Figure 8.

¹¹No comprehensive data of any kind can enumerate nonregistrants. Most efforts to measure them have used census data, but the analysis is very unconvincing. Many— perhaps most—of the individuals who never registered for the draft are the same ones who are never counted by the census. The only alternative to analyzing aggregate statistics is to sample. A sample of 1,586 males of formerly draft-eligible age was surveyed in Washington, D.C., South Bend, and Ann Arbor; roughly one-fourth of the respondents were blacks or members of other minority groups. That sample found a number of nonregistrants, distributed racially as follows:

white	0.6%
black	3.9%
other	1.7%

When these percentages are applied to overall racial data for the United States, it appears that the numbers of nonregistrants, by racial group, are as follows:

white 130,000
black 110,000
other 10,000

It should be noted that the questionnaires of nonregistrants were carefully scrutinized to assure the authenticity of the response (e.g., to screen out cases of individuals who never registered for the draft because they enlisted at a young age, or draft-ineligible aliens who were not required to register). For base racial data, see *Statistical Abstract of the United States* (1973), Table 32, p. 30.

[12]Similar data about unreported draft offenses were obtained through these questionnaires. Five such individuals were found, all of them white. Two had destroyed their draft cards, two had refused induction, and one had failed to perform alternative service as a condition of conscientious objection. This enables an estimate of 110,000 unreported draft offenders to be derived. See *ibid.* for base data.

[13]See *Selected Manpower Statistics.* The number has been derived by extrapolation and comparison with other military manpower data in that same volume. It appears that roughly 190,000 served during the Vietnam era and 60,000 before the Vietnam era. These numbers are inexact, because separate enlistment and discharge data could not be found for each year of the period.

[14]These official statistics were obtained from Women's Affairs Division of the Department of Defense Public Affairs Office.

[15]At the Clemency Board, approximately 0.1% of all applicants with bad discharges were women. At the Ft. Harrison (DOD) clemency program, 0.14% were women. These proportions indicate that women may have received about 500 of the 563,000 less-than-Honorable discharges of the Vietnam era.

[16]All of these are derivative, calculated by adding or subtracting all other displayed statistics from the appropriate base statistics.

Figure 2: Civilian Avoiders

[1]The Vietnam generation is defined here to include individuals aged 19 to 34 on June 30, 1973, yet the last persons to face induction were those who turned 20 during the 1972 calendar year. Although the 3,020,000 persons who turned 19 after January 1, 1972, could have joined the military and gone to Vietnam, possibly spurred by draft pressure, none would have been drafted. Apparently, 165,000 guardsmen and reservists and 310,000 active duty personnel belonged to this age group. The remainder, 2,545,-000, avoided military service because of their young age. See *Statistical Abstract of the United States* (1973), Table 81, p. 59, and *Selected Manpower Statistics,* pp. 38 and 108.

²This assumes that 21 was the average age of induction throughout the era. Accidents accounted for most of these deaths. For base data, see *Statistical Abstract of the United States* (1973), Table 81, p. 59.

³This tally was derived through computations based upon the statistics in the *Semi-Annual Reports* of the Director of Selective Service throughout the lottery years (1970–1972). Table 4 in each issue lists the total number of registrants, and enables a number of calculations to be made. When one subtracts the number overage or underage, presently or formerly in military service, deferred or exempted for any reason, unclassified, or in a holding classification, one can determine the number of I-A registrants vulnerable to the draft. For example, in 1970 there were 1,175,000 such individuals. In 1970, the lottery cutoff was 195, so one can conclude that those with higher numbers—47% of all those in the eligible pool—were not drafted because of their high lottery numbers. Comparable analysis was done for each year, based upon its lottery cutoff.

⁴The number of individuals with vulnerable lottery numbers (125 and below) who were benefited by this loophole cannot be exactly ascertained, but one measure is available. Using the same analysis described in note 3, one can trace the impact of the draft on all persons with I-A status on December 31, 1971. Only 153,000 were drafted in 1971 out of 1,132,000 persons with vulnerable lottery numbers who were classified I-A. After one accounts for unsuccessful induction attempts, active appeals, and draft-induced enlistments (which can be estimated as the same proportion of draft calls in 1971 as in 1969, 1970, and 1972), 633,000 individuals escaped the draft for no accountable reason. They were the apparent beneficiaries of the "lottery loophole."

⁵*Semi-Annual Report of the Director of Selective Service,* January–June 1973, App. 8 (p. 52) and App. 13 (p. 55). The tally shown includes rejections from July 1, 1960, through June 30, 1973; this assumes that the typical individual is examined during his twenty-first year. Age statistics are not widely available, but see *ibid.,* p. 54. The tally also assumes that IV-F and I-Y exemptions, once given, are not rescinded. They could be rescinded, but this was very rarely done during the Vietnam war. The rejections at the induction station usually involved volunteers who had never taken preinduction physical exams, but some individuals failed their induction physicals after having passed their preinduction physicals.

⁶Year-by-year breakdowns of the reasons for disqualification were not available, but good cross-sectional data existed for July–December of 1969 in the *Semi-Annual Report of the Director of Selective Service,* July–December, 1969, Table 5, p. 19. Data for the 1950–69 period is available in the same table, but it would include too much extraneous data. With a 46% preinduction rejection rate and a 19% induction rejection rate, 1969 was close enough to the mean for the Vietnam era to give some validity to its cross-sectional data. See the appendices cited in note 1.

⁷A "moral" defect includes evidence of prior association with subversive organizations, substantial criminal record, prior discharge from the military under other than

honorable conditions, or related reasons making an individual "not qualified for administrative reason(s)." *Ibid.*, p. 19.

[8]Assuming that the typical individual received the exemption during his twenty-first year, data from July 1, 1960 through June 30, 1973 are used for I-O classifications. *Semi-Annual Report of the Director of Selective Service*, January–June, 1975, App. 27, p. 82.

[9]Conscientious objectors were classified I-O and then reclassified I-W if they began performing alternative service. Selective Service data indicate that 59% of all conscientious objectors completed alternative service. To account for two years of alternative service, data from July 1, 1963 through June 30, 1976 are used (including the 124 individuals still doing alternative service on the latter date). *Semi-Annual Report of the Director of Selective Service*, January–June, 1975, App. 27, p. 82.

[10]It is very difficult to ascertain how many individuals failed to complete an obligation of alternative service. Before 1970, it must be assumed that all conscientious objectors had an obligation to perform alternative service, because all would have otherwise been inducted (aside from the occasional case of incipient hardship or physical defect which would warrant reclassification). After the draft lottery, many conscientious objectors did not have to perform alternative service because of high lottery numbers. An eight-month sample of 110,000 conscientious objectors with lottery numbers indicated that 43% of them had lottery numbers sufficiently high to free them from an alternative service obligation. *Semi-Annual Report of the Director of Selective Service*, January–June, 1971, p. 58. This percentage did not vary much between 1969 (when the cutoff number was 195) and 1970 (when the cutoff was 125). Assuming this same percentage for all conscientious objectors from January 1970 through June 1973, one can estimate that 29,300 individuals did not have to perform alternative service. As a consequence, it appears that some 46,000 were not certified as having fulfilled their apparent obligations. No other statistics can be found that bear upon this question. It should be noted that some local boards may simply have failed to reclassify individuals as I-W upon their completion of alternative service—but enough case examples of non-performance exist to suggest that many thousands may not have fulfilled this obligation.

[11]According to Clemency Board statistics, 13.4% of its civilian applicants had been convicted of failing to complete alternative service. Applying this percentage to the 8,750 convicted draft offenders shown in Figure 4, one gets the result shown. No statistics are available to indicate how many Selective Service complaints to the Department of Justice about nonperforming conscientious objectors did not result in convictions.

[12]Graduate student deferments were available only to students who had completed at least one year of graduate school by the end of the 1966–67 school year. In order for a graduate student deferment to be a means of escape from the draft, it was usually necessary to have one for three years (to take an individual beyond—or very close to —the age of 26). The statistic presented here assumes that the only male students who could have enjoyed this escape valve without later having to shift to other deferments

were those who completed law school between 1965 and 1969 or received Ph.D.s between 1965 and 1970. Excluding women, 69,000 law degrees and 115,000 Ph.D.s were issued during those years. See "Legal Education: A Time of Change," *American Bar Association Journal,* Volume 62, March 1967, and the *Statistical Abstract of the United States* (1973), Department of Commerce, Tables 217–18, pp. 136–37.

[13]Millions of men used college deferments to postpone their confrontations with the draft, but the only individuals who permanently escaped the draft through college deferments were students who entered college in the fall of 1969 and 1970 (the classes of 1973 and 1974) who did not have high lottery numbers or any other exemptions. Selective Service records indicate that a surprisingly small number had student deferments in December of 1972, the last month of the lottery. *Semi-Annual Report of the Director of Selective Service,* July–December, 1972, Table 1, p. 20.

[14]Prior to 1972, ministry students were accorded ministerial exemptions; thereafter, they received ministry student deferments. (See note 16 for the means of calculating their numbers.)

[15]The number of elected officials deferred from the draft to serve in state or national office fluctuated very little during the latter years of the war, indicating that the same 85 individuals may have benefited from this deferment throughout the war.

[16]To understand these occupational deferment calculations (and the alien and hardship calculations, notes 17 and 20), two points must be recognized. First, if an individual had a deferment or an exemption at age 26, he was almost never reclassified or removed from the rolls by his draft board until he reached age 35. (This was also true for those who received physical, mental, psychiatric, or moral exemptions.) Second, after June 30, 1970, draft boards began reclassifying individuals with high lottery numbers as I-H (holding classification), regardless of their earlier classifications. As a consequence, June 30, 1970, data is the most useful for calculating deferment or exemption totals. Also, on April 23, 1970, President Nixon issued an executive order preventing new occupational and dependency deferments—but the old ones still could be kept.

One can make an accurate estimate of the number of Vietnam generation individuals who avoided the draft through occupational deferments by subtracting the June 30, 1960, total from the June 30, 1970, total. This assumes that the typical occupational deferment was granted during the registrant's twenty-first year. Many individuals were granted occupational deferments only to lose them later, so the deferment did not provide them with an escape mechanism, but they would not be included in the above calculation unless they lost their deferments after June 30, 1970. Given the arrival of the lottery and the 1971 reconstitution of draft boards (which added to Selective Service's administrative burdens), it is unlikely that more than a few thousand occupational deferments were taken away after that date. For the official statistics, see the *Annual Report of the Director of Selective Service,* 1961, and the *Semi-Annual Report* for July–December, 1970, p. 7.

[17]This statistic reflects the difference between the alien exemptions on June 30, 1971 and on June 30, 1960. After mid-1970, aliens and most other registrants with high lottery numbers were reclassified I-H and could not be traced. The number of exempt aliens

might have exceeded 13,000, as some may have come to the United States, escaped the draft, and returned to their native country. See the *Annual Report of the Director of Selective Service,* 1959 and 1961, and the *Semi-Annual Report* for January–June 1970, Table 1, p. 18.

[18]The number of sole surviving sons exempted from the draft except during a congressionally declared war can be determined only for the years 1972–73, when a separate IV-G exemption was created for them. Before September 28, 1971, they were included with veterans of military service in class IV-A. The 1972–73 statistic may exclude some sole surviving sons with high lottery numbers who could have been reclassified I-H after June 30, 1970. For the most recent statistic, see the *Semi-Annual Report of the Director of Selective Service,* Table 1, p. 20.

[19]American citizens who were overseas on their eighteenth birthday and did not have a home address in the United States (e.g., were overseas military dependents), were exempt from induction from 1962 through July 1971, as long as they remained outside the United States. The exact size of this exempt group over time cannot be ascertained, but the overseas registrant draft board ("Draft Board 100" in Washington, D.C.) had 27,000 registrants in 1970. After the special exemption was removed, overseas registrants could apply for other deferments and exemptions, as well. The 20,000 statistic is a minimum tally, reflecting only the 10% who would have turned 26 between 1970 and 1971 and the 67% who would have had high lottery numbers once the exemption expired.

[20]Like the occupational deferment and alien statistics (notes 16 and 17), the hardship and dependency statistic is derived by subtracting June 30, 1970, data from June 30, 1960, data. Like occupational deferments (note 16), hardship deferments were often taken away; if so, they would not be included in the calculation shown here. Dependency deferments were almost never taken away, although they were granted with diminished frequency as the war years progressed. There is no data available to identify how many of these deferments were for hardship (economic deprivation, sole means of support) and how many were for dependency (marriage, fatherhood). After April 23, 1970, no new dependency deferments were given.

[21]All of these are derivative, calculated by adding or subtracting other displayed statistics from the appropriate base statistics.

Figure 3: Military Avoiders

[1]*Selected Manpower Statistics,* DOD-OASD (Comptroller), May 1975, pp. 39, 46, 61, and 108. The statistic is modified here to exclude women, persons of the wrong age, and persons who did not serve in the Vietnam era (as defined in these charts). Some of the era modifications resulted from estimates given by the DOD Directorate for Information, Operations, and Control, to enable the inclusion of July 1964 discharges and the exclusion of July–December 1973 accessions. Since these charts pertain to the male Vietnam generation only, most statistics shown here are smaller than total manpower statistics.

For example, the actual Vietnam-era military manpower total is about 10,300,000, (including reserves). Where applicable, the comparable total statistics are included below.

[2]*Ibid.*, p. 39, 46, and 61 (overall total: 9,025,000). As in note 1, some era modifications had to be made.

[3]*Ibid.*, pp. 39 and 61 (overall totals: 3,400,000 in Southeast Asia; 2,600,000 in Vietnam). It is assumed here that military personnel over 26 in 1964 served in Southeast Asia and Vietnam in percentages comparable to their overall proportion in the armed forces.

[4]*Selected Manpower Statistics*, p. 108. The tally covers July 1, 1964 through June 30, 1973.

[5]Binkin, *U.S. Reserve Forces*, pp. 80–81.

[6]No combat/noncombat statistics are available to cover the entire war period. In the Notre Dame survey, 75% of all Vietnam veterans answered "yes" to the question "Did you ever engage in combat in Vietnam?" The only other statistic available (Ambrose and Barber, *The Military and American Society*, p. 195) indicates that only 25% were in combat situations at any one time, without taking account of assignment rotations. That finding was made in 1967, early in the war.

[7]All casualty statistics come from *Selected Manpower Statistics*, p. 62. This includes 492 wounded in Vietnam before 1964, most of whom would have been part of the Vietnam generation as here defined. An unknown percentage of casualties was suffered by those in noncombat situations (e.g., from mortar or rocket attacks). Defense Department casualty statistics indicate that 90% of all deaths were suffered by men under 30, so—given some margin of error—it is assumed that about 90% of all injuries were suffered by the Vietnam generation.

[8]This includes 46,163 killed in action (*ibid.*, p. 62) and 10,081 who died of disease, accidents, and other nonhostile causes. Hearings before the Subcommittee on Courts, Civil Liberties, and the Administration of Justice (93d Cong., 2d Sess.), p. 340 (letter from Melvin Laird to Commander Soden). The 46,163 figure includes 120 killed before 1964, most of whom would have been part of the Vietnam generation, as here defined. Ninety percent of these 56,000 deaths, or a total of 51,000, are assumed to involve the Vietnam generation. See note 7.

[9]All of these are derivative, calculated by adding or subtracting other displayed statistics to or from the appropriate base statistics.

Figure 4: Evaders

[1]Henry Peterson, statement to Hearings before the House Subcommittee on Courts, Civil Liberties and the Administration of Justice (1974), p. 36. This statistic includes 25,382 complaints filed in the 1963 and 1964 fiscal years, assuming a two-year lag time

between violation and conviction. All but a very small fraction of these earlier defendants would have been of Vietnam-generation age—and, since draft offenses are typically considered continuing offenses by the courts, by mid-1964 they stood charged with draft offenses.

[2]"Federal Offenders in U.S. District Courts," Historical Offense Table 10: "Disposition of Defendants Charged with Violation of Selective Service Act," obtained from the Administrative Office of the U.S. Courts. Some recent (FY 1975) cases were added to these base statistics.

[3]These estimates resulted from personal conversations with Assistant U.S. Attorneys who prosecuted cases in New York City, Philadelphia, Richmond, Detroit, Milwaukee, Dallas, Los Angeles, and San Francisco. Conversations with prosecutors in Concord (N.H.), Boston, Pittsburgh, Madison (Wis.), Nashville, New Orleans, and Portland (Ore.) corroborated this overall range of responses, although they preferred not to make percentage estimates. While these estimates are imprecise, it should be noted that no jurisdiction—nor the Department of Justice, nor Selective Service—kept tallies on this question.

	Defective Cases	Acceptance of Induction	Number of Cases Dropped Between 1967 and 1970	Number of Apparently Defective Cases
New York City	25 %	75 %	5,688	1,422
Philadelphia	50	50	1,862	931
Richmond	50	50	885	443
Detroit	40	60	2,128	851
Milwaukee	90	10	359	323
Dallas	30	70	1,310	393
Los Angeles	80	20	11,884	9,507
San Francisco	60	40	3,584	2,150
			27,700	16,020

⁴The 47% failure rate at preinduction physical exams was the national average for FY 1967–73. Assistant U.S. Attorneys and draft counselors confirm that about half failed the exam as a way to avoid prosecution.

⁵Approximately 48% of military personnel on active duty went to Vietnam during the 1968–71 period when these individuals would have most often been in the service. See "Profile of DOD First-Term Enlisted Personnel Separated from Active Service During 1970 and 1971," DOD (M&RA), February 1972, Table 2.

⁶Extrapolations from the Presidential Clemency Board Survey of 472 civilian applicants, as described in Appendix C of the Board's final report. The sample included 12 convicted draft offenders who served in the military. Eight went to Vietnam (one of whom deserted in a combat situation), and 4 received bad discharges.

⁷Sentencing statistics are from "Federal Offenders in U.S. District Courts" data. Prison time data are extrapolated from the findings of the Clemency Board's survey of 472 civilian applicants, described in App. C of its final report. The sentences and the actual time served in prison do not correspond exactly, although—as the data indicate—the relationship is close.

⁸In January 1975, the Justice Department published the "Kennedy List" of 4,522 known fugitives; aside from nonregistrants, these were the only draft resisters who still faced charges.

⁹This is derivative, calculated by adding or subtracting other displayed statistics from the appropriate base statistics.

Figure 5: Military Offenders

¹See Figure 3.

²Statistics from the Department of Defense (Office of Manpower and Reserve Affairs), November 15, 1976. Statistics are available only for FY 1967–73, so FY 1965–66 data is extrapolated from 1967 data. Also, Marine Corps data for FY 1967–69 is extrapolated from the average rate for the rest of the period. The exact numbers are calculated as 1,522,000 and 563,000, rounded here to reflect their inaccuracy. The latter statistic bears no direct relation to the number of less-than-Honorable discharges, which, by coincidence, is also 563,000.

³This includes 541,800 General, Undesirable, Bad Conduct, or Dishonorable Discharges given from July 1, 1964, through June 30, 1974. Discharges prior to July 1, 1974, are presumed to have been Vietnam-related, as they usually involved servicemen inducted or enlisted before the end of the war. It also includes 21,600 "Chapter 10" discharges given from July 1, 1974 through June 30, 1975, since the overwhelming majority of those cases involved AWOL or some other Vietnam-related behavior.

⁴This is, at best, a rough estimate based upon the Defense Department's belief that AWOL offenders accounted for about 83,000 of the 204,000 servicemen given Undesir-

able, Bad Conduct, or Dishonorable Discharges within the window period of the Ford clemency program. See Figure 9.

[5]This figure is also a rough estimate, based on information which the Defense Department gave the Presidential Clemency Board. That agency reported that approximately one-third of the 34,000 Bad Conduct and Dishonorable Discharges were for civilian-type crimes.

[6]Extrapolations from the Presidential Clemency Board's survey of 1,009 military applicants, described in Appendix C of the Board's final report.

[7]This data was supplied by the clerks of the U.S. Army, Navy, and Marine Corps judiciaries. The data include only court-martial convictions for this offense, and do not include Air Force cases (for which no data is available).

[8]All of these are derivative, calculated by adding or subtracting other displayed statistics to or from the appropriate base statistics.

Figure 6: Military Punishments

[1]See Figure 3.

[2]This tally includes all General, Undesirable, Bad Conduct, and Dishonorable Discharges for the period July 1, 1964, through June 30, 1974. Discharges "for the good of the service" are also included through June 30, 1975. See *Selected Manpower Statistics,* DOD-OASD (Comptroller), May 1975.

[3]An unpublished Defense Department analysis of MARDAC data indicates that the ratio of General Discharges to Honorable Discharges with bad "spins" is about 10:7; this suggests that about 200,000 veterans fall in the latter category.

[4]See note 2.

[5]No sampling has ever been published, but Defense Department officials involved in the Ford clemency program reported that approximately one-third of all punitive discharges were for civilian-type crimes. Almost all of the rest were for absence offenses.

[6]These are extrapolations based on the Clemency Board's survey of 1,009 military applicants, described in Appendix C of its final report.

[7]All of these are derivative, calculated by adding or subtracting other displayed statistics to or from the appropriate base statistics.

Figure 7: Exiles

[1]See Figure 5.

[2]See Figure 4.

[3]Statistics from the Ford clemency program suggest that only about 12% of all deserters and 15% of all draft resisters ever took flight. However, the circumstances of those

surveys indicate that the true proportion of fugitive deserters was somewhat higher. The best way of reconstructing the fugitive population is to identify the number who went to Canada and use that as a basis for extrapolation. In Tables 17 and 18 of Baskir and Strauss, *Reconciliation After Vietnam,* pp. 135–36, Canadian immigration data is juxtaposed to estimate a total of 30,000 American exiles in Canada. (Note two errata in Table 18: 6,605 should read 1,473, and 17,614 should read 12,482.) Of that total, 20,000 are thought to have been landed, and 10,000 nonlanded (illegal).

Ford clemency program data, reinforced by the observations of knowledgeable persons, suggest that the ratio of Canadian-based exiles to other exiles to fugitives in the American underground was about 3:1:1. This projection—which is very inexact—indicates that about 50,000 persons were fugitives, 40,000 in exile and 10,000 remaining in the United States. These same sources indicate about a 3:2 ratio of draft resisters to deserters. See *Reconciliation After Vietnam,* pp. 75, 89–90, and 119; the Clemency Board's final report, Chapter 3 and Appendix C; and Bell and Houston's report for the U.S. Army Research Institute, *The Vietnam Era Deserter* (1976).

[4]In September of 1972, the Swedish government tallied 660 American exiles in that country, 71% of whom were deserters. Informed persons consider that tally somewhat low, as it excludes illegal immigrants, deserters who were not American citizens, and a small number of post-1972 arrivals. One thousand seems a reasonable approximation. See *Amex-Canada* magazine, vol. 3, no. 5, p. 7.

[5]According to a 1971 Defense Department survey, almost identical proportions of deserters were in Mexico and Sweden. See *Amex,* vol. 3, no. 7, p. 50.

[6]These tallies were extrapolated from unpublished data obtained in the Clemency Board's survey of 472 civilian and 1,009 military applicants. See Appendix C of the Board's final report.

[7]This includes 1,000 applicants to the Clemency Board, 500 to the Defense Department phase, and 500 to the Justice Department phase. All are extrapolations from available data. See note 3.

[8]Prior to Carter's pardons, the available evidence suggests that there were 3,000 draft fugitives, 3,000 military fugitives (Vietnam-era only), and 5,000 expatriates. The overwhelming majority of these 11,000 persons were in exile. See Baskir and Strauss, *Reconciliation After Vietnam,* pp. 75–80 and 88–90. The number of expatriates was calculated through annual Canadian citizenship statistics provided by the Canadian embassy.

[9]All of these are derivative, calculated by adding or subtracting other displayed statistics from the appropriate base statistics.

Figure 8: Amnesty—Civilians

[1]These figures can be calculated from the findings of an *ad hoc* survey of more than 3,000 telephone inquiries received by civilian counselors after the release of the 4,522-

name Kennedy list. This survey learned that 85% of those not on the Kennedy list were also not on the 6,200-name list previously released by the Justice Department. This indicated that more than 11,000 individuals not on either list still thought that they faced prosecution—and that 13,000 had their cases permanently dropped with the release of the Kennedy list. See the *Military Law Reporter,* Nov.–Dec. 1974, 2 MLR 1083.

[2]See Figure 1.

[3]See Figure 4.

[4]These were individuals who could not reenter the United States even though no charges were brought against them. For a precise calculation, based on annual Canadian immigration statistics, see *Reconciliation After Vietnam,* Table 19, p. 137.

[5]See the Presidential Clemency Board's final report, p. xiii.

[6]These are composite statistics combining the Clemency Board and Justice Department phases of the Ford program. See *Reconciliation After Vietnam,* Chapter 3 and Table 21, pp. 27–48 and 139.

[7]Of the 4,522 individuals on the Kennedy list, 736 applied for clemency, about 3,000 remained fugitives, and an estimated 800 had their cases dropped by U.S. attorneys or dismissed by federal judges. No precise records were kept, so this estimate was based on conversations with defense counsel and prosecutors.

[8]See Note 4.

[9]This was an actual count taken at the time of President Carter's announcement.

[10]This included the 3,000 fugitives at large and the 538 applicants to the Justice Department phase of the Ford program who had not yet completed alternative service.

[11]This included the 8,750 convicted offenders, less the 1,600 pardoned through the Ford program. The latter were also pardoned by Carter, but received nothing new of any legal consequence.

[12]See Note 2.

[13]All of these are derivative, calculated by adding or subtracting other displayed statistics to or from the appropriate base statistics.

Figure 9: Amnesty—Military

[1]See Figure 6.

[2]This statistic is based upon informal but official estimates provided by the Defense Department to the Presidential Clemency Board. An insignificant percentage of these cases involved women or overage men. The Defense Department claimed that 83,000 men had AWOL-related discharges during the Vietnam era. Most were charged with AWOL (absence without official leave), but almost all had been administratively classified as deserters for being absent more than thirty days. See the Presidential Clemency Board's final report, Chapter 3 and Appendix C.

[3]This was the final count issued by the Defense Department in the fall of 1974. *Ibid.,* p. xiii.

[4]These tallies include all bad discharges through June 30, 1974, which are presumed to include draftees and draft-era enlistees, and all Undesirable Discharges "for the good of the service" through June 30, 1975, which are presumed to include Vietnam-era absentees. See *Selected Manpower Statistics,* DOD-OASD (Comptroller), May 1975.

[5]These are composite statistics combining the Clemency Board and Justice Departmen phases of the Ford program. See *Reconciliation After Vietnam,* Chapter 3 and Table 21, pp. 27–48 and 139.

[6]About 850 fugitives were discharged through normal channels during the Ford program, and another 1,650 in the eighteen months prior to Carter's inauguration.

[7]See Figure 6.

[8]See Note 4. Of this tally, approximately half are General Discharges.

[9]*Reconciliation After Vietnam,* pp. 88–90. Of the 10,115 fugitives at the start of the Ford program, 5,555 surrendered through that program, and about 2,500 surrendered through normal military channels. See note 6.

[10]Washington *Post,* October 5, 1977.

[11]All of these are derivative, calculated by adding or subtracting other displayed statistics to or from the appropriate base statistics.

BIBLIOGRAPHY

THE VIETNAM-ERA DRAFT

"Bald Case in Point: Pro Football's Magic Immunity," *Life,* lxi, December 9, 1966.

Canby, Steven L., *Military Manpower Procurement,* Rand Corporation Study. Lexington, Mass.: Lexington Books, 1972.

Chapman, Bruce K., *The Wrong Man in Uniform: Our Unfair and Obsolete Draft and How We Can Replace It,* New York: Trident Press, 1967.

Davis, James W., and Kenneth M. Dolbeare, *Little Groups of Neighbors: The Selective Service System,* Chicago: Markham Publishing, 1968.

Defense Manpower: The Keystone of National Security, Report to the President and the Congress by the Defense Manpower Commission, April 1976.

Draft Counselor's Newsletter, CCCO, San Francisco, California.

"The Draft: The Unjust vs. the Unwilling," *Newsweek,* lxvii, April 11, 1966.

Fallows, James, "What Did You Do in the Class War, Daddy," *Washington Monthly,* October 1975.

Gerhardt, Roger W., ed., *The Draft and Public Policy,* Columbus: Ohio State University Press, 1971.

In Pursuit of Equity: Who Serves When Not All Serve? Report of the National Advisory Commission on Selective Service, February 1967.

Kendall, David, and Leonard Ross, *The Lottery and the Draft: Where Do I Stand?* New York, Evanston, and London: Harper & Row, 1970.

Legal Aspects of Selective Service, Selective Service System, January 1, 1973.

Leinwand, Gerald, *The Draft,* New York: Pocket Books, 1970.

Little, Roger W., ed., *Selective Service and American Society,* New York: Russell Sage Foundation: 1969.

Lynn, Conrad J., *How to Stay Out of the Army: A Guide to Your Rights Under the Draft Law,* 2d ed., rev., New York and London: Grove Press, 1967.

Manchester, William, *The Glory and the Dream,* New York: Bantam Press, 1975.

Marmion, Harry A., *Selective Service: Conflict and Compromise,* New York: John Wiley & Sons, 1968.

Miller, James, III, et al., *Why the Draft: The Case for a Volunteer Army,* Baltimore: Penguin Books, 1966.

Morris, Mark, *Why Draft Repeal?* National Peace Literature Service, Philadelphia: American Friends Committee, 1970.

Notre Dame survey of 1,586 young men in Washington, D.C., South Bend, Indiana, and Ann Arbor, Michigan, who were of draft age during the Vietnam war.

One Third of a Nation, Report of the President's Task Force on Manpower Conservation, Washington: Government Printing Office, 1964.

O'Sullivan, John, and Alan M. Meckler, eds., *The Draft and Its Enemies: A Documentary History,* Urbana: University of Illinois Press, 1974.

Reeves, Thomas, and Karl Hess, *The End of the Draft,* New York: Random House, 1970.

"Riots, Songs, and Fishbowls, The Hullabaloo Is Old Hat to Mr. Hershey: America's Mr. Draft," *Life,* lix, August 20, 1965.

Sanders, Jacquin, *The Draft and the Vietnam War,* New York: Walker, 1966.

Selective Service Law Reporter, The Public Law Education Institute.

Semi-Annual Reports of the Director of Selective Service, Government Printing Office, 1965–1975.

Shapiro, Andrew O., and John M. Striker, *Mastering the Draft: A Comprehensive Guide for Solving Draft Problems,* Boston: Little, Brown and Company, 1970.

Strickland, Glenn W., *The Championship Debater's Complete Sourcebook on the Draft and Its Alternatives,* Inglewood, Colo.: Championship Debate Enterprises, 1968.

Suttler, David, *IV-F: A Guide to Draft Exemption,* New York: Grove Press, 1970.

Tatum, Arlo, and Joseph Tuchinsky, *Guide to the Draft,* Boston: Beacon Press, 1968.

Tax, Sol, ed., *The Draft: A Handbook of Facts and Alternatives,* Chicago: University of Chicago Press, 1967.

Wamsley, Gary L., *Selective Service and a Changing America,* Columbus, O.: Charles E. Merrill Publishing Co., 1969.

Willenz, June A., ed., *Dialogue on the Draft,* Report of the National Conference on the Draft, American Veterans Committee, Washington, D.C., 1966.

CIVILIAN OFFENDERS

"A Youth's Reason for Spurning the Draft—A Judge's Answer," *U.S. News and World Report,* June 8, 1970.

Brotsky, Allan, "Trial of a Conscientious Objector," pp. 98–115 in *The Relevant Lawyers,* edited by Ann Fagan Ginger, New York: Simon and Schuster, 1972.

Clemency Board survey of 472 convicted civilian offenders.

Collier, Peter, "The Unilateral Withdrawal of Private Weise," *Ramparts,* February 1970.

"The Demonstrators: Why? How Many?" *Newsweek,* lxvi, November 1, 1965.

"Ducking the Draft and Dodging the Cameras: Fathers and Sons Face Charges," *Life,* lix, April 15, 1966.

"Evading the Draft, Who, How and Why," *Life,* lxi, December 9, 1966.

Federal Offenders in United States District Courts, Administrative Office of the United States Courts, annual Selective Service violation statistics.

Ferber, Michael, and Staughton Lynd, *The Resistance,* Boston: Beacon Press, 1971.

Gaylin, Willard, *In the Service of Their Country,* New York: Grosset & Dunlap: 1970.

Gooding, Richard, "An Exile in My Own Country," *Look,* February 24, 1970.

Gutknecht, David, Peggy Naas, Scott Sanovik, and Dave Wood, *Check Out the Odds,* Minneapolis: Twin Cities Resistance, 1971.

Lynd, Alice, *We Won't Go,* Boston: Beacon Press, 1968.

Peacemaker magazine, Ernest Bromley, publisher, Cincinnati, Ohio.

Rohr, John A., *Prophets Without Honor: Public Policy and the Selective Conscientious Objector,* New York: Abingdon Press, 1971.

"Sentencing Selective Service Violators: A Judicial Wheel of Fortune," *Columbia Law Journal,* vol. 5, no. 2, August 1969.

Statistical Abstract of the United States, U.S. Department of Commerce, 1973.

Useem, Michael, *Conscription, Protest, and Social Conflict: The Life and Death of a Draft Resistance Movement,* New York: John Wiley & Sons, 1973.

THE VIETNAM-ERA MILITARY

Ambrose, Stephen E., and James A. Barber, Jr., eds., *The Military and American Society,* New York: Free Press, 1972.

Analysis of Casualties by Learning Abilities, U.S. Department of the Army, Personnel Office, June 28, 1968.

Bachman, Jerald G., and John D. Blair, *Soldiers, Sailors, and Civilians: The Military Mind and the All-Volunteer Force,* Ann Arbor: Institute of Social Research, University of Michigan, 1975.

Barnes, Peter, *Pawns,* New York: Warner Paperback Library, 1971.

Binkin, Martin, *U.S. Reserve Forces: The Problem of the Weekend Warrior,* Washington, D.C.: Brookings Institution, 1974.

Binkin, Martin, and John Johnston, *All Volunteer Armed Forces: Progress, Problems, and Prospects,* report prepared for the Senate Armed Services Committee, June 1, 1973.

Code of Federal Regulations: Pensions, Bonuses, and Veterans' Relief, Office of the Federal Register.

Cortright, David, *Soldiers in Revolt: The American Military Today,* New York: Anchor Press/Doubleday, 1975.

Emerson, Gloria, *Winners and Losers: American Stories—Battles, Retreats, Gains, Losses, and Ruins from a Long War,* New York: Random House, 1976.

Fiedler, Leslie, "Who Really Died in Vietnam?" *Saturday Review,* November 18, 1972.

Glass, Andrew, "Defense Report/Draftees Shoulder Burden of Fighting and Dying in Vietnam," *National Journal,* August 15, 1970.

Glick, Edward B., *Soldiers, Scholars and Society: The Social Impact of the American Military,* Palisades, Calif.: Goodyear Publishing, 1971.

Gray, J. Glenn, *The Warriors: Reflections on Men in Battle,* New York: Harcourt Brace, 1958.

Halstead, Fred, *GI's Speak Out Against the War,* New York: Pathfinder Press, 1970.

Hauser, William L., *America's Army in Crisis,* Baltimore: Johns Hopkins University Press, 1973.

Helmer, John, *Bringing the War Home: The American Soldier Before Vietnam and After,* New York: Free Press, 1974.

Hersh, Seymour, "The Decline and Near Fall of the U.S. Army," *Saturday Review,* November 18, 1972.

Janowitz, Morris, *The New Military,* New York: Russell Sage Foundation, 1971.

Johnson, Haynes, and George Wilson, *Army in Anguish,* New York: Pocket Books, 1971.

Just, Ward, *Military Men,* New York: Avon, 1970.

King, Edward L., *The Death of the Army: A Pre-Mortem,* New York: Saturday Review Press, 1972.

Lane, Mark, *Conversations with Americans,* New York: Simon and Schuster, 1970.

Lifton, Robert Jay, *Home from the War,* New York: Touchstone Books, Simon and Schuster, 1973.

Liston, Robert A., *Greeting: You Are Hereby Ordered for Induction,* New York: McGraw-Hill, 1970.

Loory, Stuart H., *Defeated: Inside America's Military Machine,* New York: Random House, 1973.

Mantell, David, and Mark Pilisuk, "Soldiers in and after Vietnam," *Journal of Social Issues,* vol. 31, no. 4, 1975.

Marginal Man and Military Service, Department of the Army, December 1965.

Moskos, Charles C., *The American Enlisted Man: The Rank and File in Today's Military,* New York: Russell Sage Foundation, 1970.

Polner, Murray, *No Victory Parades: The Return of the Vietnam Veteran,* New York: Holt, Rinehart & Winston, 1971.

Rideau, Wilbert, "Veterans Incarcerated," *Penthouse* magazine, April 1976.

Selected Manpower Statistics, Department of Defense, Office of the Comptroller.

Starr, Paul, *The Discarded Army: Veterans After Vietnam,* New York: Charterhouse, 1973.

Tauber, Peter, *The Sunshine Soldiers,* New York: Simon and Schuster, 1971.

The Vietnam Veteran in Contemporary Society, materials collected by Department of Medicine and Surgery, Veterans Administration, Washington, D.C., May 1972.

Walton, George, *The Tarnished Shield: A Report on Today's Army,* New York: Dodd, Mead, 1973.

Waterhouse, Carry G., and Marianne G. Wizard, *Turning the Guns Around: Notes on the GI Movement,* New York: Praeger Publishers, 1971.

MILITARY OFFENDERS

Bell, D. Bruce, and Thomas J. Houston, *The Vietnam Era Deserter: Characteristics of Unconvicted Army Deserters Participating in the Presidential Clemency Program,* U.S. Army Research Institute for the Behavioral and Social Sciences, July 1976.

Boulanger, Raymond P., "The Undesirable Veteran," *Commonweal,* September 21, 1973.

Clemency Board Survey of 1,009 discharged military offenders.

Ginzburg, Eli, *Breakdown and Recovery,* New York: Columbia University Press, 1950.

Ginzburg, Eli, *The Lost Divisions,* New York: Columbia University Press, 1950.

Ginzburg, Eli, *Patterns of Performance,* New York: Columbia University Press, 1950.

Lang, David, "AWOL," *The New Yorker,* October 21, 1972.

Linden, Eugene, "The Demoralization of an Army: Fragging and Other Withdrawal Symptoms," *Saturday Review,* January 8, 1972.

McCubbin, Hamilton I., et al., *Leadership and Situational Factors Related to AWOL: A Research Report,* U.S. Army Correctional Training Facility, Fort Riley, Kansas, 1971.

Musil, Robert K., "The Truth about Deserters," *The Nation,* April 16, 1973.

Shoultz, James C., Jr., MPC Commander, "Literature Review: Research on Military Offenders," *The AWOL Soldier: A Challenge to Leadership,* vol. 4, U.S. Army Correctional Training Facility, Fort Riley.

Treatment of Deserters from Military Service, Report of the Committee on Armed Services, U.S. Senate, March 11, 1969, 91st Cong., 1st Sess.

Woodstone, Norma Sue, *Up Against the War,* New York: Tower Publications, 1970.

MILITARY DISCIPLINE

Addlestone, David F., and Susan H. Hewman, *ACLU Practice Manual on Military Discharge Upgrading,* Military Rights Project of the ACLU Project on Amnesty, 1975.

Effron, Andrew, "Punishment of Enlisted Personnel Outside the UCMJ: A Statutory and Equal Protection Analysis of Military Discharge Policies," *Harvard Civil Liberties Law Review,* vol. 9, no. 2, March 1974.

Finn, James, *Conscience and Command,* New York: Random House, 1971.

Jones, Bradley, "The Gravity of Administrative Discharges: A Legal and Empirical Evaluation," *Military Law Review,* vol. 59, Winter 1973.

Military Law Reporter, Public Law Education Institute, Washington, D.C.

Moger, Homer E., Jr., *Justice and the Military,* Public Law Education Institute, 1972.

Prugh, George S., Major General, *Law at War,* Vietnam Studies, 1964–1973, Department of the Army, Washington, D.C., 1975.

Report of the Special Civilian Committee for the Study of the United States Army Confinement System, Department of Defense, 1970.

Report of the Task Force on the Administration of Military Justice, Department of Defense, 4 volumes, November 1, 1972.

Rivkin, Robert, *GI Rights and Army Justice: The Draftee's Guide to Military Life and Law,* New York: Grove Press, 1970.

Rogers, Capt. Richard M., "The USCMA and the Involuntary Volunteer: *United States v. Catlow,*" *The Army Lawyer,* July 1974.

The Search for Military Justice, Report of the NAACP Inquiry into the Problems of the Negro Servicemen in West Germany, 1971.

Sherman, Edward F., "The Civilianization of Military Law," in *With Justice for Some,* Bruce Wasserster and Mark J. Green, eds., Boston: Beacon Press, 1970.

Sherrill, Robert, *Military Justice Is to Justice As Military Music Is to Music,* New York: Harper & Row, 1970.

Willenz, June, *A Report on the Human Rights of the Man in Uniform,* American Veterans Committee, 1968.

EXILES AND EXPATRIATES

Alsop, Stewart, "The Need to Hate," *Newsweek,* July 27, 1970.

Amex-Canada, assorted volumes.

Annual Canadian citizenship and immigration statistics.

Emerick, Kenneth, *War Resisters in Canada,* Knox, Pa.: Knox Free Press, 1972.

Fleming, Karl, "America's Sad Young Exiles," *Newsweek,* February 15, 1971.

Franks, Lucinda, *Waiting Out a War,* New York: Coward, McCann, and Geoghegan, 1974.

Hayes, Thomas Lee, *American Deserters in Sweden,* New York: Associated Press, 1971.

Jones, Douglas, and David Raish, "American Deserters and Draft Evaders: Exile, Punishment, or Amnesty," *Harvard International Law Journal,* vol. 13, no. 1, Winter 1972.

Killmer, Richard, et al., *They Can't Go Home Again,* Philadelphia: United Church Press, 1971.

Levine, Saul V., M.D., "American Exiles in Canada: A Social and Psychological Follow-up," *Psychiatric Opinion,* vol. 11, November 1974.

Levine, Saul V., M.D., "Draft Dodgers: Coping with Stress, Adapting to Exile," *American Journal of Orthopsychiatry,* 42(3), April 1972.

Noell, Chuck, and Gary Wood, *We are All POW's,* Philadelphia: Fortress Press, 1975.

Polner, Murray, *When Can I Come Home? A Debate on Amnesty for Exiles, Anti-War Prisoners, and Others,* Garden City, N.Y.: Anchor Books, 1972.

Schiller, Lisa, and Joe LeBlanc, *Exiled,* undated pamphlet published by the Philadelphia Resistance.

Whitmore, Terry, *Memphis-Nam-Sweden,* New York: Doubleday, 1971.

Williams, Roger Neville, *The New Exiles: American War Resisters in Canada,* New York: Liveright Publishers, 1971.

THE AMNESTY DEBATE

Alexander, Shana, "Amnesty, Agony and Responsibility," *Newsweek,* March 19, 1973.

"Amnesty for the War Exiles?" *Newsweek,* January 17, 1972.

"Amnesty for Whom, and How Much," *The National Observer,* March 11, 1972.

Baskir, Lawrence M., and William A. Strauss, *Reconciliation After Vietnam,* South Bend, Ind.: University of Notre Dame Press, 1977.

Commager, Henry Steele, "The Case for Amnesty," *The New York Review of Books,* April 6, 1972.

Duscha, Julius, "Should There Be Amnesty for the War Resister?" *New York Times Magazine,* December 24, 1972.

Finn, James, "The Amnesty Issue," *Commonweal,* November 3, 1972.

Reston, James, Jr., "Reconciliation, Not Retribution—Universal Amnesty," *The New Republic,* February 5, 1972.

"Veterans, Deserters and Draft-Evaders—The Vietnam Decade," New York: Ford Foundation Issue Paper, 1974.

Wyatt, Michael K., "Making the Case for Congressional Amnesty," *The New Republic,* June 10, 1972.

PRESIDENT FORD'S CLEMENCY PROGRAM

After Action Report, Department of Defense, Implementation of President's Clemency Program, prepared by Office of the Deputy Chief of Staff for Personnel, Department of the Army, October 1975, 2 volumes.

Cowlishaw, Patrick R., "The Conditional Presidential Pardon," *Stanford Law Review,* November 1975.

"Limited Program, Limited Response," *Time,* September 30, 1974.

Maxfield, David M., "Clemency Program: Should It Be Extended?" *Congressional Quarterly,* September 20, 1975.

"Outlook for Amnesty," *Newsweek,* September 2, 1974.

Pearman, William A., "An Analysis of the Impact of Clemency Discharges on Recipients' Employment Opportunities," in *Report to the President,* Presidential Clemency Board, p. 403.

Reeves, Richard, *A Ford, Not a Lincoln,* New York and London: Harcourt Brace Jovanovich, 1975.

Report to the President, Presidential Clemency Board, GPO, 1975.

Report to the Service Secretaries by the Joint Alternative Service Board in Support of Presidential Proclamation 4313, Department of Defense, 1975.

CONGRESSIONAL HEARINGS AND REPORTS

90th Congress: Senate Armed Services: Amending and Extending the Draft Laws; April 12–19, 1967.

————: Senate Armed Services: Military Deserters; May 21 and 22, 1968.

91st Congress: House Armed Services Special Subcommittee on the Draft: To Amend Military Selective Service Act of 1967; September 30, 1969.

————: Senate Judiciary Subcommittee on Administrative Practice and Procedures: The Selective Service: Its Operation, Practices and Procedures; October–November, 1969.

————: House Armed Services Special Subcommittee on the Draft: Review of the Administration and Operation of the Draft Law; July 23, 1970.

————: House Armed Services Committee: Hearings and Special Reports on Subjects Affecting the Naval and Military Establishments; 1970.

92d Congress: House Armed Services: Hearings on H.R. 523, Administrative Discharges; June 2–8 and July 7, 1971.

————: House Appropriation Subcommittee: Department of Defense Appropriations for 1972—Morale and Discipline in the Army; September 23, 1971.

————: Senate Judiciary Subcommittee on Administrative Practice and Procedures: Selective Service and Amnesty; February 28–March 1, 1972.

————: Senate Subcommittee on Drug Abuse in the Military: Drug Abuse in the Military; February 29, 1972.

————: Senate Armed Services Subcommittee on the Volunteer Armed Force and Selective Service: Volunteer Armed Forces and Selective Service; March 10 and 13, 1972.

93d Congress: House Judiciary Subcommittee on Courts, Civil Liberties, and the Administration of Justice: Amnesty; March 8, 11, and 13, 1974.

————: Senate Judiciary Subcommittee on Administrative Practice and Procedures: Clemency Program Practices and Procedures; December 18 and 19, 1974.

94th Congress: House Judiciary Subcommittee on Courts, Civil Liberties, and the Administration of Justice: The Presidential Clemency Program; April 14, 17, and 18, 1975.

————: House Judiciary Subcommittee on Courts, Civil Liberties, and the Administration of Justice: report on the Presidential Clemency Program; August 1975.

————: Senate Committee to Study Governmental Operations With Respect to Intelligence Activities, *Intelligence Activities and the Rights of Americans;* April 1976.

95th Congress: King, William, "Achieving America's Goals: Rational Service or the All-Volunteer Armed Force?" report to the Senate Armed Services Committee, February 1977.

————: Senate Committee on Veterans' Affairs: "Eligibility for Veterans' Benefits Pursuant to Vietnam Era Discharge Upgrading," Report to accompany S. 1307, June 28, 1977.

INDEX

absence offenses (AWOLs), 109, 113;
Defense Department study, 116, 232;
deterring, 148, 149, 153; long-term,
121–2; Project 100,000, 127, 128;
punishment, 135, 145, 160–1, 163–6;
short-term, 121, 143, 144; in
volunteer army, 240, 242; *see also*
deserters
Abzug, Bella, 208
Addlestone, David, 144
administrative discharges, 139, 160–1,
240
Agnew, Spiro, 168, 207, 208–9, 211
Air Force (U.S.), 10, 14, 54–5, 120,
135, 138, 139, 158, 241, 246; *see also*
armed forces
Alder, Thomas, 71
Ali, Muhammad, 63, 79, 97
Allen, Paul, 98
Allison, Larry, 183, 186, 187, 193
alternative service: as condition of
amnesty, 92, 212–13, 215–22; for
convicted draft offenders, 74, 80;
CO's and, 40, 41, 246; refused, 96–7
American Civil Liberties Union, 136,
225
American Deserters' Committee, 192,
196, 225
American Friends Service Committee,
38
American Legion, 10, 188, 209, 225,
229
America's Army (Hauser), 238
Amex-Canada (magazine), 181, 190,

192, 200, 205–6
amnesty: Australian approach, 205;
Carter's view, 229–30, 231; compared
to pardon, 226–7; Congressional
opposition to, 233–4; exiles' view,
205–6; Ford program and, 213, 224;
future wars and, 235–7; as ideological
issue, 206–10; Justice Department's,
220–1; Kennedy hearings, 228; Nixon
view, 203–5, 208–10; precedents for,
204, 214; *see also* clemency; pardons
amnesty lobby, 204–13 *passim*, 224,
229–30, 231, 236
antiwar activists, 6, 23; accelerated
induction for, 25, 63, 72; as amnesty
lobby, 206–9; deferments for, 25–6;
guidebook, 173; in high schools, 85;
in service, 139–45, 183; underground,
167, 171–3, 178; veterans' view, 249;
see also resistance movement
armed forces: all-volunteer, 237–42,
245; antiwar activism in, 139–45,
183; combat avoidance in, 51–61;
discharge review boards, 240–1;
discharge system, 152–66; enlistment
standards of, 122–31, 137, 139;
generation gap in, 132; morale and
discipline crisis in, 110–52;
recruitment practices, 122–31, 137,
238, 239–40, 241; reform of, 238–42;
rehabilitation programs, 122–31, 133
134–5; in War on Poverty, 122–31;
see also enlisted men; officers;
servicemen; *and individual services*

ABOUT THE AUTHORS

LAWRENCE M. BASKIR served as General Counsel and Chief Executive Officer of President Ford's Clemency Board. WILLIAM A. STRAUSS was Director of Planning and Management for the Clemency Board and was director of the staff that prepared the Board's final report. They both live and work in Washington.